St. Louis Community College

Forest Park
Florissant Valley
Meramec

Instructional Resources
St. Louis, Missouri

OF WOMAN CASTE

OF WOMAN CASTE

The Experience of Gender in Rural India

Anjali Bagwe

Zed Books

OF WOMAN CASTE
The experience of Gender in Rural India
was first published by STREE,
16 Southern Avenue, Calcutta 700 026, India, 1995.

This edition published by Zed Books Ltd.,
7 Cynthia Street, London N1 9JF UK,
and 165 First Avenue, Atlantic Highlands,
New Jersey 07716, USA, in 1995

Cover designed by Andrew Corbett

This edition is not for sale in South Asia

A catalogue record for this book is available
from the British Library.

US CIP data is available from
the Library of Congress

ISBN 1 85649 321 0 hb
ISBN 1 85649 322 9 pb

To my parents, for giving me my roots

Preface

WOMAN CASTE is a literal translation of *bayanchi jaat* from Malvani, the dialect of Marathi spoken in Masure, the research village. Similar terms are used in many Indian languages: in Hindi, for example, as *aurat jaat*. They naturally evoke the inferiority of women as a separate subgroup. The converse, *mardanchi jaat,* or 'men's caste', evokes machismo as a much desired manly trait, which sets men apart from mere women in matters of courage, skill, dominance, aggressiveness and overall superiority. *Jaat,* in common Indian usage (as distinct from the interpretation of caste in contemporary academic discourse on the Indian social organization), lends itself to women and men also as ideologically constructed subspecies. Women and men are seen to occupy separate spatial and psychological dimensions of existence. They are subject to different prescriptions of conduct, work roles and ritual functioning. Jaat, in common perception, is thus seen to subsume both women and men as distinct subgroups with gendered patterns of existence. Women's studies literature also points to the prevalence of unique subcultures of women and men in traditional societies around the world.

'Woman caste' is generally used as a derogatory term to justify patriarchal definitions of women's place in society, deriving from a biased view of gender differences. It evokes an entire range of myths and stereotypes about women from the men's point of view, to explain little understood aspects of the world of women. Those women who are indoctrinated to such terminology may use it to acknowledge overtly the wholesale inferiority of women as the weaker sex. It is immaterial that ʾhis alleged weakness may itself be a function of the system of unjust male oppression and exploitation of women. Besides using the term in this sense, men also use it to express subliminal fears of the seeming inconsistencies and irrationalities of women's behaviour—often beyond men's control. This may serve to undermine their superior status, in the context of gender struggles (see the old man Nana's comment on the recently widowed Kaki, p 84). Such fears rationalize the use of further repressive measures to subjugate rebellious women. Thus, on the one hand, this term alludes to women as a special group in need of male control and protection. On the other, it is used to disparage manifestations of those aspects of the women's subculture that constitute active resistance to the restrictions imposed on them by an unjust patriarchal system.

By using 'Of Woman Caste' as the title, I have attempted a 'reification' and revaluation of the term in a very positive sense, in the light of women's own subjective experience of their world. The title, then, is a celebration of the distinctive self-affirming aspects of women's subculture; of their resistance to dehumanizing patriarchal injunctions; and of the creative and nurturing aspects of women's work and self-expression in village society.

As it evolved, writing the dissertation in Berkeley was a very cathartic process, underlined by nearly a year of acute homesickness for the research village. It was not possible to include all the data covered in my research, given the paucity of time and space. The second stage was that the writing of this book which was based on the dissertation and yet was also separated from it, did not make much progress until I could spatially detach myself from the research village over the past year. At that time I faced the daunting task of turning the 500-page dissertation into a much more concise book. Thus, I had to leave out a great amount of interesting material on the village, including the historical and cultural background of Masure. I excluded the colourful legends of the people, constituting their oral tradition of an almost cinematic genre in folklore; also the village ghostlore; a description of the temples and deities, and of the unique traditional ritual hierarchy in the Kokan, as evident in the village. The 60-70 page case studies were also condensed to less than half the size, leaving out a wealth of material on the various aspects of women's creativity in mundane tasks such as preparing and decorating mud floors. I also omitted some social work perspectives to provide greater space to women's studies as an evolving interdisciplinary concern. Finally, an update was provided to bridge the gap between 1989-1995. I am grateful to Stree for its support and for closely sharing an exacting process of revisions with valued insights and infinite patience. I would also like to thank Sonal Mansata of Compuset International for the design and the typesetting, and especially for the care she took over the Appendix.

Many people and organizations have helped me tremendously in my research and in writing this book. I am grateful to the Lady Meherbai D. Tata Educational Trust Scholarship for Study Abroad, the University of California Travelling Fellowship, the Jacob and Mary Kemler Seitz Scholarship and the American Association of University Women, International Fellowship, which supported my doctoral research with generous grants.

I wish to thank Professors Eileen Gambrill, Arlie Russell Hochschild and Ruth Dixon-Mueller, members of the Dissertation Committee at Berkeley, and also Professor Jewelle Taylor Gibbs of the School of Social Welfare. I am grateful for their consistent support and personal interest in my work. Among many friends who offered special interdisciplinary insights and practical help are Gloria Bowles, Smadar Lavie, Jane Singh, Maresi Nerad, Dorsh Marie Devoe, Claire Papapavlou, Ellen Gunty, Vatsala Basrur, Myrna Garcia, Prabir Burman, Anilkumar Gupta and Ramesh Ganeriwal. I also wish to thank Martha Chang, Foreign Students' Advisor at Berkeley.

Special thanks are owed to Gopal Krishna Modiji for his encouragement and also to the following: Vandana Karambelkar, Meeratai M. Jadhav, Gurunath Kulkarni, President, Sindhudurga Saunskrutik Kendra, Swapnagandha Kulkarni, Dnyanesh Deoolkar of the Nath Pai Sevangan, Bhai S. S. Khandalekar, P. A. Kambli of Apna Bazar, Y. B. Bagwe of the Bagwe Samaj Seva Sangh, Ashok Patil, former DSP, Sindhudurg, Rajendra Desai and Thomas Fernandes of the Malvan Taluka Mitra Mandal. I remain obliged to Vijaya Chauhan, Sonal Shukla, Vibhuti Patel, Vidya Bal, Nilima Kanetkar, Prakash Kushe, S. G. Bagwe, K. M. Parab, Shivram Sukhi, Aparna Bagwe and Parag Mhatre.

I am grateful to the women and men in Masure who shared their lives with me in the process of research and organizational work and ultimately made this such a meaningful task.

In mid-February 1995, I had completed twelve years in Masure, and the writing of this book. It seemed a good time to leave my ancestral home, though my commitment to the village and to the Kokan region continues. I wish to thank the Prabhu-gaonkars for accepting me as a part of their extended family of Masure. I also wish to thank my mother, Dr Urmila N. Bagwe, for bearing with me through all the anguish I caused her during my strange quest into the unknown while carrying out my research.

I would like to offer my affection and respects to the memory of my father, Dr Narottam Shridhar Bagwe (1913-1968) and to my sister, Dr Mangala Dattakumar Mhatre (1945-1994). I would like to add that I am eternally grateful to Param Pujya Shri Gagangirinath for bringing me to a new realization, and for thus setting me free from the past.

Masure and Bombay, 1995   A B

Contents

Introduction

MASURE IS LOCATED slightly inland on the Kokan coast in southern Maharashtra, roughly at a distance of 450 kilometres from Bombay. If all goes well, the journey from Bombay takes almost fifteen hours on the state transport bus. A part of the Malvan taluka in Sindhudurg district, Masure is about fifteen kilometres away from the once prosperous harbour town of Malvan, which has declined with the silting up of its historic natural harbour. The village has a rich historical tradition. It used to be a centre for flourishing arts and crafts. Little of that remains today.

The village includes a part of the estuary of Gad River, salt marshes, fertile river plains and forested hills. It has a population close to 9,000, distributed over twelve main *wadis*. The wadis in turn have several smaller hamlets containing clustered neighbourhood groupings separated from each other by streams, farms and hilly grazing pastures. Women constitute over 65 percent of the village population because of male outmigration to the cities.

While the largest population group is Hindu, there are smaller groups of Muslims and Roman Catholics. Among Hindus the majority group is of the dominant Maratha caste, who are Kshatriyas, followed by the Kunbi peasant caste who are slightly lower in the caste hierarchy, and the Pujari caste, both also referred to as Marathas in contemporary usage. There are a few landed Saraswat families, and even fewer, but relatively prosperous Bramhan families. There is a group of the Bhandari community of cultivators, and another group of carpenters, the Mestry community, both categorized among Other Backward Classes (OBC). The Devli families comprise the temple servants, much lower in the caste hierarchy. Then there are separate hamlets housing groups of people from the Scheduled Castes. These include the Chambhars and the Mahars, as they call themselves even now. The latter are divided into Hindus and neo-Buddhists.

The village has a primary health centre, and two or three doctors run private practices. There are two higher secondary schools, a technical school, and several primary schools, at least one for each major wadi. Depending on the number of young children in each wadi, there are several anganwadis, or pre-primary schools. There are also three or four mahila mandals or women's associations in a few wadis. The village is now well connected by public bus service to Malvan, to other towns and villages in the district and to Bombay. It has a post office, a police out-post, branches of a nationalized bank and the district co-operative bank. By now most of the village wadis have been given electricity connections, although power failures are common. What is striking is that there are more temples all over the village than all the institutions and services put together.

I was almost totally unacquainted with the village and with the Kokan region or its distinctive culture before I began my research. My family had migrated to Bombay at the start of this century, and only minimal contact with the village was possible as the years went by. My parents and their siblings were born in Bombay, and were the products of an urban upbringing, through their lives as city professionals.

When I began to delve deeper into cross-cultural studies of women as a postgraduate student in the United States, it became clear that very little material on this region was available for doctoral research. A year later, I was on my first state transport bus to the Kokan, a journey that seemed so innocuous then. A progression of events, described in a later chapter, led me to my own ancestral village, Masure.

The research was initiated in 1983, and discontinued from the point of view of the dissertation by mid-1988. At a certain stage the force of circumstances ensured that I gave up being an outsider and simply took over the persona of a village woman, although from an unabashedly privileged position compared to the poor women farmers who became friends and family. I had given up the vantage point of professional neutrality and research objectivity; otherwise I would not have lasted in the village beyond the first two weeks. This book, which is based on my doctoral dissertation, attempts to portray the inner world of village women. It delineates their affinities and interactions, particularly their responses to oppressive male domination in the prevalent social system. The impact of modernization within a depressed economy unresponsive to genuine needs and concerns of poor villagers engaged in subsistence agriculture, male out-migration in search of jobs, ecological devastation of a prosperous subtropical rainforest region, and the forces of religion and ritual are vital factors that form the backdrop to this study.

Research Methodology

The core part of the research consists of an exploration of the world of four women farmers and their interactions with their families, community and the village, to experience their subjective view of their lives and struggles. Interwoven within this fabric is my own story of awakening and transformation as a part of a long process that culminated as I wrote the book. The major part of the book is formed by four extensive case studies of village women. These women became friends who readily shared their lives with me without any reservation. That I was allowed to become a part of the farmers' community, both women and men accepting me in their fold as one of their very own, was a valuable lesson to me. I would like to hope that the case studies take the reader beyond restrictive stereotypes and dehumanising clichés to the real world at the grassroots.

The main protagonists' true stories are presented in a narra-

tive style, in a deliberately circular, rambling manner of story-
telling that is an integral part of the Malvani language. I have
made all reasonable efforts to conceal the subjects' identities. I
wish particularly to emphasize that I have tried to restrict my
own biases and judgements while presenting the women's stories. I consider it very important to understand the value of
narrating crucial events in the women's lives from their own
perspective. I appreciate the fact that they have made themselves vulnerable to negative criticism, having shared their
lives with an uncharacteristic level of openness and detail. I
have also tried to remain true to the central characters' own
biases as these affect their interactions with others. Thus at
times the interchanges appear to be too harsh, but the village
world at the subsistence level, given all the insecurities and
oppression in the lives of the residents, is itself fairly harsh. If
any person appearing in a case study seems too unsympatheti-
cally delineated, it is not because that is my view, but is rather
a reflection of the protagonist's own prejudice, which I have
reported as a subjective representation of the reality.

These women are friends who lent themselves to me during
my stay in the village. They were thus subjectively and almost
automatically selected for inclusion. Their life stories present
fascinating and valuable facets of farm women's existence
through various life stages, areas of ritual and work functioning, and through fine class distinctions within an almost homogeneous grouping. Apart from reasons of accessibility and
acceptance, there are no theoretical and methodological issues
involved in selecting these particular women for the study.

The factors of caste and class are not central to the present
study except that they intrinsically determine the nature of
interactions in the village. Three of the women belong to the
dominant Maratha caste in the village, while the fourth belongs
to the group of carpenters who also have small farms. They are
all more or less from the same class category of poor farmers,
owning less than five acres of cultivable land. Small parts of
their land lie fallow in peak agricultural seasons because of lack
of labour. Very fine and subtle distinctions prevail amongst

themselves in terms of class, as described later. Very few, the lucky ones, get regular money orders from migrant labourers in Bombay, and even then the sums are very small.

I have had the privilege of observing at close quarters many other women's lives in several neighbourhood communities in the village, sometimes across all caste and religious groupings. Any woman's story could have become a legitimate part of this study, and there are as many variations in styles of functioning and creative adaptation to their environment as there are women in the village. This is a crucial observation, since we often tend to generate invalid stereotypes about a whole people from very individualistic and subjective presentations. While I believe that my observations of these four women's experiences, as interwoven with vignettes of contrasting styles of other women and even men flitting through the passages of this study are fairly accurate representations of the reality, I also wish to assert the need to respect a divergent world-view, individual opinions and differing choices exercised by each woman. This perspective can get submerged under suffocating portrayals of a homogeneous village society with a rigidly hierarchical system of interrelations.

Besides participant observation, the process of data collection included several indepth and open-ended interviews with the four main protagonists of the case studies: Kaki, Akka, Parvati and Savitri. The women were very frank and forthcoming in their responses, a result of the trust and confidence assiduously built up during my stay in the village. I was not required to pressurize them in any way, and the credibility of the research was never in doubt. At each stage, a clear explanation was given about why a particular aspect of their life was being probed and how such information would contribute towards developing a greater understanding of the issues at hand. This included explaining the connection between research and policy formulation as it might influence their lives over a period of time. Such information was given in a simple, easily understood manner. It reaffirmed the purpose of this research in the context of gender studies. I also emphasized that reasonable efforts would be made to protect their names and identities.

Once the personal histories were noted in a draft format, separate individual sessions were conducted with each respondent. These were used to provide feedback, to reascertain their consent on including sensitive personal information voluntarily shared by them during previous interviews, to obtain further clarification about controversial statements, and in general to probe their ideas and attitudes towards specific issues arising out of the case studies. Later joint focused group interviews were held with the four women. These excluded sensitive personal information because sharing this could be very threatening when acquaintances were present. Group interviews helped to clarify the commonalties and divergences in their experiences and attitudes. Similar joint exercises were scheduled over the draft on folklore. All the individual sessions perhaps allowed for safe ventilation and they also helped the women to develop a long-term perspective on their own lives and relationships. These sessions were sometimes painfully cathartic and were at other times tinged with humour. This was often a two-way process, especially in joint interviews, when the women did not hesitate to comment on my own life as they saw it, especially over my own transition, as revealed over a period of several years spent in the village. This of course involved a great amount of good-natured ribbing as well as compassion for my predicament.

Data collection for this research included discussions about individual perceptions of various aspects of village life and its culture, including matters of fine caste and gender distinctions, discussions with close kin of the four women protagonists and other residents of the village. There were easily more than sixty such respondents, women belonging to the Muslim and the Christian communities, and the Mahar, Kunbi, Pujari, Bramhan, Saraswat, Sutar, Bhandari and other OBC groups, as well as with the dominant Maratha caste households, including the ruling clan. Other such respondents included some of the teachers, nurses, doctors, para professionals, big landlords, tradespeople, *gram panchayat* members, village-level officials and the local police. I also interviewed over twenty-five district- and taluka-level government officials and administrators, professionals, journalists and socially committed organizers who were mostly from the district towns of Malvan, Kudal, Sawantwadi and Kankavli. Among all of them, I found a great extent of misconceptions about life in the village and its people. They spoke frankly and perceived me more or less as a person sharing their own urban, middle-class-to-wealthy status with concomitant values, in addition to being 'highly educated' and 'foreign-returned'. They never failed to express astonishment over my single status and my commitment to living in the village.

Besides these respondents, significant information was obtained from more than twenty-five migrants who had left the village for the city and were mostly from the working class. I also discussed important issues with intellectuals, organizers and trade union activists who belonged to the migrant working class. Finally I must mention eight city politicians who were involved in the Kokan and who belonged to the established political parties in the state. I received little resistance from all the above groupings particularly because I was a Kokani and was living in the village for a protracted period. Moreover, the credibility of my research was helped by my organizational work in the village. I had developed a fair amount of rapport with each respondent by following an unobtrusive, gradually evolving approach. This helped ultimately in obtaining special insights into the issues and problems of the region from various perspectives. My thesis evolved as a careful synthesis of salient points emerging from these discussions, interviews, group activities and my own experiences both as a researcher and as a daughter-come-home.

Amongst the group of four women protagonists there exists a variety of strategies of compromising with, yielding to, subverting or transcending the traditional system of male dominance. These educate us about the ways in which individuals cope with rigid definitions and prescriptions of behaviour, and about the considerable loss to society in terms of wastage of so much creativity and intelligence expended in manipulative efforts to combat counterproductive systems like patriarchy.

The book points to the awesome wages of a monstrous mutation of traditional, ritualized caste and kinship-based patriarchy on the one hand, and, on the other, modern capitalist patriarchy as it prevails within the interconnected nexus of male out-migration for city jobs, myth of a money-order economy and increasing marginalization of the primarily female subsistence economy of the research village. It describes in particular how this system undermines life structures and identities of both women and men.

Review of the Literature

Berkeley, circa 1989. One of my professors has just bought a book on women and childbearing in India (Patricia Jeffery et al 1988). She makes a brief detour at a copy shop before she meets me. She waves the book at me with a broad smile. It has a nice cover photograph of four North Indian girls sitting in a small room, in a domestic vignette. The blurb says 'agrarian relations in North India cannot be understood if women and their activities—including biological reproduction—continue to be marginalized. The "private" act of childbearing cannot be divorced from its social and economic context, for women's experience of work and childbearing are deeply influenced by class and household politics'. But the professor has an interesting anecdote to report, which makes the whole issue leap out of the two-dimensional pages of the book into our relatively distant lives in the Western Hemisphere.

Do Women Work?

An Indian employee at the copy shop who sees the book in the professor's hands demands to know what the book is about. As she begins to explain about the theme of women and work, he flings both his arms dramatically in the air, cutting her short as he grandly proclaims, 'Women in India don't work. They sit around the house doing nothing but gossip to idle away their time, while hard-working husbands bring home money for their livelihood.' She tries to remonstrate about the condition of poor women but he ends the brief conversation saying, 'all women, all women'. He points to the book as he walks away, 'They get pregnant so they can sit at home and do nothing, demanding this and that from their poor overworked husbands.' Such is the view of the 'ordinary man in the streets'.

Indeed, it is not just the ordinary man in the streets who bears this dismissive attitude towards serious women's issues. When I returned to India with my research proposal on women and work in rural India my former boss quipped at a meeting of upper class bureaucrats, 'Do women work?' There was no need to say more about finer theoretical aspects amid the ensuing laughter. When I reached the village, petty officials were surprised that I had chosen village women for research on women and work. 'You won't find working women here in the village,' they patronizingly explained. 'Those are all in the cities. Village women don't do any work.'

These are significant examples of how a prevailing cultural ideology not only shapes reality but also serves to distort perceptions and attitudes in a manner quite contrary to the realities of existence. Whether expressed in blandly ignorant terms, with exaggerated mannerisms that heavily underscore the power of machismo, or when expressed in a gentle, witty style delicately laced with sarcasm, usually as the last word on gender, such quintessential patriarchal arrogance marks the everyday reality of women all over the world. Even while feminist scholars have disproved the myth of the male breadwinner and the dependent housewife model across all cultures, the harshest stereotypes persist where patriarchal oppression is at its crudest in terms of the denial of basic human rights and protection to the largest group of vulnerable citizens.

Socioeconomic Studies on Village Women

The issues of women and development, women and poverty, women and agriculture were basically non-issues until Ester Boserup (1970) arrived with her landmark study based on data from Africa, Asia and Latin America, drawing attention to a badly neglected area. Arriving a few years ahead of the International Women's Year in 1975, which began with an unprecedented international conference to discuss the status of women around the world, Boserup's study proved to be a catalytic factor in opening up the field of women and development to critical inquiry. This further revolutionized our understanding of issues related to rural women, their work and their lives.

In her study, Boserup traced the marked decline in women's economic status under colonial and postcolonial states. What made governments around the developing world sit up and take notice was her clear thesis that the lack of understanding and consequent neglect of women's role by economists and development planners had itself led to the marginalization and pauperization of women and their families. She contended that biases, prejudices and misunderstandings related to women's labour force participation had eroded the household economic base, thus contributing to an overall increase in poverty. Thus integrating women into the process of socioeconomic development was of vital importance in achieving overall development.

The Report of the Committee on Status of Women, Government of India (1974), presented startling facts and figures of an overall decline in women's status in India in all areas. Their most shocking finding was regarding the steady decline in the ratio of females to males in India over the decades, in sharp contrast to corresponding figures in developed societies. This indicated that female mortality was very high for infants and for women in childbirth and was caused by severe malnourishment. Asok Mitra's detailed analysis of census data (1980) agreed with the findings of other researchers: there was a sharp decline in labour force participation of women in India, particularly in agriculture, with a corresponding rise in female unemployment over several decades up to 1971. The issue of including women's work in a subsistence economy, in the grey area between domestic and farm work, and in the unorganized sectors of the economy merited close attention. For example, a particularly vexing issue was whether and how to include women's part-time or seasonal work in agriculture.

On the other hand, Dixon (1982) and Beneria (1982) address-ed the issue of invisibility of the woman worker in third world agriculture. They raised questions concerning problems of defi-nition and procedure in data collection that lead to gross under-counting of women's farm work in labour force statistics. Rogers (1980) documented the extent to which sexist biases of planners misrepresent and distort women's economic participation in planning for development. Charlton (1984) has emphasized the fallacies in assigning women to 'special projects' rather than aim-ing for the full integration of their economic roles in rural devel-opment programmes. Dixon-Mueller (1985) has assessed many issues on sex-based task specialization and access to agricultural resources, showing critical features in intervention which would help improve women's participation and their benefits.

Of particular relevance are the studies dealing with important issues concerning rural women, especially regarding the status of women in rice agriculture (Chakravorty 1975; Omvedt 1978; Mencher et al 1979; Mencher and Saradamoni 1982; Miller 1982; Sen 1982; Gulati 1983; Mencher 1983, Jan 1985, April 1985; Krishna Raj and Jyoti Ranadive 1984; Agarwal 1984; Bardhan 1984, 1985; Mies et al 1986). Researchers generally agreed that women, and not men, are the mainstay of subsistence agricul-ture in paddy cultivation areas. Women in these areas constitute a vast pool of agricultural labour, and thus serve to suppress overall wages for women. Women usually work longer hours at more tedious, low skilled and underpaid jobs.

They also agreed that women in these regions contribute in greater proportion to household consumption needs, thus giving the lie to the general assumption that women are at best sup-plementary providers. They highlighted the increase in de facto female-headed families in the rural areas, along with an overall increase in poverty for those households where women were primary providers. With the ingress of capitalist farming in rural areas, the researchers also witnessed large-scale margi-nalization of women in agriculture and their consequent pau-perization. They warned that neglecting women's economic role in development planning would lead to an increase in rural poverty.

Agarwal (1986, 1988) linked the important issue of depletion of natural resources, and the increasing appropriation of what remains by a few, questioning the long-term viability of agricultural yields under the present agricultural policy. The issue of ecological conservation is conversely tied up with that of capitalist agricultural development and marginalization of women in the economy, and needs to be given special attention in studies of rural women. Mies (1976) and Beneria (1982) forcefully argued that the problem of the deteriorating status of women in the third world will not be resolved by greater inclusion of women in the process for social change nor by the integration of women's needs in development assistance programmes. These very programmes foster economic and political dependencies that serve capital accumulation. According to them, the roots of female marginalization are structurally embedded in the capitalization of third world economies, and a radical transformation of capitalist patriarchy is necessary to bring about positive change.

In her study of women lace-makers, Mies (1981) also highlighted the polarization of economic interests between men and women within the household. For example, she found that men tend to have interests that may be sharply divergent from those of women and their families, leading to a schism in the family in terms of utilization of money and joint resources for the benefit of all rather than just for the men themselves. In the lace-making business, where the producers are all grossly overworked 'housewives', it is a hierarchical chain of men in the household acting as middlemen, local traders, and international entrepreneurs who profit from the enterprise. This was made possible by the displacement of women from agriculture brought about by the capitalization of farming, and their subsequent 'housewifization'. The effect on women themselves is a lowering of their autonomy, health and overall status, and even destitution at times.

Rubin (1975) and Hartmann (1976) provided important

theoretical perspectives on how the work of men and women—both in and outside the household—fits into a complementary interlocking pattern within the broader economic system. They stressed that gender-based division of labour, involving women's domestic labour and men's labour force activity is directly or indirectly linked to the economic system. Both types of activities are essential to economic production and reproduction of the workforce.

Of special relevance here is Burawoy's (1976) study of migrant workers in South Africa and the USA. He discussed the impact of spatial separation of the units of production and reproduction, that is, the workplace and the permanent home. He asserted, with particular reference to black workers in South Africa, that the payment of marginal wages, coupled with inadequate living conditions ensures the dependence of the worker on his rural kin, by making it impossible for him to achieve any kind of permanence or security in the city. This observation is equally true in the case of seasonal migrant villagers from the Kokan, who continue to depend on their rural families in spite of working in towns and cities for a major part of the year. The Centre for Science and Environment (1985: 179-82) also draws attention to the general fallacies concerning male migrant labour and the myth of the money-order economy, as to how the latter generates false stereotypes about rural women.

Zeidenstein and others (1979) discussed general methodological aspects of research on women in agricultural production in developing countries. They discussed the use of specific instruments for data collection and analysis, including charts for rural women's time use, individual and household labour and income modules, and pictorial charts for self-reporting respondents. They also underscored the need for high quality microlevel data for a better understanding of rural women as a prerequisite to planning for social change. Binswanger and others (1980) discussed interdisciplinary methodological issues in rural household studies in Asia.

Jain (1976) and Dixon (1978) presented fascinating studies of existing innovative programmes to assess avenues for organizing and employing rural women in India. These include a diverse range of small-scale regional programmes and activities, including dairy cooperatives, women's cooperative banks, self-employed women's union, traditional groupings of women artists and organized militancy by women on social issues such as prohibition of liquor sales.

Traditional Social Hierarchy in India

Srinivas (1962, 1987) made a radical departure from the earlier views on the Indian caste system as a rigid hierarchical form of the fourfold typology of *varna*: Brahman, Kshatriya, Vaishya and Shudra. He provided ethnographic evidence that revealed the fallacies of this belief and formulated the concept of the dominant caste. Raheja (1988) has developed this concept further through painstaking documentation of a North Indian village, grounding it in a central-peripheral configuration of castes rather than a hierarchical ordering. Advancing a view of caste as constituted of contextually shifting set of meanings rather than one overarching ideological feature, she gives the lie to Dumont's work (1980). Dumont offers a controversial interpretation of caste as a rigid hierarchical system based on the 'purity' of the Bramhan priest and the 'temporal power' of the Kshatriya ruler. The theory of the dominant caste as well as the central-peripheral configuration dependent on ritual gift-giving is strongly borne out by my own observations in the village.

Ethnographic Studies of Women and Villages

Among earlier village studies, Wiser and Wiser (1971) described life in Karimpur, a village east of Agra, and delineated the process of change in a study that portrayed the lives of villagers they encountered and interacted with as missionaries. Marriott (1955) raised the question of the interrelation of an Indian village with the larger society and with the civilization of which it is a small and local part. He talked about the critical issue concerning the dual process of interaction between village-level, indigenous ritual and belief which exists as a part of the 'little tradition', and the 'great tradition', which is the larger Sanskritic tradition of India.

Beteille (1965) described the process of contemporary change in a multi-caste village in South India. A later book (1974) discussed significant aspects of interdisciplinary research in village India. Also pertinent is Rosenthal (1977) who showed the evolution of the present political leadership from the capitalist agricultural lobbies of western Maharashtra. In his classic memoirs of research in a South Indian village, Srinivas (1976) took the reader on a sensitive and humorous journey through a typical multi-caste, traditional village, as a young Bramhan ethnographer, a bachelor, living as the guest of the village headman. He provided valuable insights concerning caste interrelationships and conflicts, and also regarding the status of the researcher. Srinivas and others (1979) presented a collection of papers on the trials and tribulations of field research, which I found particularly insightful in view of my own experiences in Masure.

However, while reading a majority of these earlier studies on village India, one wonders if women are at all important to the village structure and systems of social interaction. Descriptions of economic organization leave out women altogether, as Boserup pointed out so emphatically, without any admission of biases and limitations inherent to the study. This is a serious omission particularly in regions where women play a very significant role in supporting their households. Specially addressing these issues Rosaldo and Lamphere (1974) and Reiter (1975) in their edited collection of papers by women anthropologists provided the necessary boost to women's studies, with valuable insights in the field of cross-cultural studies of women. In an unconventional ethnography, Burgos-Debray (1984) introduced Rigoberta Menchu, a young Guatemalan Indian woman and national leader, recreating the whole ethos of the socio-political struggles of the Guatemalan Indian community through her life story. The study by Murphy and Murphy (1985) on the Mundurucu Indians in Brazil is also a valuable eye-opener in this regard, with its detailed description of women's activities within and outside the household.

Jeffery (1979) gave voice to secluded Muslim women from a Pirzada community in North India, sensitively portraying their concerns and aspirations in a very restricted setting. Ursula Sharma (1980) presented an ethnographic study of two North Indian villages, looking at women's roles in agricultural production and its effect on their overall status. She discussed the interaction of cultural norms controlling women's behaviour, economic constraints and kinship roles and obligations. She found that economic change per se led to very little improvement in the relationship between men and women in the household. Women depended more than ever on men, as holders of property and earners of cash.

Islam (1982) presented an interesting collection of papers by women researchers who described their experiences of fieldwork in Bangladesh. They raised important methodological and practical issues in field research on and by women in a traditional setting. It was an insightful adventure to sail through the excellent collection of personal reminiscences of several renowned women anthropologists compiled by Gold (1986).

Recent Research

There is now a wealth of material in gender studies since the period of my research, and I discuss some selected titles that are relevant to this study.

REVIVALIST-REFORMIST RESTRICTIONS AGAINST WOMEN UNDER BRITISH COLONIAL RULE

O'Hanlon (1994) has presented a fascinating translation of a radical essay by an unlikely firebrand Marathi author, Tarabai Shinde whose book was published in Pune in 1882. In her introductory critique, O'Hanlon sets the essay within the context of caste, class and gender in Maharashtra in the nineteenth century. Dwelling on the peculiar blending of Bramhan and Victorian prescriptions on the appropriate behaviour of women in society, and their implications for women across all castes and classes, she has speculated that social and religious identities in colonial times may have become more caste-bound than they were in pre-colonial India. Gender relations emerged as a powerful new means for the colonial hegemony itself. Shared idioms of femininity provided key groups of Indians and British alike with a common language in which they were able to discuss and agree on important aspects of the Indian social order.

Tarabai discussed a range of practical matters of particular relevance to the Maratha caste, including marriage mores and conventions concerning widowhood and purdah, women's education and personal mobility, domestic politics and problems in everyday marital and family relationships. She was concerned about the ways in which women were represented in texts of classical literature, newspapers, novels and plays, and with the process through which these textual norms and models of women's behaviour came to be invented and imposed.

Srinivasan (1988) had earlier described a similar coming together of religion, politics and state power in the late nineteenth century in Tamil Nadu in domesticating women and controlling their sexuality. He has delineated the process by which a community of women, the devadasis—deputed as slaves of Gods for service in temples—were deprived of their singularly privileged social and economic position in the name of community reform by mostly male, upper caste Hindu professionals who were strongly influenced by Victorian Christian missionary morality and religion. Yet the classical dance form of Bharatanatyam that the devadasis had preserved and practised exclusively was destigmatized, coopted and popularized by Bramhan women. Moreover, male relatives of the devadasis were offered patriarchal property rights that further deprived the women.

GENDER-SENSITIVE HOUSEHOLD STUDIES

Borooah and others (1994) have offered critical insights in the matter of gender-sensitive research. They have argued that data on women need to be grounded in the context—local, household and socioeconomic—and therein lies the problem of integrating these complexities and variations in the national data. We need more sophisticated conceptualizations of the interconnections among individuals, activities and structures. The three central arguments are that special research methods are necessary for obtaining quality and quantity data on women; household studies can capture the complexity of factors that affect individual behaviour and choice; and that because the field of women and development is by its very nature interventionist, such information is critical to the formulation of more efficient programmes and policies. They also emphasize the need for improving research methods and for training students to undertake gender-sensitive and policy relevant data. Together, the various authors make a persuasive case for in-depth household-level research, the use of multidisciplinary and even interdisciplinary teams of researchers. They also caution against equating development of the hinterland with commercial and industrial development, which invariably leads to ecological destruction.

Sinha (1992) has explored how gender roles in India are embodied in space. She has used two case studies of a Muslim community in a village and a predominantly Hindu community in a newly constructed housing project on the fringes of a city in North India. Analysing the linkages between spatial organization of both the house and the neighbourhood and gender-appropriate behaviour, she found that space contains a clue to behaviour and is instrumental in communicating social norms.

Allen and Mukherjee (1990) have presented an interdisciplinary collection of papers in an attempt to understand the seeming paradoxes in the social life of women in India and Nepal as expressed in rites and rituals. Pointing to the cultural practice of lumping together women and Shudras, that is, the untouchables, who are often jointly referred to as prime pollutants—the former temporarily on account of menstruation, and the latter permanently because of their lowly caste and occupational status—Krygier (1990) has discussed menstrual seclusion, as it affects the hierarchy between the sexes within all caste groups.

In his analysis of Chetri women in Nepali households, Gray (1990) has sportingly confessed to the ethnographic bias in his study since he talked only with men about women and men in the domestic sphere. According to him, in a society where there is overt and formal acknowledgement of the superior status of men in both the public and domestic domains, women may be posited as an anthropological problem on the methodological level. Also the symbolic ambiguity about women—as good and evil, powerful and weak, and the wife's progression from being the bearer of sons to the divider of the joint household—creates a double-bind context. This constitutes a problem both on the analytic level of explanation and on the folk-level of pragmatic action. Gray had investigated the patrilineal joint family wherein there is status differentiation between all the household members, particularly a hierarchy separating the *chelibeti*, that is, women who are born into the family, and conjugal women, that is, women who have entered the clan through marriage.

Allen (1990) has described and analysed rites performed by the Newars of Nepal, highlighting their similarities and differences with comparable rites of the Nayars in South India. He has argued that among those castes that are fully committed to the ideology of 'purity', a strong emphasis is placed on male control of female sexuality. As castes perpetuate lineage-based structures, high value is accorded to those women who maintain the lineage by producing sons. Allen suggests that the solution to the problem of sexuality and reproduction lay in the development of three customs: the betrothal of girls prior to menstruation, the absolute control of sexually active women by their husbands, and the prohibition against widow remarriage.

Kumar (1994) has presented an excellent interdisciplinary cross-cultural collection discussing methodologies for conceptualizing women. Women, like other underprivileged groups, present a challenge because of the total dominance of the repressive structures within which they exist. Women as subjects are deployers of alternative discourses who manipulate normative signs and create new spaces for themselves. Thus protest can take the form of evasive tactics, counter-cultures of language, genres of song and dance, myths full of double entendres, private correspondence, diary writing and many pressure tactics. In her chapter, Raheja (1994) has examined several aspects of the speech of rural North Indian women, focusing on two genres of oral expression in which aspects of patrilineal kinship are commented upon, critiqued and resisted.

Women's ritual songs and proverbs make visible the contradictions within dominant North Indian discourses concerning kinship, marriage and gender, and in doing so begin to subvert their authority. Raheja has stressed that she views such discursive forms and the alternative normal sensibilities encoded within them as 'a condition of political resistance rather than a substitute for it'. She has outlined the terms in which these forms expose and critique the contradictions within North Indian kinship and indicate the ways in which they articulate a subversive moral perspective that is invoked within the constraints set by patrilineal kinship in North India.

WOMEN AND WORK AND THE FEMINIZATION OF POVERTY

Papa (1992) has presented nine case studies across various caste groups belonging to the poverty population in an Andhra village. She found that female participation in agriculture was higher than male participation for all farm sizes, including both progressive and non-progressive forms. Women's work roles include agricultural work, and there is clear non-recognition of their contribution. Wage discrimination is also commonly practised against women. Papa has stressed the need for developing the cultural and social reform base for improving the lives of women, especially through education.

Lingam (1994) has argued that although marital dissolution by death of the spouse, divorce, separation and desertion are the most common reasons why women become heads of households, there is also growing evidence of wider causes contributing to their increase. These include changes in the occupational base, agricultural policies, landholding patterns and patron-client relationships along with population growth. She has highlighted the structural constraints faced by women in their status as household heads with low literacy, low asset holdings, lower productivity of lands, lesser access to avenues of income-earning and government assistance and declining community support systems. Ganesh and Risseeuw (1993) have provided valuable insights into the dissolution of kinship systems. In many developing countries, it is assumed that kin networks will continue to take care of social security needs. On the one hand, the state does not purport to assume welfare functions in any comprehensive sense. On the other, macro-political and economic processes and policies are transforming those kinship structures and their caretaking functions, leaching out vulnerable categories of people—mainly women—from the security of the kinship net.

Ram (1992) has presented a micro-study of Christian Mukkuvar women from a fishing village in Tamil Nadu. She analyses the relationship between the economy and culture, including kinship, marriage and household formation. She has looked at the linkages between the family, the household economy and the economics of fishing and marketing. Describing the erosion of subsistence and artisanal fishing because of the growing use of foreign technology and the internationalization of the fishing trade, she points to the alienation of women from outdoor work, from the sea, and from trading activities. Thus women are in charge of the household economy, and the enhanced period of absence of the men enlarges this role. At the same time, women become increasingly dependent on money sent home by the men. This has given rise to the ambiguity of women's economic power. Sexual control cannot be easily enforced because of male absence which leads to the ambiguity of femininity in the cultural and religious spheres.

Gothoskar (1992) has edited an important collection of papers by scholars and activists involved in trade unions and in organizing women in the informal sectors of the economy in India. Although these papers are largely centred on the urban milieu, they contain valid implications for rural women workers in agriculture, in trades and crafts. They point out that women's participation in ongoing struggles is influenced by the diffuse boundaries between women's work and leisure, paid and unpaid work, and in work and non-work relations. These wider struggles often base themselves on the day-to-day ongoing struggles of women, usually alone and sometimes in smaller and bigger groups. Without these unceasing individual struggles, not only are collective struggles not possible, but the very survival of women depends on these. The basic struggle for women revolves around trying to get enough for their families and for procuring the most basic necessities of life such as food, water, fuel, fodder and shelter. This struggle is made even more grim because as women they have very little control over the conditions and products of their labour. Moreover, they have almost no say in deciding who gets how much of the family's meagre resources.

Kulkarni (1994) has provided the background for understanding the rural economy. She has conducted a very interesting statistical comparison among the major states in India, based on the figures available from the 1981 and the 1991 census surveys, indicating the dependence of rural workers on agriculture. She has offered special perspectives on the gender-based distinctions in this area. She suggests that Maharashtra is in no way better than some of the backward states. Maharashtra, which is the most industrialized state in India, has shown a decline of only 0.13 percentage points as far as the dependence of rural workers on agriculture is concerned, which clearly reflects the excessive concentration of industrialization in big cities, not accompanied by a corresponding economic transformation in rural areas. Maharashtra also shows a substitution process in the agricultural sector in which male workers, who are possibly favoured in the matter of jobs in the non-agricultural sector, are replaced by female agricultural workers. A study of the percentage of the total increase in rural workers absorbed into the agricultural sector between 1981 and 1991 shows that the increase in female work   is as high as 94 percent. It can be conjectured that the corresponding figures may be even higher in districts like Sindhudurg with a higher overall proportion of women to men, although the latest district data of the census are not yet available. The proportion of female agricultural labourers compared to that of cultivators who work on their own family farms and rural non-agricultural workers is also higher in Maharashtra. Among the cultivator group there is a substantial change in the sex ratio in the last decade, favouring women, which has risen from 49.31 women per hundred men to 64.94. There is sufficient basis to suggest that there has been an even greater increase in Sindhudurg district. It should be noted that the reporting of women workers from cultivator-families belonging to the upper castes may continue to be suppressed because of the patriarchal biases among both cultivators and census-takers.

THE NEW ECONOMIC POLICY IN INDIA (NEP)

Vyas (1993) has offered a general analysis of the new economic policy in India. He has suggested that if the poor are to participate in the growth which the NEP promises, concentrated action is needed in several directions. Increased investment in infrastructure and human resource development, emphasis on programmes that will provide them with an assets and skills base, strengthening the public distribution system catering to their basic needs, and devising timely social security measures for the 'new poor' are urgently required.

Sharing important ecological perspectives, Kumud Sharma (1994) has asserted that the effect of fiscal and monetary policies on women is determined by social and gendered patterns of resource use and control in rural households. Implementation of Structural Adjustment Programmes (SAP) sharpens the conflict between the use of land and other resources for food production and subsistence needs and use for commercial exploitation. It is crucial to realize the role rural women have played in providing households with food security. Women also make significant contributions to maintaining biodiversity, sustainable agro-forestry systems, water management and innovative management of community resources. They are also hit harder than men by environmental degradation and can be helped by changes in the public distribution system of food grains, provision of drinking water, fuel and fodder, health care and education.

Joy Ranadive (1994) bolsters the arguments of Vyas and Sharma, suggesting that the interface between macro-politics such as the Adjustment Policy Programme (APP) and the micro-unit of the household lies in the latter acting as a buffer that absorbs shocks released by the former. Whatever happens within markets in agriculture and industry, the repercussions reverberate at the household level as they affect demand, supply and price variables. There is an inherent male bias in the formulation of the seemingly gender-neutral macro-APP in that it does not account for the cost and investment of time and effort on the part of women in the production and maintenance of human resources. Policies often affect men and women differently, which is not given due importance by policy makers. The formulation of the safety net, part of the APP, should also take women's needs into consideration. Unless the unit of the household is opened up for investigation, the true impact of the APP cannot be identified, without which an effective safety net cannot be devised.

Shah and others (1994) have attempted to link the political and social implications of these economic policies on women's lives and work with the development of strategies for survival and empowerment. They suggest organizational strategies in relation to women's paid and unpaid labour to improve the quality of their lives and lay the basis for empowering them towards the transformation of the structures of their subordination.

THE POLICY FOR WOMEN IN MAHARASHTRA

Gothoskar and others (1994) have provided an excellent section-by-section critique of the Government of Maharashtra's proposed Policy for Women, announced in 1994, which covers its plus points as well as its inherent contradictions. The policy is designed to contain popular dissent and to diffuse the discontent expressed by popular social and political movements, particularly in an election year. In order to legitimize itself in the eyes of the electorate, the policy provides a populist programme to coopt women's long-standing demands, but it has its own agenda. It makes no comments on the sexual division of labour and the rights of minority women. It does not mention the amply documented details on the oppression of women, and there is no recognition of the women's movement. Among the contradictions is the proposal to generate revenue for the policy of closing liquor shops by a cess on liquor. All the policies that would help women, for example, on property and inheritance rights, are mostly applicable to Hindu women in the absence of a uniform civil code in place of the personal law of each religious community. Moreover, the policy concentrates on reproductive health alone, without providing for an integrated women's health programme.

OF WOMEN AND MEN

As a lone woman researcher in a traditional village, I was interested in learning about personal experiences of other single women doing research in similar circumstances, but none of the books just discussed touch on this aspect of research. More significantly, I discovered that a majority of women ethnographers in these studies were accompanied by their husbands. Their insights about their work and travel, facilitated or hindered because of this fact, would have proved very valuable in understanding the process of interaction and acceptance between researchers and village communities. It is surprising that very few studies pay attention to this critical aspect of the research process.

This book has evolved out of a concern for understanding the dynamics of the status and the role of poor woman farmers in the Kokan, about whom very little is known in the social science literature. The studies included in the foregoing review of literature have helped to provide very little information on the wages of research and the toll it takes on the researcher, particularly when a study is located in a strange milieu or when it involves a relatively lengthy duration of stay in a traditional community. This is a matter of concern because I know that at least on a couple of occasions very fine cross-cultural research proposals never took off because the student researcher developed cold feet just before taking the final plunge, after considerable investment of time, money and energy. Perhaps a primer on how to get introduced to a community in a traditional society, how to gain acceptance for purposes of research, giving practical guidelines and morale boosting advice, as well as tips on what pitfalls to avoid, would prove of immense help to the itinerant ethnographer at the point of take-off.

Many studies undertaken by women have focussed on the exploitation and oppression of women in a rigidly hierarchical traditional society as it prevails in the villages of India, with a view of women as passive subjects of gross discrimination. While discussing change and deterioration in social relations in the rural agrarian milieu as a result of the ingress of the capitalist economy, researchers of gender relations have paid scant attention to the ways in which the traditional male power of individual men in the village is also undermined within the overarching patriarchal system. The discussion on domestic atrocities in villages, which are thankfully less frequent than in the cities, ought to point out that not all village men are drunkards and wife-beaters. The very issue of the use of muscle power by local landlords and increasing police atrocities in the countryside point to psychological 'emasculation' of poor village men. Thus corruption and elite terrorism, or threat of the same, deprive village men of traditional male power, while the inexorable forces of a depressed economy take away their economic power. The important issue of how these factors themselves influence the nature of gender relations within rural households has not been attended to sufficiently in studies on women.

This book touches on this subject even while maintaining its focus on the subjective world of village women. It goes beyond viewing women as passive recipients of derogatory treatment and explores the dynamics of strategic options exercised by individual women in coping with the daily struggle for survival.

An exploratory, micro-level research study, its goal is to gain fresh perspectives on the lives of poor farm women at the grass-roots. It seeks to understand the extent to which observations of life and work of poor village women, particularly in other rice growing regions of India, are also validated in the Kokan. It also seeks to understand the impact of macro-factors such as male out-migration and male dominance from their own subjective point of view.

Note on Usage

I have preferred to use Malvani and Marathi words to reflect the language as it is used in Masure. For instance, I use *Kokan* and not the colonial 'Konkan' for the region, *Kokani* and not 'Konkani' for the language, *Bramhan* and not 'Brahmin'. Similarly, the *Ramayan*, the *Mahabharat* and the *Kashi Khand* are spelt the w   that regional people speak of these texts and not as the Rama   na', the 'Mahabharata' and the 'Kashi Khanda' as is more usua_ _n academic literature in English. Also, words like *Bhain* and *Dhaikala* are used in keeping with the farm women's speech, rather than 'Bhavin' or 'Dahikala', as spoken by educated people in the region.

CHAPTER I

The Woman Researcher

IT IS ALMOST three o'clock as I walk through the fields in the
sultry summer afternoon, making my way across the dry
stream bed strewn with sand and pebbles on the east side of
the wadi. As I head towards the Bharateshwar temple, the short
cut involves climbing over the permanent breach in the useless
concrete dam. It is an hour of stillness with not a soul in sight,
and the very palpable heat surrounds me like a sheath of comfort as I walk on the cracked earth full of parched rice stalks.
The sky is blindingly white with the severe subtropical sun still
almost directly overhead. The earth is a dry and dusty red ochre
in colour. The lonely walk provides a few surreal moments in
a spaced dimension apart from the regular bustle of village life.

An occasional light breeze stirs the leaden air. The ground
underfoot may be of a dusty dryness, the sky ruthlessly ablaze
with the white light, and the surrounding air a cloak of extra
warmth in the hotness; but on the fringes of my vision there
are tall swaying coconut palms with dark green shadows of
fronds, waving me on my way. There is always some lush greenery by the dry stream bed, drawing succour from a deep spring
well invisible to the eye. Distant trees provide a cool soothing
contact to my burning, almost vaporizing vision.

In the Seasons of My Mind

Always, there are signs of life around, even in the afternoon
stillness. There is a brood of poultry pecking in the soil under a

hedge for worms. A mother hen lets out a loud squawk, fluttering around her hatchlings with wings beating the air, perhaps alarmed by the approach of a predatory jungle crow. It could be a snake slithering in the underbrush. There are vultures circling over the horizon, scouting for the carcasses of dead cattle deposited near the burning grounds.

The dogs are all cooling off in the shaded mud porches, and it is too soon for cattle to venture out in the heat. Yet an occasional buffalo may be seen dipping in a stagnant pool left behind by the stream waters long gone on their way to the river. There are little boys playing hide and seek behind old mango trees, waiting for the ripe mangoes to plop down at their feet every few minutes. It is questionable whether children or even adults need much food in the brief summer months in the village. Even in that godforsaken dryness, when water becomes scarce, the earth is ever-gracious with her bounty of treasures, flung freely at willing adventurers. These include mangoes, cashew fruits and nuts, jackfruits and a myriad other gifts.

A year-round spring well in the courtyard, unblocked by rocks deep in the womb of the earth, is a special boon that only a few households enjoy. For the rest, particularly the womenfolk, come April begins the long dreary labour of fetching water from distant wells, and an additional stretch of time spent in the washing. At a time like that the few wells still left with water become public property according to respected village traditions. For there is no greater sin than to deny water to the needy, as old Madhgya once tells me. Of course, the lower castes and menstruating women must stand by respectfully for other women to draw and pour out water for them—a task never denied—since they must not pollute the water supply at its source.

From then on the soul longs for nothing but an early start to the monsoon showers bringing sufficient floods and deluge to fill up the deepest of dry wells, spring water rushing with mad abandon over the previously dry pebbles. One more turn of the wheel of life, and it is the urgency of farm work that overwhelms the mind, great anxiety over drought and famine receding far for at least one more year.

It is hard to decide which is the best part of the year in
Masure. The fondest of childhood memories may belong to these
hot and 'fruitful' summer months spent as vagabonds adrift
from the dreary bondage of school life, during the long vacations
at the end of each academic year. There are always compensations and amusements, as hordes of visitors from Bombay are
off-loaded by the frequent summertime buses, crowding markets and meeting places in a swirl of red dust. In the overly
wet monsoon months from June to September even as the damp
sometimes seeps to the bones, there is the joy of flowers and
vegetable gardens through the whirl of a heavy farming season.
There are many school holidays during which chilling rains fall
in a nonstop downpour lasting several days, when huge trees
come crashing down, obliterating electric poles and wires, and
rivers and streams flood in swirling eddies. Roads and walkways are invariably washed away, isolating each hamlet and
the village itself from larger civilization. The whole space containing the sky and the air lowers in an intense passionate
greyness hovering amidst the jungle treetops. A heart-stopping
lushness of green vegetation runs riot with not a square inch
of the earth left bare. The grounds teem with all kinds of new
life, from coral-red splashes of baby millipedes, to lavender coloured orchids and huge mushrooms in the rotting forest soil.
When the sun peeps out occasionally from behind glowering
black clouds, the whole world turns into a glimmering rainbow
prism of light and warmth. Then we have to watch out particularly for the scores of varieties of snakes, big and small, deadly
poisonous or harmless, as they come out of damp quarters to
stretch out languorously in the brief grassy warmth.

The winter months, roughly around November to March, are
at times exceedingly cold in the forest elevation of this particular
hamlet. Enchanting mists arise from the stillness of streams in
the early mornings. Old people walk around like shivering
wraiths with arms tightly drawn across their chests for what
little warmth can be summoned from their aging selves. Houses
lack insulation, with open spaces between the roof and the walls
and between each row of roof tiles. Bodies huddled together pro-

vide some warmth in the coldest part of the pre-dawn hours, even as whatever little warmth from the day long kitchen fire has totally dissipated. Many people then gather around their re-kindled kitchen hearths to warm for a while before going back to bed. There are still a few hours left to go before it is light. It is a special time of peace and tranquillity, as the previous crop has been harvested and a lighter round of winter farming is underway. The main excitement of these days is the bountiful seafood, particularly mackerel, that is generously available in the local markets. Spicy hot and sour fish and coconut curries or fried fish savouries are eaten with rice almost on a daily basis for the few months that seafood is so cheaply available.

Then there are the festivals, plenty of occasions for laughter, merry-making and good food. Even ancestral spirits, appearing in the form of crows, and cows are fondly given special offerings of consecrated food from the frequent feasts through the long festival season beginning in June and ending around April each year. In each distinct season of the year there are definite perils and pleasures that make living in the village such an exciting and sensuously gratifying experience. Each season offers full satiation of effort and reward, joy and heartache. One then looks forward to the next riot of refreshing surprises that spring out of forgotten memory into village reality, almost at the turn of a conjurer's wheel.

Always there is the anxiety of work piled up in a never-ending stream of survival tasks. Yet once you accept the supreme primacy that all this work has in the consciousness of an ordinary villager, and particularly for a farm woman—so unquestionably her reason for being—it is easy to understand the near-mystical connection that people have with their habitat, within the natural cycles of changing seasons amidst varying harvests, despite the grinding poverty. For most farmers there is no boundary line dividing their cognitive selves and their habitat, in an obvious symbiotic relationship with mother earth. I have also become a part of this strong inter-connectedness between nature and human beings. That is why I am so miserable at other times, living in concrete or synthetic housing, when the smell of earth mixed with fresh cowdung is missing from my life. I probably then share at a subliminal level the misery of the typical village migrant cut off from his roots.

The Village of My Dreams

My first visit to the village is in January 1983. It is not long past the yearly monsoons, and the alluring red of the village earth has not yet dried enough to fly in clouds of dust at the approach of vehicles. Under a clear violet sky, lush greenery overhangs the narrow winding roads hewn into the mountain sides. This is the village of my dreams, and the search is over even before I get acquainted with the site. There is more green here than my eyes have known in a long time. Houses with red country-tiled roofs in barely discernible hamlets neatly camouflaged amidst all the vegetation quickly pass out of sight. The hamlets seem cocooned in the forests. Further down, the road passes through open green fields with clusters of swaying coconut palms here and there. Dark patches of ploughed earth yet to be sown provide the contrast against variegated greenery of different crops growing in little plots of land, side-by-side. There are definite criteria for selecting a research village, such as population size and mix, and no doubt this one fits the bill. But at the back of my mind I know that it is something else that has settled the issue for me. It is the sense of belonging, before I have met even one villager. The site has selected its researcher, and I am home.

Armed with references and an assistant, I have extensively toured the district over the past three months, in repeated sorties from Bombay. The assistant is expected to introduce me to travelling over an unknown terrain, particularly because travelling alone entails certain risks for single women. This is a justifiable apprehension since I do not know if I will find myself alone without shelter in a strange district at nightfall. The assistant is also expected to help smooth my passage since I don't speak Malvani as yet. Malvani is a version of Kokani that derives its name from the town of Malvan, and it is spoken throughout the entire district. But my assistants keep changing, because none can stand the dreary boredom of dusty village tours for more than a few days.

I am busy familiarizing myself with the terrain, the texture and the culture of the region. It is a curious self-directed adventure which is supposed to culminate in a year-long process of data-collection for the doctoral dissertation. I carry the research proposal—a neat twenty-page document—with great reverence in a backpack slung on my shoulder, at least while the going is good for those first few weeks. The villagers see a peripatetic pair of strange city women, my assistant and I, making the rounds, and scores of rumours are rife in the various hamlets. The story doing the rounds of the village varies in fine detail. I am a policewoman, on a secret assignment. The villagers are warned that I am a government agent collecting data on them, so beware! As I later find out, that story soon circulates even among the migrants in tenements in Bombay.

I move into my dilapidated ancestral dwelling in a particular hamlet. Soon I am alone, my assistant having departed following the death of her brother in a rickshaw accident in Bombay. The caretaker who has keys to a couple of houses on the wadi, and the untrammelled use of lands and produce that only he has access to, disbelieves my pious intentions. He is convinced that I am there simply to do him out of his privileges in the ancestral property.

With typical misogyny he tries to make things as difficult as possible for me, unused to village ways as I am. In a fit of spite he even takes away the pot for storing drinking water. One of my neighbours lends me a spare new pot that she has purchased in anticipation of her monsoon needs. The caretaker does not mend his ways despite well-meaning intervention by a scandalized group of community elders. Ultimately his fears prove true, since his efforts merely serve to harden my resolve not to leave except of my own volition. 'You will have to live under a waterfall during the heavy downpours, under that roof,' he warns me with great satisfaction. He has shrugged off total responsibility for the old building in the hope that without his assistance I will not last many days.

I learn all the backbreaking survival tasks by trial and error.
I have learnt to draw well water for my personal needs, and
am proud of being able to light a kerosene stove for the first
time in my life, and of the very 'masculine' task of lighting a
petromax lantern in the darkness sans electricity. I find a young
girl of the barber caste to help me in the washing and cooking
chores. This is a careless act that has already scandalized the
village since it is a serious transgression against the strict rules
of commensality. But they do make allowances since I am a
city-bred woman with no knowledge of village ways. At that
early stage, I cannot rely on my neighbours for directions. It is
supremely important that I assert my independent ways or I
will soon be reduced to the status of a typical housebound non-
farm woman. But my helper from the barber caste vanishes as
the rains begin, perhaps to shore up farm labour with her
mother, and I am left alone once again.

It is a very ramshackle dwelling that I find myself in. The mud
plaster of the walls has gone crumbly, and the roof is termite-
eaten beyond repair. The windows are just holes in the wall without panes, with rusting iron bars fixed vertically. They stop
humans, but not snakes, and stay open night and day. The roof
has not been cleaned for an age, and baby scorpions occasionally
drop from the skies. Then there are floating black wisps of stinging hairy moth larvae that continue to settle down from the roof
in a steady momentum.

After a while, little children happily surround me in my home
in the daytime, but I do not understand why they run away with
exaggerated shivers just before nightfall. I discover later that
the house verges on the crematoria, the burning grounds, amid
the forest vegetation that I have been exploring with joy all these
days. My house is supposed to be a regular haunt for the forest
spirits that roam the region at night and in the afternoon hours.

There is fear also because mad Baburao from the neighbouring clan had leapt to a violent death in the dry rock-bottom well
some ten feet away from my back door. That was some fifteen
years ago. It was rumoured that he had driven himself thus
out of quiet desperation over repeated harassment from his sis-

ter-in-law. He was an orphan after his mother's death. The widowed sister-in-law had refused to care for him after that. She had deliberately starved him on occasion, ranting at him for being such a good-for-nothing. One day the sensitive soul had taken the only way out, as it must have seemed to him. It had been difficult to get his remains out, but good old Mangya from the neighbouring wadi had undertaken that task with love and deep sorrow for the dead man. We no longer drink water from that well, using it only for the washing. We bring drinking water from one of the spring wells a short distance away. Thankfully I do not discover this legend during those first few months of living in that house.

Then begins a season of one of the heaviest recorded rainfalls in a century, bringing surging floods in its wake, particularly down by the riverside. The first night of the storms is the worst. I have nothing but a powerful torch by my side when a limb of the mango tree looming over the house crashes down by an outer wall, which develops two huge craters, leaving the house open on the forest side. The roof exists only for moral support; droplets of water splash on my face no matter where I move the wooden cot in the big living room. Water rushes over the kitchen walls from a big hole in the roof, and I have strategically placed buckets and mugs and little pots and pans around the living room to catch the water as it streams down from the roof. My sad belongings left on the floor of this house without furniture have begun to float. I creep up to an open window and yell for my distant neighbours, calling out the few names that I know. I do not dare to venture out on to the porch at that late hour in the night. The thundering storm and the rushing gale drown out my voice. I resign myself to a watery night and eventually fall asleep.

The community elders are very solicitous the next morning as they go around the wadi assessing damage from the deluge. There is news of roads being washed away, of some people even managing to traverse the central plains in little boats for urgent tasks that cannot be put off. The central part of the village has experienced the worst flood of the century, and many people are marooned in their houses. House walls come crashing down, and the angry river has washed away precious paddy kept aside for transplanting, causing untold damage in the most fertile agricultural lands in the river plains. On our wadi the stream level rises in the flood, but the houses have been built on steep elevations precisely for such an eventuality, and there is little damage except for old Baygya's tamarind tree being uprooted right next to her house.

The Daughter-Come-Home

It is a surprise, of course, that my house survives that season. The neighbours have patched up the craters in the walls. They have gingerly patched some of the big holes in the roof with thin strips of bamboo. All this is for free. It provides some relief, although it does not stop the main cataracts during heavy downpours that continue over five months that year. At least the mud walls and floors will stay reasonably intact. That experience considerably heightens my respect for the resilience of the ancient mud dwellings. They generally put up with a lot of abuse and neglect at the hands of termites, humans and the inclement weather before finally succumbing to the forces of disintegration. There are many such deserted ruins of houses around the village, a mute testimony to changing times.

The residents despise the former caretaker for wishing such a watery misfortune upon me, for not having done anything to prevent it from happening despite my earnest entreaties to him that summer. The kindly Bramhan woman from the neighbouring hamlet sends two of her young children to keep me company at night. That emboldens two more from my own wadi to join us, so it is a merry group that sings *bhajans* and braves the storms in the sorry haunted house on its last legs in my first year in the village.

We even begin to celebrate the festival of Ganpati after a gap of nearly fifty years since the death of my great aunt who lived alone in that big house. The wadi residents are very happy about this, and they are proud to guide my fumbling attempts at religiosity for the first time in my hitherto atheistic adult life. But first of all, I get a carpenter to fit some makeshift panes to the open windows and to replace some totally termite-eaten apologia for doors in the house. We then paint the walls afresh with the ochre mud, and in parts even with bright washes of anil-stained lime. Old Aba, a neighbouring kinsman who has taken me under his wing to guide me to village ways, very solicitously instructs me to paint pretty squiggles on all the walls. They have been sadly bare in mourning all this while through years of neglect, against village custom.

We welcome the Elephant-Headed Harbinger of Goodwill and Happiness, the Dispeller of Gloom and Misfortune, the Great Pot-Bellied, Crooked-Trunked Giver of Knowledge and Wisdom, the Lord Ganpati, with a sense of community sharing in the house that year, and the ghosts never come back. The Lord too overlooks my strange fumblings at worship, starving without complaint into the late afternoon until I am ready to offer Him much-delayed, spartan fare, after all the single-handed ritual responsibilities as the mistress of the house. I am yet to develop village epicureanism, and the food must taste very strange to Him, although He bears it with good grace.

A house has to be given its due. In the eyes of the villagers, it is not just the love and care lavished on a home that sets it apart from a mere cattleshed. There are certain sacred duties towards an ancestral abode, just like those towards the departed ancestral spirits and the Gods. More particularly, it is the performance of certain rituals for pacifying the spirit of the dwelling itself, and then the celebration of at least a few festivals in the year, which bring that aura of peace, protection and sanctity to make it a decent home. Only then can you expect to go about your worldly tasks without hindrance. Such celebrations include worshipping the cobra, the Lord Ganpati and celebrating the Marathi New Year on Gudi Padwa day in April. Then there is Diwali, the festival of lights, and the marriage ceremony of the *tulas* herb planted at the entrance to each house. I am tutored to each and every ritual that I am capable of performing, and it brings a great deal of gladness to the hearts of the wadi residents, even as the occasions serve to acquaint me with their concerns as a part of my research. Religion serves as the line of least resistance, the easiest medium for my interactions with the villagers who were strangers until then, even as I begin to change in fine gradations from a decultured, westernized city dweller into a village woman highly attuned to the ethos.

I am compelled by the force of necessity to set aside my formal research concerns and to undertake a major roof overhaul and a general restoration of the huge old dwelling with its nine rooms, in a spirit of thanksgiving for having held up despite the deluge. From that point on, the flow and rhythm of village life takes over, and the research evolves and unfolds as an unresisting, natural outcome of my life in the wadi as a daughter-come-home. My very persona begins to change. My self-image changes as I compromise in little ways, while still insisting on having my own way in matters where I cannot change. I begin to apply the little red dot on my forehead. I even resurrect old traditional designs, such as the crescent moon or the tulas motif, and I am gratified to see some other woman following my example. I grow my hair long to satisfy their wish. I wear nice feminine bangles on hitherto naked wrists, pretty ear studs on hitherto plain earlobes, and even a chain around an otherwise shockingly bare neck. All this meets with smiling approval from the women wherever I go. They are proud of having reformed me to village ways.

There are other ways that I do not change, and then they have to bend their firm beliefs considerably to accommodate my strange behaviour on good faith. I refuse to follow menstrual taboos; they do not ostracize me, and continue to share their lives closely with me. There are other big and small issues. The obnoxious caretaker had taken the trouble in those initial days to warn me not to smile or talk to men in public. When the jungle contractor begins his harassment in earnest, even though I have not given him cause for any misapprehension regarding my affections, it is the carpenter lads who patiently explain to me that it must be because I may have absentmindedly smiled at him sometime. 'It is enough if you just smile, Tai, and a man may imagine himself at your feet with calf-love,' they say with grins. Yes, I have forgotten what it is to be a woman. I have begun to explore a new persona of a glowering dowager as I travel around, in case someone gets the wrong ideas. The village continues to grow on me.

Village Methodologies: Pray Hard, Build a House, Start a Riot

Many co-residents work free of cost on the exacting roof repairs through the hot March afternoons, helping to move huge logs of timber down to the waiting carts on their way to the sawmill, and other such tasks. The whole wadi shares in my pride at the end of it all. I have never known the difference between bamboo strips and good timber before, and trust my kinsmen to guide me through the whole effort. It is also a strange experience for them to have a major task such as this accomplished without any misfortune, any heart-burning, within the allotted budget of time and money, and that too by a woman totally strange to village ways. They are convinced that I was then possessed by the spirits of my long-departed ancestors who must have inspired me in the first place to return to the village in time before the house came crashing down to obliterate forever their name from the village. Sometimes I even hear tales told of my being the Goddess-Incarnate, but that is mere flattery, village-style.

Earlier, before I leave for Bombay, towards the end of that first summer in the village, old Dada, who knows that I come from a family of doctors in Bombay, requests me to bring some useful medicines for the monsoon damp when I return to the village the next time. I gather free samples of cough, cold, and fever remedies, medicines for diarrhoea and dysentery, anti-helminthics, some ointments, eye drops and vitamins in the city. Little have I imagined the advantages and perils of such an undertaking.

From the day after my return to the wadi, news has spread far and wide about my skills as a healer. Within a few weeks,

women with sundry aches and pains and migraine come and
inform me how their visits to thirteen doctors in the district
had left them dissatisfied, but that my medicines have cured
them instantaneously of their myriad ailments. I am reputed
to have the healing touch, and soon there is to be the kind of
daily crush on my veranda that leaves me time for little else.
It helps to establish my credentials in the village as a woman
of some use, and also to get past the initial suspicion of my
being a secret agent for the Government of India in New Delhi.
Needless to add, had I only been the hectic 'paper-pusher' or
'note-taker' kind of a researcher, that rumour would have
proved to be a masterly stroke of genius which would have suf-
ficed to establish my guilt in the eyes of the villagers, neighbours and kinsmen alike. There would have been no research.

For a single woman to practise the scholarly art of a kind
that requires a prolonged sojourn in the village is beyond the
frame of reference of the most seasoned villagers. In their savvy
reckoning it is perhaps more appropriate if I am indeed a spy
or an informant who is envious of their peaceful subsistence
living in the village. To that extent, the fears of the middlemen
and their corrupt backers are no doubt justified. But the medicines serve well initially to validate my presence in the village,
as the kind of direct service that is essential to overcome barriers to communication as an outsider. It might be even better
if you are a rope-walker, fire-eater or monkey-trainer, but I am
sadly devoid of these useful skills. The medicines serve well for
a while.

The Rhythm of Changing Seasons

I realize soon enough that if I am to do any indepth study at the
micro-level, I will have to suspend my rigid time schedule as
stipulated in the research proposal. To achieve this, I must not
push the process. It will have to evolve very naturally as a part
of the ebb and flow of the wadi inter-connectedness, within the
rhythm of changing seasons and work pressures. I have much to
learn in the meanwhile.

Conditions of subsistence living vary sharply from year to year, even as sons get jobs, migrants lose jobs, through sickness and calamity, and as additional stresses arise due to drought, famine, floods and sundry crises. Values and attitudes are extremely different, and without a critical self-awareness along with respect and acceptance towards the villagers' own world-view on the part of the researcher, it is very easy to abuse and misrepresent the total gestalt of village women's existence. A pointer to such sharply divergent perspectives is the fact that many women, for example, even when close to starvation and bound to inhuman conditions at times, are sorrier for my unconventional state of singlehood than I am for their miseries and toil. As I discover for myself, it takes a long time to get on free and easy terms with the women. Initially it is the men who visit me regularly, asking questions and sharing flippant information that provides me with little understanding of the village and its customs. A little later the women too visit casually to satisfy their curiosity. But again, there is little meaningful interchange at that level. Probing their work, attitudes and relationships requires time, a commodity they are genuinely short of.

Even otherwise, at that level, there is no way of checking out the validity of the replies they give to the simplest of queries, since parrying questions, answering in strange paradoxical proverbs and in general concealing information is a finely honed Malvani art. Often my own artlessness provokes a great deal of mirth. I suspect that the joke is at my expense, but smile along because the answer will come only if I am patient. Worse, I may never know when I may be committing a solecism in terms of probing personal wounds, secrets or taboo areas. Understanding the subtleties of village interchange takes time. In the meanwhile I may have done a lot of damage to my plans for data collection by an intrusive ignorance of the very different definitions of time and space and codes of conduct in the village. It is not seemly to whip out questionnaires and conduct research heedless of village conventions, simply because I am in a hurry. There is no guarantee that such data are at all going to serve

the interests of truth or will benefit the villagers in any way.
It is only after I begin to participate in wadi rituals, often joining
the women in communal cooking sessions at weddings, gradually developing meaningful relationships with individual
women, that I begin to get a feel for the distinct structures and
meanings of existence in their lives.

I discover that like the medicines that I have been distributing
for free, my camera and tape recorder are great ice-breakers.
These gadgets appear particularly magical in the hands of a
woman. Soon I have invitations from old women of the fortunate
married status to come take their pictures, bedecked with all
their heirloom jewellery that one time before they die, so that
their families may have a photograph to frame and worship
after their passing away. Then there are even more ghoulish
assignments of taking posthumous pictures of dead old men on
their last journey so that their families can frame the pictures
for ancestor worship. Like practising medicine, I have no inten-
tion of setting up a photography studio either, even as the hope-
fuls keep asking me to take photographs for their pension, job or
relief applications.

A certain level of mutual exploitation is inevitable in the
wadi when living in terms of cooperative coexistence with a
high level of give and take. I have to be very firm where money
is concerned. I refuse the role of a moneylender, particularly
since crises of all kinds are very common in the lives of the
villagers at the subsistence level. Yet the villagers always
speculate about who is ripping me off, and how. Wild rumours
come to my ears until I am furious. Each acquaintance imagines
that she or he is the only pure one on the wadi, while old so-
and-so and all the others must visit me only to demand money
or to partake of the delicious viands cooked just for them.

Testing Times

Then there are other times of testing, like cattle being let loose
on to my beautiful vegetable patch. I learn to raise my voice in

a pitch hitherto unknown to me, flinging loud decibels at the owners to get them out or else, while at the same time running barefoot, waving a large stick to chase the cattle off my grounds. They naturally lead me to a chase several times around the yard and the house before finally quitting in good humour, and it does not take me much more impetus to improve upon my Malvani vocabulary, spouting in colourful staccato bursts. I have begun to earn the admiration of the villagers, at least those who have the good fortune to be within earshot. They never fail to mention later, with humorous winks at each other, how truly a daughter of these parts I am. That is one of the greatest compliments a native outsider can hope to get, and I share in the humour of the situation.

I reach an important milestone when a gang of petty criminals who live outside the neighbouring wadi illegally cut down a teak tree belonging to my family. Everyone except I know the minute details of my lands and trees, and I immediately receive an urgent message to go and stop the thieves. The latter are of my own distant kin group, of a long-estranged branch of my own family. I have no choice but to intervene, since the theft of ancestral property is a serious challenge in the eyes of the villagers, and to ignore the call is to be stamped an irresponsible wastrel. I do not like to be side-tracked from my research, but there is really no choice.

The scene of the crime is near a distant stream by other burning grounds. Old Putlabai grazing her buffalo shakes her head mournfully from side to side, 'Sad life for a single woman to live in these wild parts,' she calls after my retreating back. I run headlong into my first clash with the middleman. The initial rounds go to him as the police refuse to take cognizance of the crime. The middleman has even taken hold of the piece of paper from the revenue office, showing the details of ownership of the land from which the tree is stolen. I do not know then that the revenue official can very well issue another form. They give me the merry run-around the village, over four kilometres walking distance away from my own wadi, even as nightfall approaches. I have one intrepid old farm woman by my side along that walk. Besides the issue of theft, it is illegal even to cut down a teak tree without permission from the authorities. The officials are usually very quick to threaten honest farmers with dire consequences for a lesser transgression. But unless the police search for the tree secreted away by the offenders, there is no crime to speak of.

It is a different matter that it is not easy to secret away in the village a single log of teak wood nearly thirty feet long. There must have been literally scores of witnesses. The police cannot be moved. One of the criminals has publicly bragged about 'seeing what that slip of a woman can do'. They are betting on the local bus on how the middleman will take money from both parties, while the thieves will go scot-free. It is my fate as a single woman to stew in silence.

All villagers are very territorial in outlook, by village custom. This act of provocation is outside the wadi bounds, so my neighbours cannot intervene. It is not as if my life were under threat. I am on my own. Providence comes to my aid. A visiting kinsman from Bombay, a retired police administrator from the top rungs of the state police, has dropped by unwarily to enquire about my well-being during a flying visit through this village of shared ancestry, just as the village constables arrive to tell me that they cannot trace the stolen tree. He gives them some rivetting 'shop talk', after which the police are galvanized into action. Within twenty-four hours I march triumphantly in a mini procession with twelve lusty lads helping to carry the retrieved log of teak to my house. Putla watches with an open mouth. 'Not this woman,' I say to her, remembering her earlier message of despondency, giving her a sweet smile as I can well afford to then.

We have solid evidence. I have possession of the stolen goods; and the police are happy, under pressure, to log a successful resolution in their statistics. I file charges. The criminals are harassed in compulsory court attendance for almost a year, as the hearing keeps getting postponed. Some of them are 'chapters' in village lingo, which means they are recidivists, or habitual criminals who have several cases pending against them.

It is certain that they will be sent to jail for adding one more crime to their already heavy records. The roof of their house collapses in the heavy rains that year, and they come to me begging for forgiveness, being told that it is the revenge of my family's deity! In future they are careful not to harass me openly, at least for a few more years.

An unmentioned fact about women doing research in isolated spots and in rural areas in general is that the appearance of male protection is fairly essential, in whatever token a manner. It can be a husband, or it can be co-workers going on their independent quests, but women must be seen to be under the umbrella of a common group or organization. A single woman undertaking a prolonged stay in a village finds that her presence is somehow validated and legitimized if she is seen to be under the protection of a man in whatever way. I am lucky to find kindly protective men in my neighbourhood who take over that role before I even realize what is happening. Old patriarchs and chivalrous young men alike come forward to educate me in village ways, until eventually a couple of them come to take over the halo of being 'my men'.

Actually, my house comes to be known as their house, in terms of 'managerial' capacity. Much as I try to assert myself as an independent individual, strangers and village men in general require male intermediaries to talk to. There is much embarrassment and avoiding of eye contact if I take the initiative in arranging work that I am paying for. It is not so much because of a gendered shyness, as out of deference to the feelings of my men. On other occasions the same men have absolutely no compunction in ordering me to bring them the *paan* tray as they ruminate over the state of affairs in the village world, agriculture, livestock and the seasons.

Whether I need coconuts to be taken down the trees, have my fence mended, or arrange for ritual celebrations, it is my men who make all the outside arrangements. Gradually my men grow impatient and out of sorts with me if I infringe on their rights in this matter. It is an issue of masculine pride for them, and my interference only serves to diminish them in the eyes of envious co-residents. I learn my lesson the hard way, when my men walk off in a huff, and I have to go beg their cooperation to get emergency tasks done that no man will touch without their consent. I have to give in on this important issue particularly since men of work are so rare in these parts, and there is plenty of work to be done around the house, preparing for each season. Every single woman on the wadi has these appointed men who take care of the male 'preserves' for her, and these are valued relationships, almost extending into families. That is the way of the village.

Wishful Thinking

During those initial weeks of exploring the village, I decide to maintain a low profile as I go about the task of getting acquainted with the village. Curious college-going youngsters ask me if there are any trees in America. It is with typical 'decultured urban naivete' that I imagine that my caste, kinship or class status is of no major concern to the villagers. That is self-delusive ignorance on my part because I am ill-equipped to understand these issues as they define both the structural framework as well as the fine-webbed matrix of inter-connectedness in traditional society. My 'airy-fairy' modern notions of equality and individual self-actualization are soon to fall flat on their faces as I am confronted at each step, for the first time in adult life, with rigid definitions about my ordained place in the hierarchical village society.

I have lived a strangely cocooned life in the city, to the extent of being distanced from the harsh realities of caste and gender. It is the kind of progressiveness and maturity that is very common among activists and reformers in modern India. I have believed until this point that my denial of a caste consciousness or sexist conditioning will somehow cause the problem itself to disappear from my environs. All that I have achieved is to insulate myself from a stark cultural reality. I am handicapped in the village in terms of being unable to identify the very fine distinctions and gradations in caste hierarchy. I do not possess the magical knack of intuiting caste and clan membership from mere surnames, like most people do even in the city. I generate misunderstandings with my free and easy, decultured, degendered ways, and it takes a long time to get over those initial months of bumbling. No grouping is impressed with my self-proclaimed egalitarianism. They look on it with suspicion or distress.

My atheism is a rebuke to existence, as even kind Muslim and Christian acquaintances do not hesitate to tell me. We all have our assigned designation in life, as they patiently explain. It is to be our path, our *dharma*. To deny that is a crime against divinity. Moreover, there is a lot besides my physical parameters that goes to determine the shape and the crystallized structure of my identity for the villagers. It cannot be a fluidity expressed in spontaneous ways of interaction, at least not yet. The villagers are not going to come forth to me in the sense of a meaningful exchange until I have firmly established my identity, particularly in terms of ancestral connections.

Banyan, not Orchid Roots

Without realizing it, I have been working at cross-purposes for a long time, and there is little progress in my work. I then understand that it is providence that has unerringly led me to select my ancestral village for this research, despite some time spent on needless reconnoitering in the districts for a suitable site. For it is only here that the villagers will ultimately shrug off all my seeming eccentricities in behaviour, overlook my mindless transgressions—even the brash stubborness—once they know that I am a daughter-come-home. Then they even set about polishing and refurbishing old memories to give me back my rightful place within the ebb and flow of village living.

In any other village or community I would have been exceedingly vulnerable as a single woman without the natural protection of being a sprout of these ancient roots. The smallest rumour or suspicion would have been sufficient to end my research in a village other than this one, and I would have been at the mercy of the powers-that-be. Moreover in my own village, I can flaunt my egalitarian ways with impunity, even at times thumb my nose at the village elite, and hope to carry the day through sheer gall and effrontery. It is dangerous living of a kind I have never known before. As a small town lawyer informs me with great bitterness and regret, 'You are lucky to find yourself in these parts. Any place else in the district and they would have "finished" you long ago. Don't fool yourself about the protection your natural charm gives you. It is the meek of the earth who people this Malvan taluka. You should consider yourself lucky.'

Yes, I have been lucky. I have not come to the village to garner long-lost estates. It is not my fault that the neighbouring middleman happens to be thriving on farm produce off my ancestral lands, as his estranged brother pointedly informs me one day during a special visit. I have made powerful enemies in the village simply by virtue of being who I am. In the eyes of the corrupt elite and the middlemen operatives, I should have no other business in the village except as a spy, and they have much to hide. Providence has been undoubtedly kind to me. But all this is revealed much later.

The medicines soon become a hindrance to my life and peace of mind, particularly, as the kindly postmaster warns me, since I am inviting the wrath of the village doctors. In any case I have blundered into that strange role willy nilly. I have to be extremely firm with the villagers to divest myself of that imposed role. It is only after I stop bringing any medicines to the village for any distribution whatsoever, that they finally accept that denial. By then I have become a part of the community.

Healer, Exorcist

I do continue occasionally to hand out free medicines in times of epidemics, even out of my personal supplies, but I have to be extremely discreet so as not to revive the old deluge of ailing patients. Sometimes, I arrange for free check-ups and medicine dispensations to coincide with visits of doctors from the city, when villagers are welcome to take advantage of the service.

There are some rewarding moments from that period of imposed medical service, like the time I saved old Malgya's two-year-old grandson, suffering from malnutrition, literally from death's door. He recovered completely within a few days of my attending to him, with sound advice to his nurturers. The old woman never fails to attribute her grandson's life and health to my efforts, and it is gratifying when he later turns out to be one of the brightest children in the pre-primary schools or bal-wadi. Another such occasion occurs when I 'cure' young Malati, Manya's wife, of spirit possession. Manya had been living like an invalid for the past few months, weak from a mysterious illness through the heaviest part of the agricultural season. Some old residents identify his ailment as jaundice, and he is on herbal remedies with no relief. It is right on a festival eve that his heavily burdened wife, Malati, stumbles and falls down while fetching water at sundown.

There is much work to do. With two small children to look after, she can hardly afford to be ill. Besides, she has a big household to tend to. Her sister-in-law is of no use. She is anae-mic and has imaginary aches and pains all the time. The entire burden of that household is really on Malati's hard-working shoulders. She cannot hold her head high while her husband is suffering from an unexplained chronic illness. No doubt some evil-minded person has cast a hex on her happiness, and to fall and hurt herself at such an ill-opportune time is a shock she cannot bear. She is seized by fits of shaking, and it does look like some invisible spirit has caught hold of her.

The terrified kinfolk run helter skelter, some to consult old women for sage advice, others to get benediction from the Lord of the Underworld at His temple. Her brother-in-law comes to ask me if I can provide some relief, while another man speeds to the temple priest. I visit the woman with a couple of my personal palliatives, and even as I calm her down, I sternly warn the evil spirit to get lost, or else. Her shaking ceases magi-cally even before she has barely swallowed the medicine with a draught of water. I then talk to her soothingly about her husband's illness, explaining the need to get him qualified medical attention. She recovers soon after that as a result of the Lord's blessing. The next day she produces her sole gold ring before her elder brother-in-law. 'This ring is not of greater value than my husband's health,' she tells him. 'Please sell it off, and take him to a good doctor in Malvan before it is too late.' The doctor successfully diagnoses Manya's ailment as being the result of an excess of worms in the alimentary canal, and he is a new man after a few days' of treatment. Poor Malati probably has the evil spirit to thank for the crisis that has lead to her husband's cure at last.

These happy tales of the strange days of imposed healership go down in my treasure chest of cherished memories. Yet I am glad to be free of the heavy demands on my nonexistent skills based on ordinary common sense and a working knowledge of health aspects and issues.

The following year, once the house is beautifully restored, I have to propitiate the long-neglected ancestral spirits. Old Aba, my beloved guardian, is dead. I have suffered a bout of indifferent health. That brings on rumours that I am undergoing a spell of being spooked by the evil spirits myself, as a result of my carefree wanderings through the haunted terrain of the village. It also brings forth the next major test I have to face, and then an avalanche of them.

Community Organization: Stumbling into 'Reserve Territory'

Meanwhile I am firmly entrenched in the village, particularly on my own wadi. The co-resident kinsfolk have no doubts and suspicions about me beyond such as are invoked in the usual travails of sharing a neighbourhood for a long duration by hereditary right. After initial fumbling efforts, we have succeeded in establishing a women farmers' organization, duly registered with the government.

The rules of registration require an administrative hierarchy. Earlier efforts to work even with a nominal hierarchy provoked major fissures in the organization. Villagers from the Kokan are very rigid about egalitarian forms of interchange, particularly within in-groups. After all the levels of exploitation and undermining in traditional ways of village life, they cannot take any more hierarchies, even of the most limited kind. At various times my efforts in organizing the women are sabotaged because of malicious subversion of the work of the 'democratically elected office bearers' by the farm women.

Government rules remain inflexible since administrative hierarchies look refined and modern on file. Indeed, that is what the government is all about. So I am the president since the women refuse to confer this title on another fellow farm woman. The vice president puts her thumb imprint on the application form, evoking tremendous consternation on the part of the representative of the Bombay Charity Commissioner. The treasurer puts her signature amidst great giggles. This one experience has made her hardships as a farm woman seem worthwhile. The secretary keeps scratching an exposed leg to the disgust of the bureaucrats in the district headquarters. We are a merry group, but we suspend the hierarchy once we are back home. The wadi men are intensely jealous because mere women have stolen a march on them in forming a government-recognized organization.

I have also initiated a marketing programme for *kokum* processed by village women, having found a reliable sales outlet in Bombay. The prices are linked to retail prices in Bombay, revised on an annual basis. It is a risky venture, but catches on like wildfire. The taluka middlemen have reasons for the visceral hatred they show towards me.

We organize an International Women's Day camp for farm women on the eighth of March each year, bringing in outside resource persons to talk to farm women, along with entertainment which includes a film show at night. Up to one hundred farm women, lugging their children, participate with great enthusiasm on each occasion. The wadi residents beam with pride, for it is a matter of honour to become the centre of attention.

In the teeth of strong opposition from the bureaucracy, I shelve my plans for starting a village women's marketing cooperative. I had not understood then that the arena of people's cooperatives is a jealously guarded political preserve. I am also constrained by my research interests, particularly the time restrictions of the university for completing my degree requirements. Working with the men, I am instrumental in getting the entire wadi of forty-five households electrified, through sheer persistence lasting over four years. We also put in backbreaking work over widening the narrow wadi walkway, confined as it is by abutting granite rocks. We also get an effective wadi residents' forum going to deal with village-level harassment by government officials. So I have truly succeeded in stirring up a hornet's nest, it seems, through my ingenuous efforts at community organization.

Organizer, Activist

My role as social worker was secondary to that of researcher at least until the completion of my doctoral studies in 1989. Participation in community affairs itself evolved into a more active role than being just an observer. It was not until 1990, however, that I began to be involved primarily as a community organizer and activist. I lived on a modest inheritance through these years. At first I served as a resource person, interceding on behalf of villagers within the taluka and *jilha* authorities in matters of family pensions, relief assistance, and miscellaneous petitions. I proved a nuisance to local officialdom since my intervention implied bypassing a well-oiled machinery of graft and petty harassment. The higher authorities, including district collectors and tehsildars were usually cooperative in rendering prompt assistance.

I also organized special services and programmes for women and the community whenever the need arose, as described earlier. Even this miniscule activity was threatening to local politicians, cocooned in their world of everlasting jealousies and intrigues. In an impoverished region, it is development schemes for the poor that are the only source of corruption. Within a quasi-feudal structure, accountability to passive villagers is almost unheard of. I tread on sensitive egos by lending myself thus to the peasants. A backlog of undelivered funds for backward regions over years of development planning continue to pile up at the state headquarters in Bombay. At the same time, unused financial allocations are sent back from the district because of mismanagement as schemes go abegging for want of proper implementation. There is little congruence of interests between a self-serving nexus of politicians and officials on the one hand, and the ignorant peasant populace on the other.

My simple questions to officials concerning the implementation of projects in the village appear very threatening within an entrenched system impervious to local demands. Even more threatening are my studied attempts to clarify pertinent issues, focus on priorities, and organize men and women in an effective manner so that their demands cannot be side-stepped. Disaffected villagers have begun to monitor village-level functionaries closely on fair implementation of rural schemes. This is contrary to the earlier etiquette of near-feudal benevolence and patronage on the part of the authorities and docility on the villagers' part. Local attempts to block just demands are counteracted through seeking intervention of higher authorities, who are always willing to help in the face of organized pressure. This is more so when I have facts and figures at hand to justify such intervention. Goodwill earned from district journalists and editors plays its part in convincing the authorities of the need for speedy action.

In all this, my work of mobilizing mostly illiterate farm women becomes a sore point with the lower level functionaries and politicians. Their control over the public domain is threatened by women organizing in a solid phalanx, also backed by their men. Patriarchal powers of persuasion and coercion have conventionally operated through amenable men in the community while women remained passive. Women who were totally ignored in the matter of governance have remained unindoctrinated to the finer rules of village etiquette while dealing with the authorities. On its part, the village elite is grossly ill-equipped to address women directly. A certain amount of in-built chivalry prevents overt harassment of village women by the elite. Authority in the village is no longer the preserve of a single dominant caste. A motley group of village officials and elite individuals have to tread warily so as not to offend sensibilities of caste and kinship while dealing with organized women. Their fear that the men might openly revolt and rally behind their women in the event of a conflict, further eroding their control, does indeed work in the women's favour.

While men can be silenced by liquor or threats of imprisonment, there is no possibility of such blandishments or threats in the case of women. Women are more practical in public affairs and less prone to ego hassles. They have a greater emotional stake in the well-being of their families and communities. Women are also naturally much more militant than men in voicing their demands, and less amenable to being fobbed off with typical administrative obfuscations, especially in my presence. As I serve as a conduit for local demands and aspirations, I also become the focus of considerable ire on the part of the powers-that-be.

I take care to involve men in all stages of community action projects, even as I ensure that the initiative is seen to rest with the farm women. This strategy pays off rich dividends so that subversive action to sabotage our work from within the community is kept to a minimum, and both men and women derive psychological gains from our practical successes. Women need tremendous support from their menfolk in order to participate wholeheartedly in community action programmes. This is not only in terms of morale building, but also in the practical accommodation of their absence from the home for an extended period. Thus, farm women egg me on to intercede with their men in a diplomatic manner to overcome possible opposition to their joining the task at hand. Men's support is vital at a time when there are few precedents to women playing a wider social role in village affairs. The men probably see me in the light of an honoured colleague, since they associate with me in a free and easy degendered sense of camaraderie.

There is a specific revealing incident: a hundred villagers, among whom there are more women than men, court arrest and jostle with a large posse of police to draw attention to a longstanding demand for a paved road through the larger neighbourhood. Well-managed community action along with good publicity results in total success. The paving of the road is undertaken almost overnight. Looking back, I am proud to see an emerging sense of responsibility and confidence on the part of village men and women in their ability to organize community action to solve their own problems even in my absence. This is in sharp contrast to their earlier manner of being passive and fatalistic.

By mid-1988 I am preparing to leave the village for a six-month visit to the United States. This will culminate in a PhD degree after ten-long years of change and transformation, of death and rebirth in a cyclic process as I flit from world to world. When I return to Berkeley, following years of intense living in the ancestral village, my friends stare at me intently for long intervals to pronounce as if in a daze, 'You've changed'. So I have, in a fairly pronounced way. It is the combined result of becoming a villager, surviving some intense harassment as an assertive single woman in the village, of going through some difficult life passages, and of growing up at last. There is an additional edge to the determination to finish the dissertation after such a long gap for the purpose of field work. A successful anthropologist pats me on the back, adding, 'You're now an anthropologist.'

I feel the same way that I did earlier, with a knot tightening somewhere in the gut, when I had to take over the mantle of being the medicine woman or the photographer in the village. I feel like that when someone remarks about my doing things for the 'masses' in the village. I do not wish to be identified as a 'do-gooder'. I suffered in the village because my identity did not fit any previous frame of reference. I was a product, an image, of each person's projected ideals, fears or fantasies. As I see it, *being there* was an important accident, the rest followed as a process of interaction between my sensitivity, stubbornness and receptivity to the challenge of village living as a learning experience. So maybe I am an anthropologist, like I am so many other things, and I do owe a debt of gratitude to many anthropologists with whom I unknowingly shared the difficult experience of becoming a part of the field, if only for strongly validating and legitimizing my personal journey.

Meanwhile I have been harassed like few other women, threatened with imprisonment, and dragged through the courts under false criminal charges. The whole district administration, including the police and the courts seemed to have been tied up into neat knots by the Machiavellian politicians and their henchmen. But they keep tripping over each other in their blundering arrogance, adding to my prestige in the eyes of the villagers. It has been a curiously strengthening span of existence, and I cannot imagine a life away from the village any longer.

I leave India with a supremely valuable judgement from the Bombay High Court that unambiguously states:

> Having regards to these facts the Magistrate should not have immediately taken cognizance. If issue process orders are asked for the mere asking as has been done in the instant case no person's life, liberty or reputation would be safe. Litigation is increasingly used as an instrument of oppression by the evil-minded and it is time Courts exercise their duties with extreme caution.

But then I hear of charges being tossed around in other courts in the district. That is what awaits me upon my return to my ancestral village, degree in hand.

All this is a fine challenge for me, as it even allows me to fantasize about lost connections to a long gone ancestral warrior woman. She was called the Raibaghin, or the jungle tigress, and she is said to have led her group of warriors on their chargers into many a violent reckoning in these wild parts. But this is the latter part of the civilized twentieth century, and I can only hope that they will let us get on with our own schemes for change and development. I am a fourfold fool: first to reject a glamorous living in the USA; second, I leave the joys of TV and video in the city to set out for the filth and deprivation of village living; third, of course, that I stay unmarried, callously rejecting the professed honourable intentions of my wealthy tormentor, the jungle contractor; and worst of all, that I identify with 'them' rather than with 'us'.

Outsiders are not welcome to the village. Now that I have the temerity to have survived it all and become an insider, I must be taught a very tough lesson, and an example must also be set before 'them', lest they should forget the dangers of 'crossing us'. It is not such a rare occurrence. Change and transformation involve upsetting the status quo, and that is a very foolhardy thing to do unless you are sure of your ground. I am sure of my ground now.

CHAPTER II

Folklore and the Malvani Ethos

FOLK SONGS have a place of pride in the village, particularly as an integral part of the women's subculture. Men have their songs too, and a special cultural mode to voice these. But they are borrowed from the larger Marathi *bhakti* tradition, not exclusive to the Malvani milieu. They do not reflect the essence of the men's ethos as the women's songs do theirs.

When men arrange their singing sessions, or bhajans as they are called, the women of the house are expected to provide tea and ladoos or homemade sweets to eat. Women cannot demand such things. They are happy if the hostess offers them paan and *supari* to chew on. Men use musical instruments which are expensive, and also cost money to repair. Women's songs are accompanied by the grinding stones; they are expected to work when they sing.

Malvani Folk Songs and the Gender Divide

There used to be Malvani songs which the men sang, but it is beneath their dignity to do so anymore. Only the most naive young lad will publicly sing a Malvani men's folk song. These are simple songs of defeat and laughter. '*Nay nay nay, nay ge bay; aslo kadhi baghlo nay,*' 'No, no, no, no, never seen such a one.' The songs tell of deserted, barren villages, and 'hopeless' boys playing pranks. The songs draw parallels between their own delinquencies and the much adored mythical Krishna's juvenile pranks. Typical Malvani irreverence demands that we don't call him Nandakumar Krishna, which means, Krishna, son of Nanda. He becomes instead, with added emphasis, that Nandya's brat.

Malvani has now become the language of uncouth peasants. The Bombay sophisticates speak Marathi. Village men have given up their own songs. But it is harder for the women to do so, and they do not want to. At least, not the older women. They continue to spin out their songs, yarn after yarn, weave after weave, although the colours are fast fading, and will soon be gone like all the rest. Symbols of Malvani creativity, they have begun to vanish with the changing days.

There is a vast body of literature on folklore in India. Bhagwat (1941) traced this genesis of Marathi folk songs to a period as early as A.D. 600. She developed a typology of the *ovi*, as 'Maharashtrian folk songs on the grind mill', and has comprehensively documented a rich collection of 507 couplets with English translations. She also alluded to the strong influence of the Kokani culture on the oral traditions of Maharashtra. Narayan (1986) has presented wedding songs of Kangra women, discussing the role of friendship between young girls and the folklore, as part of a shared tradition and collective experience that enables individual transition through marriage as a major life passage. I have found that Malvani folk songs emerge as a creative device that enables women to ventilate their derision and anger through stylistic genres of verbal expression and serve as an aid to cope with the daily frustrations and oppression in an unjust system.

Women's songs are sung at the end of the daily grind, to the tune of the heavy stone grinding the grain in a ceaseless, droning, rotary movement into the early morning. Hands keep interchanging rhythmically. The work does not stop, because weddings or festivals, there is always work to be done, feasts to be readied for Gods and men. Women do not sleep, they sing.

Sometimes there is excitement, like when 'Anjani' as the villagers call me, brings the recording tape. With broad smiles and beaming faces they listen to their own voices. Of course the men snigger, they always do. Imagine wasting good gadgetry on women's songs. But there is Ravgya the brat chiming in with the women in an exaggerated swagger, because he is dying to hear his own voice when she plays it back. He has never had his voice immortalized on tape before. Just like listening to the radio! Everyone laughs at his antics for a while, and then forgets him, for the work goes on.

SONGS OF THE GRINDING STONE*

There is to be a special wedding feast. It is Aba's youngest son's wedding tomorrow. It is so shameful to have to get flour from the mill, as they did at Ani's Baygya's wedding. They had to rush. Then it rained torrents and the groom's party could not cross the river. It was such a fiasco. The *wade* they made from the mill flour . . . what a waste of good grain. When it is hand-ground, with stone, the flour is of an exact coarseness. You can tell the difference as each morsel rolls around the tongue. Akka is so proud of the wade she serves. She has never failed with anything. Poor Akka. Her daughter-in-law! Hush. If she gets to hear, she will have some real coarse words beating on your eardrums. Keep quiet, I will tell you later.

The women's folk songs are called *ovya*, also known as songs of the grinding stone. Ovya are simple, unselfconscious couplets that the women improvise and go stringing along like beads in a necklace. Usually wedding songs, these songs are sung late into the night as all the women of the community gather to prepare for the huge wedding feast, to the steady grating accompaniment of heavy stone grinding on stone.

Pairs of women sit facing each other, with legs spread-eagled, saris drawn up to the thighs, to make room for the grinding stone in the middle. A piece of cloth is spread under the grinding stone, to collect all the flour which overflows between the two stones. The stones are heavy, round and

---

* The Appendix provides the original Malvani songs in *Devanagari* script along with the romanization.

flat, each about three to four inches thick and about twelve inches or more in diameter. The interface is chiselled into measured grooves for roughness to grind the grains as finely or as coarsely as required. The top slab has a cuplike hollow centre into which the grain is fed, one small fistful at a time. While one hand feeds the grain, the other hand holds a long rosewood bar fitted into the top stone, pulling on the stone in a circular motion. Two women working together, each with a hand on the bar, indeed make the task lighter, and the songs provide disciplined emotional release.

While the women are doing their work, the old man of the house may be sitting on a chair in a corner, quietly ruminating over past wedding feasts, going over a mental checklist for the next day's arrangements, or engaged in a muted disagreement with another elder. The old woman and other women of the house may be bustling around providing extra grain for the grinding, collecting the ready flour, and may also sit down to sing. 'Shri Krishna, groom beloved, why were you so late . . .'

There are infants asleep in the melee, and little girls all agog, holding on to their mothers' saris or eagerly joining in the singing. Then there are young lads busily walking in and out; or remarking on the quality of the flour or the singing, with an exaggerated supervisory air, giving rise to mock gender battles. And there is always gossip, plenty of *gajali* making, as it is called.

WIVES OF MIGRANTS: ALIEN DAUGHTERS

We should have called the Bhain Malgya, the lone old woman left from the temple servants' caste, who still has a reserve of women's folk songs. She is much admired by the farm women for her songs. They even overlook her snootiness, which they would not have taken from a younger woman of this lowly caste. But she has all the songs. She is getting old, and rarely leaves her house these days. We will take Anjanitai to visit her one day. Actually, she was asking to be introduced, and she does know all the songs.

There is old Akka. She is late because she had to finish washing all the vessels. The daughter-in-law is *baherchi*, on leave because of her periods. Akka! sing for Anjanitai. Akka puts her lantern down, smiles at old Aba sitting in the chair smoking his bidi, yells at all the brats to get lost, smooths over her nine-yard sari before sitting down, pats her hair in place, and begins to sing with a happy smile. One by one, other voices join her, and the song begins. The song always begins with a slow, measured, deliberate, and muted tempo. In the silence of the night, the first voice has an intense, resonant edge to it. As other voices join in, there's a softening, a lilt, and then a definite rhythm. The heavy work of grinding flour gets lighter as they go along.

ALIEN DAUGHTERS

> Four of us, let's go to the temple.
> At the temple we found father-in-law,
> Let's bend to his feet.
> Let's go to work, we will go to work.
>
> Mother-in-law, father-in-law,
> They're like sheltering *tulshi* trees,
> But we're alien infants.
>
> My mother, my father,
> Raised me from infancy,
> Raised me from infancy.
> Caressed me from infancy
> And gave me into mother- and
> father-in-law's care.
>
> Nurtured me like the jasmine flower,
> Nourished me like the plantain tree,
> And added to alien wealth.

An oft-repeated theme is that of the daughter-in-law's nostalgia for the natal family, expressing grief over the loss of warm and caring relationships experienced in the mother's house, in contrast to the isolation and loneliness at the in-laws' home.

CROW'S LAMENT

> Listen, the crow laments,
> Listen, the crow laments,
> There's too much anguish at my in-laws.
>
> Why, beloved parents of mine,
> Did you send your girl so far,
> Send your child so far . . .
>
> Had daughter not gone far enough,
> Would the bangles have run back home,
> Would my bangles have run back home . . .
>
> Had daughter not gone far enough,
> Would the necklace have returned,
> Would my necklace have returned . . .
>
> Had daughter not gone far enough,
> Would the *mangalsootala* have reached you,
> Would my mangalsootala have walked back . . .

Another common theme of women's songs is that of a covert, or shyly expressed, longing for the much-absent migrant husband. It is indecorous to voice romantic sentiment at other times, whether in the natal family or at the in-laws. A stress on modesty, as well as the element of teasing expectancy implies that any reference to the husband comes at the very end of a song. The sense of anticipation and of being naughty is considerably heightened as all other dutiful relationships skilfully woven into a song are exhausted, and the mention of the dearly beloved husband can be no longer put off. In sad songs, however, the husband being left to the very end could also be indicative of the hopelessness of the situation, since a major portion of the couple's youth is spent in separation and longing, and a wife can never really depend on the husband's presence.

THE EMPTY VANSA

Vansa means a winnowing fan, ritually used in fertility rites. It is filled with fruit and grain, and worshipped by married couples. Another meaning of the word indicates genealogy, past, present and future. The incidence of childless couples is very

high in the Kokan, owing to male out-migration in the reproductive years. What follows is a typical lament of the wife of
the migrant worker. She is cut off from her natal home, and
lonely in the house of the in-laws. This is to be her only home
until death. She has already decorated and ritually filled her
new vansa, but nobody can tell her what to do with it.

(Note: Sister-in-law here refers to husband's brother's wife,
while little sister is husband's young sister.)

> My new vansa is full, tai, to whom shall I give it?
> To whom shall I give it?
> Father-in-law's gone to the bazaar, tai,
> To whom shall I give it?
>
> My new vansa is full, tai, to whom shall I give it?
> To whom shall I give it?
> Mother-in-law sits on the bed, tai,
> To whom shall I give it?
>
> My new vansa is full, tai, to whom shall I give it?
> To whom shall I give it?
> Sister-in-law's left for the fields, tai,
> To whom shall I give it?
>
> My new vansa is full, tai, to whom shall I give it?
> To whom shall I give it?
> Little sister's gone to play, tai,
> To whom shall I give it?
>
> My new vansa is full, tai, to whom shall I give it?
> To whom shall I give it?
> Brother-in-law's gone to school, tai,
> To whom shall I give it?
>
> My new vansa is full, tai to whom shall I give it?
> To whom shall I give it?
> My husband's left for work, tai,
> To whom shall I give it?

Within the songs is a permitted stylized range of grumbling
over the in-laws' demands, otherwise unthinkable. The songs
reveal the hierarchical nature of relationships and interactions
amongst the women in the household, for example, between the
daughters of the family as compared to the daughters-in-law,
or between the various daughters-in-law themselves.

PHUGADI-PHU

The other form of folk songs are a part of women-only song and dance recreation ritual called *phugadya*. Some of the songs for ovya and phugadya may interchange, but the latter rarely have sad songs. The enthusiasm with which the farm women throw themselves into these fun and dance sessions at the end of a long and tiring workday should be seen to be believed, with the middle-aged women generally excelling at the energetic horse-play these sessions often evolve into. The younger women present a more delicately modest mien, while the older women and the widows may sit around and sing the songs. City and town women and girls watch with mouths agape the sheer energy that village women bring to the dancing, with endless pirouettes until they literally collapse on the floor with exhaustion.

On festival days, women often visit each other's houses to dance phugadya well into the early morning. Men, of course, are banished from the vicinity then. While dancing the phugadya, middle-aged women in particular may draw up their nine-yard saris to crotch-level, interlock their legs in a sitting cross-position, and twirl around on the floor like fast-spinning tops. These games are competitive, and it is great sport to watch two middle-aged women trying to outspin each other, or engaged in assorted acrobatics to the accompaniment of songs! Some phugadya take the form of exaggerated, slow-moving stylistic gestures, even using household utensils to add a touch of novelty to the dances. These sessions are called phugadya because the dances are often accompanied by a *phu phu* sputtering at the mouth.

SESAME FLOWER

(All women link hands and dance in a slow-moving circle)

'Sesame flower, pretty sister-in-law
He's coming to fetch you.'

'Let him, but who?'
'Father-in-law.'

'Let him, if he will, but what does he bring?'
'He brings bright bangles for your wrists.'

'Bangles for the wrists I will not accept.
I will not go with father in-law.'

'Sesame flower, pretty sister-in-law,
She's coming to fetch you.'

'Let her, but who?'
'Mother-in-law.'

'Let her, if she will, but what does she bring?'
'She brings a fine necklace, rubies and pearls.'

'Rubies and pearls I will not accept.
I will not go with mother-in-law.'

'Sesame flower, pretty sister-in-law,
He's coming to fetch you.'

'Let him, but who?'
'Brother-in-law.'

'Let him if he will, but what does he bring?'
'He brings you a nose ring.'

'Nose ring and jewels I will not accept
I will not go with brother-in-law.'

'Sesame flower, pretty sister-in-law,
He's coming to fetch you.'

'Let him, but who?
'Husband darling.'

'Let him, if he will, but what does he bring?'
'He brings you a piece of coconut kernel.'

'Coconut kernel, I shall eat like a rabbit.
With husband darling, I shall traipse along.'

The insouciance of the daughter-in-law, tiny though she is, is much appreciated by all the dancing women, who collapse on the floor in a giggling heap as soon as the last word of the song is out. The expected denouement is prolonged until all possible improvisations in terms of the identity of the person coming to fetch the child bride and the pieces of jewellery brought as blandishments are thoroughly exhausted. This is a song of older times, when child marriages were fairly common. The child bride grew up in the in-laws' house, and she was sent to the husband immediately after menstruation began, anywhere between twelve to sixteen years of age.

Daughters are in fact viewed as temporary keepsakes in their parents' house, to be held on 'trust' until claimed by the rightful owner. Thus in weddings the women sing with a sad lilt: '*Jyachi hoti, tyane neli; amchi maya yata geli*' ('He to whom she belongs took her away; our affection is wasted'). Besides affection, another meaning of the term *maya* is wealth, or material investment. *Maher* is the mother's house. The mother does not have any customary property right, neither does the daughter. But the daughter does have a tremendous stake in the wealth of affection and pure belongingness, in the sense of uncritical acceptance that the maher represents, which she can never hope to find with the in-laws. The dwelling of the latter she must refer to as *ghar*, which means home. The first is a place of sunshine, of joy, warmth, and caring, while the second is where she must tread carefully, conscious of her duty and obligations; a cold, alien place. In common village idiom, at one place she picks flowers, at the other she must gather dried cowdung cakes for fuel!

Earlier, little over a generation ago, as the older women tell, the villagers practised *dej* or bride price. There is even a popular proverb, *pahili beti, dhanachi peti*, which associates the first daughter with a treasure chest. The groom's father or older male relative would pay 'compensation' to the bride's father or relative, in acknowledgement of the economic loss suffered by him in giving his daughter away. Such dej compensation would generally include a mutually agreed sum of money, anywhere from Rs. 40 to Rs. 150 (a lot of money in those days), depending on the groom's or his relative's capacity to pay. Now, of course, the malaise of the cities has spread far and wide, so daughters have to await marriage until a decent dowry can be got together, either through their own efforts or by their male relatives.

While a lucky bride may find doting in-laws after marriage,

a more common experience is to meet with irritable people who have little patience amidst their own burden of work, to teach her the ways of the new household that she finds herself in.

DAUGHTER-IN LAW THIEF

(This is acted out with one woman chasing another, broom in hand—broom of course, being the instrument of chastisement—while the rest join hands and dance around in slow motion)

CHORUS: Daughter-in-law thief, where did she go?
Following after you, mother-in-law.

Daughter-in-law thief, who ate the curds?
Swear on your feet, mother-in-law,
Swear on Lord *Ganoba's* feet
I'm the true daughter-in-law,
I'm the true daughter-in-law.

Daughter-in-law thief, where did she go?
Following after you, mother-in-law.

Daughter-in-law thief, who ate the plantains?
Swear on your feet, mother-in-law,
Swear on Lord Ganoba's feet,
I'm the true daughter-in-law,
I'm the true daughter-in-law.

Daughter-in-law thief, where did she go?
Following after you, mother-in-law.

Daughter-in-law thief, who ate the coconut?
Swear on your feet, mother-in-law,
Swear on Lord Ganoba's feet,
I'm the true daughter-in-law,
I'm the true daughter-in-law . . .

Thus the most appreciated theme in the Malvani women's songs expresses the ill-concealed hostility between the mother-in-law and the daughter-in-law. The former is usually permitted to be used as a target of malicious lampooning by the latter in the songs. It should be noted, however, that both mothers-in-law and daughters-in-law among the singers, old and young women alike, empathize with the misery of the bride or the daughter in-law in each song, and not with the mother-in-law, even though their real-life roles may justify reverse identification. Thus mothers-in-law in the singing group probably visualize their own dutiful youth spent in loneliness and longing, and perceive no need to extend that same sense of empathy for the plight of their own errant daughters-in-laws.

It is a curious twist then, that in such songs all women transcend their respective roles to find an uncommon solidarity against the mythical mother-in-law. It is to be acknowledged in any event that the songs provide a sharply subversive element of release in the face of an oppressive reality of grinding poverty, exhaustion from overwork, loneliness, sexual and emotional repression, and petty conflicts, bickering and jealousies among all the women in a household. It is no wonder then, that all women, young and old, look forward with undisguised eagerness to these sessions, which have a cherished place in Malvani folklore.

UKHANE

Besides ovya and phugadya, there is the sport of *ukhane*, or name-taking, when women get together in a gentle spirit of fun and sharing to speak out their husbands' names. This is a liberty otherwise prohibited in a culture that de-emphasizes the closeness and free and easy interchange between spouses. This is a much loved sport for Malvani and Marathi women, and to a much lesser extent for the men, particularly after a wedding. It involves the creative recitation of simple couplets within which the spouse's name may be cleverly transposed. It is accompanied with an exaggerated air of shy modesty and jocularity on part of the listeners. Traditionally, a husband and wife may never address each other by the first name, at least in front of witnesses. It is not seemly to do so.

The ukhane sessions involve much giggling and elbow nudging and a keen sense of competition. Couplets are honed and pared in advance, prepared just for this session, though always preceded by a few minutes taken up by gestures expressing shyness so that the woman is not thought to be shameless.

Some women excel at fishing out unheard of couplets through cross-cultural gossip with women from other villages. Others may always reach the middle of a couplet and forget the critical part containing the husband's name. There will be a lot of kind prompting, of course.

The act of 'name-taking' is an extremely subtle way of expressing the tenuous bond between husband and wife. It also emphasizes the feminine virtue of duty and devotion. It adds to the mystique of the marital relationship, where often none exits in reality.

> Piles of snow
> On ranges of Himalayas.
> Spoken 'Gangaram Rane's name',
> To keep the assembly's word.

Characteristic Malvani irreverence is active here too, easily subverting what is meant to be uplifting and mystifying. Thus bitter wives are known to replace shy, poetic verses honouring their husbands in the name-taking with shocking bursts of rhymes that achieve the opposite.

> At edge of the yard, brambles and bushes
> 'Gangaram Rane' mouths nothing but curses.

> To the post at the door
> Tied a gaggle of geese.
> A cheapskate like 'that'
> Let me go, please.

> Cleaned mountains of bowls
> With black soot and grease.
> Folks laughed at my face,
> Wife of 'Gangaram Rane'.

A husband may feel quite helpless to retaliate in such an event, since the Malvani sense of economy and decorum does not permit him to use a grinding stone to remedy a pinprick. The wife is aware of this. A subtler way of expressing similar angst is by mouthing an entire delicate couplet without saying the husband's name at all. In doing this the wife maintains a sense of

public decorum, while at the same time insisting on her right
not to forgive her husband his trespasses.

The ukhane said by men, of course, are more often just a
matter of formality, a ritual that a bridegroom goes through
when he escorts the new bride into the house for the first time,
at the end of the wedding ceremony. As in most other spheres,
they are brief and much less creative.

> Dish of dishes, spinach I adore
> For wife beloved, Lalita, I adore.
>
> Stick of sticks, cane plain
> Wife of mine, plain, plain!
>
> Who's afraid to speak a name
> Lalita's in my satchel!

An insolent lad may dispense with any sense of mystique by
boldly pronouncing the bride's name when pressed to do so by
a swarm of giggling females of all ages. This leads to a mild
sense of betrayal and deflation, which is altogether intended.
Womanly nonsense! On the other hand, each bride shudders in
anticipation of this ordeal. For the sobbing young bride, recently
torn away from her natal family and delivered into this horde
of strange and frightening in-laws, elocutory panache is not
readily available. For the assembled listeners, it is an occasion
of fun and excitement not to be forsaken out of mere kindness.
It is a rite of passage, an essential stage in transition from a
carefree young girl to the role of a dutiful wife. It is one of the
many wedding rituals that are such exquisite torture for a brief
period, before the daily grind takes over.

A long ukhana like the one that follows demonstrates considerable mental facility and verbal panache, when delivered
in a fast, faultless way as old Akka does, with words rolling off
her tongue, so that her husband's name strung at the very end
seems cleverly concealed in all the verbiage. This is 'name-taking' at its creative heights. A skill like this is much envied by
all the women.

> Dig spade dig, shovelfuls of earth,
> Plaster the walls, paint the columns,

In Mother-in-law's womb,
In sister-in-law's steps,
Born was Ram; didn't say Ram; didn't speak the name;
Measureful of betel nut, thirty-two-leaves
Applied lime to thirty-two leaves.
How can I walk with anklets on my feet?
How can I speak before so many men?
Assembly of gold, stares of the youth,
Beggar woman's tangles, cobra's hood.
Let pass by the open window,
Palanquin of 'Gangaram Rane'.

Malvani Gajali

Gajali, as gossip is called in plural, have a place of pride in Malvani folklore. To talk is to make gajali. It is a pure and simple fact of life in the village. If the target and cohorts are absent and much despised, there are raucous and ribald gajali. Otherwise, it is gossip in hushed undertones with heads bent low. A man may launch into a colourful account of the latest drunken brawl in the neighbouring community. Certain aspects of the tale may be set right by other listeners in the know. Women quietly resolve to check out the tale from the horse's mouth, or rather from the horse's wife's mouth, or even from the horse's neighbour's wife's mouth the next day, under the pretext of taking some odd rice to the flour mill conveniently located in that community.

Often there are swift one-liners, masterly caricatures of the target, rarely malicious. A mother hen gets startled by something. She lets out a loud squawk and flutters busily around her brood, beating the air with spread wings. Ani's younger sister-in-law nudges a comrade with her elbow, 'Look at her; bossy, just like her mistress!' There is much absurdity, and fountains of laughter, women wiping their streaming eyes with the edge of their saris. Few people have raised gajali to the state of art that the Malvanis have.

In Malvani society, there are no secrets. The ferreting out of private, hidden information is a finely honed art; information is power and prestige. A person with enough information is to be envied; of course speed is of the essence in this game. Just as is the skill of embroidery. It is not the measly article itself, but what you can add to it, with what style, where, and when, that imparts glory to the deliverer. Any talent at swift repartee is to be cherished.

Gajali-making, or the satiation of natural curiosity about the state of being of the fellow villagers and the kinsfolk, and the nosing out of information of potential worth is perceived as a matter of Malvani pride, a cultural treasure. So also is its converse, which is the hiding of wanted information. This latter state is characterized by a multitude of stock expressions, such as the head bent low over some busy chore, saris drawn close to the bosom, or the fixed stare, hands rolling the paan or scratching at an irresistible spot in the middle of the shoulders. Voices fall silent with a hasty switch in the subject of conversation. The fluidity envisioned at times of gajali-making gets crystallized into a bovine stoniness.

Expletives Undeleted

The importance of expletives is not to be denied as a crucial part of Malvani folklore, an undeniably creative expression of the right to free speech of Malvani men, women and children. A famous dramatist, Machhindra Kambli, has immortalized for all times the Malvani penchant for profanity, by making it the raison d'être of all his wildly popular plays in Bombay in the last decade. He succeeded in creating a new dramatic genre in this heartland of Indian popular theatre, and the success of his plays was not only due to enthusiastic support from Malvani migrants, but from all sections of theatre enthusiasts.

The colour of Malvani curries is bright red, the proud colour of home-grown chilli peppers. The peppers add the spice, while kokum peel or tamarind adds to the mouth-twisting sourness of the broths. The weather is hot and humid, life is stressful and intense. One cannot envision mealy-mouthed decorous speech in these circumstances. People engage themselves with pure abandon in the task of developing an added zing to the much enriched lexicon, with the use of multicoloured subtle and not-so-subtle to outright stunning abuses. Timely knowledge of the target's weakest spots is of considerable help while homing in. There are times when a bombastic delivery achieves best results. At other times a low key effort, with a honeyed delivery may be best appreciated. There is a very wide range of variations available to the cognoscenti, and there are acknowledged and much envied practitioners. Imprinted on the Malvani psyche is the fundamental truth that the twist of a wicked tongue is mightier than a thousand lashes.

Proverbs

Malvani lingo is profusely peppered with conventional aphorisms of days gone by, in the form of proverbs that succinctly sum up a situation with great economy of expression. There is a particular staccato style of delivering these proverbs, and it often serves as a tool for linguistic obfuscation when engaged in one-upmanship with neophytes to the intricacies of the language. They may also be used as special shorthand to avoid lengthier forms of speech in their busy lives.

More than any other group, it is the old women who are especially fond of using a constant barrage of proverbs instead of communicating in a more normal way of speaking. The proverbs are strongly rooted in the common cultural experience of villagers in the entire region, and are an important part of the folklore. A famous proverb, *tuka nay, maka nay, ghal kutryak,* succinctly sums up a contentious character trait which the locals sportingly own up to. Loaded with sarcasm, it refers to a spoilsport attitude whereby something of value is thrown to the dogs rather than allowing another person to use it.

Conclusion

A special feature of Malvani women's folklore is the extent of rebellion and ire expressed by the women against oppressive conditions and despotic authority figures, particularly the mother-in-law, the sister-in-law, and the husband. Within the broad area of folklore exist specially gendered genres for men and women. These include group devotional songs, or bhajans, sung mostly by men, to the accompaniment of musical instruments. They include the *double-bari* or question-and-answer sessions of competitive ad-libbing based typically on conundrums and paradoxes from the ancient Hindu epics of *Mahabharat* and *Ramayan*. They also include men's *dhaikala* or costume mythological dramas enacted by travelling actors in temple premises before large audiences. It is usually young boys who enthusiastically enact the female roles.

Men in many neighbourhoods also regularly present plays based on contemporary 'social' themes, usually stories modelled on narratives popular in the cities. More often than not, they are tear-jerkers on the theme of feminine suffering and self-sacrifice in the face of male depravity. Enthusiastic local talent is available for the plays, while the heroine is usually a specially invited free-lance actress from urbanized centres like Goa. Though not an essential part of village folklore, these plays often serve as a striking contrast to the oral tradition, as vehicles of indoctrination to the urban middle class values, and modern patriarchal values, in particular.

Even though the various forms of folklore are generally gender-specific, it is not rare for women to organize their own bhajan groups, for men to participate in 'name-taking'; or more rarely, for an envious bunch of men to organize their own phugadya patterned on the women's dance sessions. This is a tribute to the covert egalitarianism, or perhaps, 'laissez-faire' as it prevails in rural Malvani society, under an overarching rigidly traditional patriarchy which stresses sharply gender-divergent modes and customs of behaviour.

CHAPTER III

Aba and Kaki, a Village Couple

THE BHAJAN *mandali* of the wadi is assembled on the porch after dinner. First come several noisy young boys with the long nal drum and little bronze cymbals, cooing and shouting in the dark of the jungle night, if only to ward off fear of the haunting spirits. The racket they set up is a reminder to the wadi men to set forth from their respective homes for the bhajan at my house. I have performed a long neglected rite of propitiation by offering worship and food to ancestral spirits that day.

Aba is ill. He wheezes with a hand on the chest, and officiates as the 'host', overruling all protestations of concern for his health. He does not approve of my selection of the priest for such a momentous occasion. He has pulled the proffered chair very close to the ritual fire, and follows every action of the Bramhan with great concentration. He has taken it upon himself to make sure that my ancestors will not have to return in disappointment after such a long wait because of the uncouthness of the priest, who in his secular role is a cart driver. It is also his responsibility to act as the prompter to me and the Bramhan so that the names of all the departed worthies of several generations ago are correctly given.

The Patriarch Who Stayed Behind

He may have never stepped into a school, and may never know *ga-ma-bha-na* of the Marathi alphabet, but none can challenge his undisputed authority over matters of religious propriety. He has got a very sharp eye, honed over years of tried and tested apprenticeship as the eldest surviving son of his clan. He stayed behind in the village to tend the ancestral lands, while others enlisted (if only for a few years, but their pensions were secure) in the Maratha Light Infantry of the British Army, the British police force, the Grand Indian Peninsular Railway, or in the Bombay textile industry. He had in fact tried a few temporary jobs in Bombay for brief periods, but he felt defeated by the harsh pressures of city living. He was not suited to heavy farming either, in his youth. All those days his large brood had barely managed a hand to mouth existence.

While I am new to the village, old man Aba takes me in his personal charge in matters of education to village ways. He is a friend, not a patriarch. This is our mutual conspiracy, as are my relationships with all other villagers I grow close to, both men and women. We relate with the kind of nonhierarchical and open sharing of ideas and opinions which is way beyond the pale of sanctioned interaction in the village. A precious bond of trust and affection grows between us as each day goes by. He watches the goings-on with an eagle eye as workmen repair my dilapidated ancestral home. He walks into my kitchen as I sit on the floor by the mud *chool* or cooking stove, rolling chapatis. 'I'll sit here and quietly watch you,' he says. 'I like your kitchen. This is always the heart of a house, in all ways. The rest of the house does not matter. A kitchen is the most important room in a house . . . Me, old fogey that I am, I'll sit in this corner and chat with you. If you leave your cooking to talk to me, I know you'll go hungry late in the afternoon. Please don't mind me in your kitchen.' He always speaks to me in this gentle, modest manner.

Mentor, Guide, Gajali-Maker

The Aba I knew and remember with such heartache, was the most gentle, diligent of all teachers, introducing me patiently to village life. He overlooked my strange ways, my irreverence, and indulged my thirst for information. The stories would roll off his tongue. His eyes would narrow into slits, as his hands gestured to flesh out village ritual hierarchies, roles and duties that only he knew with such painstaking accuracy.

I knew I had touched a special chord in Aba's heart as the sole descendant of a 'progressive' family returning to pay homage to ancient roots. My professed purpose of field research did not gel in his eyes. It did not matter. What mattered was that I was re-establishing long-lost connections. It was impressive for a woman to restore the ancestral home with such panache, while even city men had to shed tears of bitterness and frustration over this. Also, for a woman to undertake this ritual of ancestor propitiation was unheard of. But the men of the wadi were happy and proud of the fact. There were no usual detractors with their gloomy faces and laundry list of previous failures, as there were whenever I proposed a venture in community action. Very unknowingly, I had served to reaffirm their pride in their identity as villagers.

Though I had initially laughed at their strange superstitions and fears, and still continue to mock at some of their impositions in matters of feminine decorum, fulfilment of neglected responsibilities towards ancestral spirits in the ancestral home is the very foundation of their faith in existence and in religion. Besides, they are the people who stayed behind to nurture this simple faith, out of choice or necessity. They are the butt of ridicule as mere peasants in the world. But here was a 'learned' woman of a fine, wealthy family who had returned to live amidst them, trying to speak their *maka-tuka* language instead of the Marathi language spoken by people of culture. She had even learnt to eat paan and tobacco like them, and joined them in muddy farm work instead of turning up her nose at them like other city women. They made it clear to her and to visitors to the wadi that she was *amchich*, their very own.

The Haunted Dimensions

The men, sitting on the rug spread outside on the porch, are almost all there. A few late stragglers are walking up the narrow pathway by the light of little hurricane lanterns, sticks in hand in case there are snakes or other wild creatures in the dark. Usually bhajans are sung indoors, but this occasion is for the ancestral spirits, so the porch is an appropriate place. It is a clear, cool night, and it is very pleasant outside. With so many people around, the single petromax lamp pierces the dark with an unusually bright light, and even the little children are unafraid and excited. We do not have electricity in the wadi yet.

Vijgya walks in amidst the women gathered in the living room with an air of authority. 'What is this? Haven't you had the good sense to get the ritual lamp lit yet?' This is permissible male authority, and allowed to pass, although Madhgya's mother mutters under her breath with a long face. He stares hard at her and raises his voice even louder, 'Hurry, hurry. We don't have all night. And don't delay getting the tea and ladoos when it is time.' Another deliberately raucous voice from outside calls out to hurry. The men know that once they are out in full strength they have a culturally sanctioned importance that the worst battleaxe of a subversive woman may not undermine. They must not be made to wait.

These damned women are very impudent. Give them a good few inches, and they will grumble in public that it is not a yard's worth. But now that all the men are here in full solidarity for the bhajan, a purpose of great devotion and piousness, the women can be shown their place: indoors, silent, respectful and also appreciative. The tea had better be good after all that singing. The women got together the previous night to make the sweet ladoos specially for the bhajan men because our men need to be propitiated too, just like the Gods and the spirits, as Akka says to the women amidst a lot of tittering.

The lamp is lit, and incense wafts on the air. With great clearing of throats, after repeated testing of the nal drum, the men begin to sing. The bhajans are conducted with a lot of faith, and the men do not make mistakes in singing. Today the men feel really moved. These particular ancestors have waited too long.

The men have sung for almost two hours now. I did not send for the battery-operated loudspeaker and it seems quite unnecessary now. It is a hauntingly beautiful, still night, the dark woods looming behind the porch silhouetted against a starry sky. As we all know, the emotions expressed in the devotional songs are wafting away to the other dimension where they will reach the souls of the long-departed ones. The men are in no hurry to end the singing, and the women listen transfixed, from inside the house.

Aba's wife stands glued to the tiny window with wooden bars, watching the men sing with a rare thirst. They know she is there. They can see her, but her sixty-year status allows her that liberty. I watch with fascination the deep glow of the petromax lantern outside reflected on her serene unlined face. She is very small, barely four feet in height, with a slim girlish waist, her brood of six children notwithstanding.

Today she has worn a small garland of jasmine flowers in her hair, and she has the gentle poise of a woman content towards the end of her toil. She is lost in the bhajans, and it is a joy to behold such magical immersion in the songs of devotion that the men are singing outside. The biggish red dot of *kunku* on her forehead, a proud symbol of her piety and her husband's well-being, stands out like a challenge against her round moon face, big dreamy eyes lost in a far-away look as a half-smile curls her pinkish paan-stained lips.

This is how I prefer to remember old Aba's widow. Did she have a premonition of his death a week later? She had never in all her timid life forgotten herself so at a public get-together. It was the last occasion of such childlike enjoyment in her life.

The flowers in her hair, the coloured dot adorning her face, the simple black beads round her neck attesting to her married status (black, to ward the evil eye off her husband's mortality), green glass bangles around her thin wrists as symbols of fertility, were all very simple adornments centring her to the earth as a blessed woman, a joy to behold. She had not neglected her duties, tough as her life had been. So today she stood secure in the glow of those adornments. She knew she had earned that serenity, and nobody could point fingers at her because she stood framed in that window, lost in the music bridging the two worlds.

Take Her Fertility into the Burning Grounds

A week later, they hold her frail wrists tight, as someone hits on the bangles gently with a farm sickle to separate them from her widowed wrists. Fire crackers are set off, in three distinct bursts, to let the villagers know that someone has died. To her, they serve as a dreadful explosive warning that her status in life has changed. She has heard these bursts all her life, causing her to shudder mechanically at the thought of just another death. Today she does not shudder. The sound of the crackers is inside her head, exploding her poise and serenity for the last time. By then, half the village knows that Aba of this wadi is dead. Men and women put aside tasks at hand and set forth, to console the bereaved or to help with the funeral tasks.

Women have gathered inside, wailing. His wife is sobbing, *'Karmachandalin me, nashib phutka maja'* ('I am a woman cursed, destiny has cheated me'). She is using all the worst abuses of widowhood for herself, slapping on her forehead with her palms. Aba's much loved youngest daughter, twenty years old, hangs on to her mother and keens aloud, 'Baba, Baba . . . why did you leave us like this,' in the pauses between her mother's wailing.

A great number of people are milling around by then. They have washed Aba's body and clothed it in the clean crisp clothes that he had proudly worn at his youngest son's wedding, a few months earlier. They have even seated him in a chair, looking lifelike in the usual pose he struck while telling his famous tales. Someone has already tied bamboo poles to the chair and decorated it with plantain stalks, and they will carry him thus to the burning grounds marked for his clan.

The Kunbi man Manya, who always officiates at such times, and is almost one of us, gently grasps the thread stringing the beads at Kaki's neck, ever so respectful, while severing it with the farm sickle so it falls into dead Aba's lap. Other women hold her so that she doesn't collapse to the ground at Aba's feet. They have remembered to make a garland of flowers and tie it in her hair before leading her out to Aba, and someone now tears it off her hair and drops it into his lap.

They have filled her *oti* one last time, the triangular pocket made out of the loose end of her sari, clutched at the stomach, filled with fistfuls of rice and a coconut. Today she has to bend over her husband's dead body, weeping silently as she lets the contents of that oti spill into his lap, in a parodied reversal of the fertility theme. He will take it away from her into the burning grounds.

All the assembled people have paid homage to his body before it is burnt to ashes. Now they pick him up and carry him swiftly away to the burning grounds, while the women, mostly old widows who are now left with her, take her for a symbolic bath to clear away the pollution of the dead body before she can be taken in the house.

Into the Dungeons of Widowhood

She is brought in with a covered face and shoved into the corner room where she is left on the floor, weeping as they shut the door on her. God forbid the woman who catches sight of that awful 'white' forehead without the red kunku. Who wants to be punished with a similar fate? Married women should stay away from her because the widow's evil eye cast at their own blessed adornments might be powerful enough to take away their husbands' lives. Rough old Ani even remembers to push Kaki's married daughter out of her newly widowed mother's path, to protect her from the evil eye.

For the twelve days that she was shut in that room, she could not bring herself to eat, despite urgings from her loving daughter and a few solicitous kinswomen widows. Somehow the shame went deep. How could she eat? For twelve days, an important period of transition, she did not step out of that dark dank room into the fresh air of daylight. This was perhaps to facilitate her inner world to adjust to the outer constriction that was her fate from then on. To ease herself, she had to steal out to go by the stream in the pitch dark of the pre-dawn hours, with the dutiful daughter for company since it was never safe to go out alone. She was ashamed in case some unsuspecting passerby saw her accursed face. But her body refused to yield. She was totally constipated for six whole days until one of the neighbours procured a laxative powder for her. When she emerged from that room on the thirteenth and the last day of severe pollution after the death, she was no longer the same woman. Her physical appearance had changed. Gone was the innocent softness of her glowing face on the night of the bhajan. It was replaced with a strange bitter harshness. She had visibly shrunk to the bone in those twelve days of self-imposed starvation. She had walked with her head bent, eyes to the ground, all her life. But the earlier look of piety and devotion was replaced by a sullen rage. She felt herself to be a victim of the whole callous world. Her sense of betrayal was total.

Through a life of suffering and hardship, this was the eventuality that she had feared the most. She had probably anticipated it several times over through Aba's repeated bouts of illness caused by high blood pressure, asthma, and general debility. Then, as he recovered, each time, she had come to believe in her own powers to prolong his life. All those stories of devoted wives bringing their husbands back to life through the force of their piety had made a very powerful impression on her when she was young. Where had she gone wrong? How had she sinned? Her demented fevered brain would not release her from this agony, and she continued to blame herself. For a year after that, during the period of extended mourning for the household, she had refused to leave the house except for the most unavoidable tasks. She continued to lurk in the shadows even much later; it had become a habit. She almost became the invisible woman. She gave up going to the fields. If the crops shrivelled, they might blame her, she reasoned.

'She's too much,' old Akka muttered, pulling on her oldest granddaughter's hair as she braided the thickly oiled mass. 'Nobody expects her to carry on so. Remember when Nangya's father died? All the kids were this high,' she points to the little girl squatting in front of her. 'Poor Nangya's mother covered her head with a rag and set forth to the fields. Some nasty women had

ventured to remark on the "shameless" sight after she had
passed, but that was in those days. Even then our old Bai had
yelled at them, "Will you go and feed all the little mouths for the
entire year, pious that you are? How are they all to eat if she
doesn't tend the crops?" They had shut up after that.'

Of Woman Caste

Aba's wife and son have never cared to maintain his old connections. All the people on the wadi are pained by this neglect. We
feel slighted. Old Nana mutters under his breath one day, an-
grily tapping his stick on the mud floor: 'Don't be taken in by all
her pious ways. See how she carries on. She did not give him a
minute's peace when he was ill and dying.

'He had been a very timid, gentle soul for most of his life,
once he had settled down with his wife and children. He often
refused to get involved in wadi brawls, and was much in pain
if ever falsely accused. Remember the time drunken old Natha
had yelled obscenities at him over a petty disagreement, and
he had quietly shed tears and refused to touch food for several
days because of the hurt? He was like that. But you can never
trust these women. They wait until you're down, and then they
slit your throat. *Bayanchi jaat*, of woman caste!

'She used to continue with her nonstop ranting, theatrically
touching her forehead to curse her own fate. "All through my
life you never ceased to cause me worries and troubles. Now
give me some peace in old age . . ." It had not mattered to her
that he was ill beyond repair. There was no need to put up any
pretense then, with all the wadi residents watching. Then why
does she carry on so now?'

Kaki is upset by my presence, and I have stopped visiting
her too. She feels pressured by my questions, my probing. She
does not like me to ask why. She feels uncomfortable about my
urging her not to punish herself so, that times have changed,
that people are not really talking about her all the time behind
her back. She does not want to be cheated of her sentiments,
her crisis, just because the times have changed. She has locked

herself into this role, and does not want to let go of the security
it offers. She is the long-suffering pious woman. She is very
different from old Bai, Shamgya's mother. I was away in
Bombay when her husband died. She refused to accept sundry
advice on getting her husband's family pension continued in
her own name. 'Let Anjanitai return, I can wait,' she had insisted. 'They will give you only half the monthly pension; it will
take two years to get hold of the money, look at Nandu's mother
in the other wadi,' those in the know had warned her. She had
held her peace and brought all the papers over to me on the
day of my return.

First, she had sat in a corner, and wiped her eyes with the
end of her sari at the memory of her departed husband. It was
only after that that she had broached this other matter. She
had no problem in getting the full amount of his monthly pension continued for herself from the next month itself. We had
an important meeting scheduled, and some women from Bombay had come especially to address the farm women. I hesitantly
asked Bai if she would want to remain present. It was barely
a month after the husband's death. 'Of course, I will come,' she
had replied with asperity, 'but you'd better warn those others,
in case any of them decide to accuse me of lack of decorum.
That will be your responsibility, and I will come.' No one had
said anything, and she had attended all the meetings after that,
participating in the goings-on with real interest.

Worlds of Fear

Kaki knew that she could visit me whenever she wished, although I had largely suspended my visits to her house sensing
her discomfort. I respected her wish to deal with her widowhood
in her own way. When she understood this, she began to sneak
into my house once in a while, at odd hours, when she was fairly
sure that there would be no one else around. She would visit me
to ask if I had any message about her son and his family in
Bombay, or to keep up contact in general. She always walked
with slow measured steps, with a mournful air, even five years

after Aba's death. Any query would bring tears to her eyes. Her heart bled for her poor farmer son, working so hard in the hot sun, without comfort. She would recall each current misery and cry.

Gradually I pieced together her story, over several months, as we met at each other's house on sultry afternoons when the rest were away at work on the farms. Kaki had retired from farm work since Aba's death, and her chief preoccupation was taking care of her infant granddaughter at home. 'Farm work is too heavy for me nowadays. I leave it to them. I don't try to instruct them about it. My mind is happy with the *porgya*, the child. I do go help if "she" [meaning the daughter-in-law] is not well, like I went to do the transplanting for a month last year, but otherwise, I leave it to them.'

Kaki has this curiously exaggerated trait of referring to people indirectly. Once you are tuned into the conversation, it does not take you very long to understand who the 'he', 'she' and 'them' happen to be in Kaki's world. It is a wise habit, born of caution. It probably serves to prevent false accusations of gajali-making if the person thus alluded to should be within earshot. It soon becomes second nature. It serves to underscore Kaki's extreme sense of insecurity and defencelessness within her household and beyond.

She was the eldest of her mother's two children, with a brother three years younger than herself. Her father died when she was about five years old. Next year an aunt by marriage who lived in the same house was also widowed. There was great sorrow in the house. She remembers her grandmother weeping. She had lost four grown up children in one year: two sons and two daughters. Kaki does not know the cause of the deaths. What she does recall is the sense of shock, numbness and confusion she had then experienced. She remembers her great puzzlement on seeing her widowed mother's hands, bare, without bangles. If she ventured to ask why, her mother would cry. She remembers thinking to herself, 'What a strange way to be.

s this how housewives conduct their affairs?'

Kaki recalls her great terror when all these women started veeping, particularly her mother. Sometimes there were point-dly callous remarks directed at the widows. 'Whose inauspi-ious face did I see first thing this morning?' The speaker had robably experienced some misfortune that day, and it was nec-ssary to find a target on whom to vent all the frustration. The vomen would cringe with shame. 'I never forgot these things. was convinced that I would invite a like fate if ever I saw a voman's face within twelve days of being widowed. I took care ever to be near such a woman.'

She remembers great fear as a little girl. There were no men n the house. The doors were useless, termite-eaten. Their day-ime visitors would reassure them, but once they left, the vomen felt lonely and insecure at night. Of course there was o electricity, and poor households could not afford to burn 1uch oil, so it was always very dark in the night. The grand-1other would say, 'thieves will come and kill us all.' Kaki in-ernalized the terror. This is one of her earliest memories. 'I ad trouble sleeping, I would worry so. I would wake up scream-1g and shouting, but the sound would be locked in my chest.' he became a confirmed insomniac since then.

She did not go to school. She remembers her grandmother aying, 'Women who go to school reincarnate as bhains.' Bhains r Bhavins) are women belonging to the caste of temple ser-ants. They were often kept as concubines or sexually exploited y upper caste men in earlier days. 'When I was little, the re-gious *buwa* would come to our wadi for *kirtan*, citing stories f great suffering and misfortune from ancient religious epics nd tales. That is all I learnt.'

She started accompanying her mother to the fields, learning rming tasks. She recalls her mother talking to women while ansplanting paddy, expressing worry about her daughter's ture. 'I've only got this one girl. Once I get her happily arried, I should be free of all my worries.' Kaki never rgot those words. Through all her humiliations following arriage, she reminded herself of the great misery she would cause her mother if she returned to her.

An elderly kinsman took the initiative and began to pressur
ize her mother to marry the daughter off. He brought a proposa
from his own distant relatives. She was not yet fourteen, and
she had not attained puberty. Her mother was reluctant to
marry her that early. But the kinsman cajoled and threatened
'You and your daughter look well after yourselves. Don't ask
for my help later. This is a good match, from among my own
relations. Two men alone, father and son. There's nobody to
cook for them. They won't wait very long, and you'll lose a good
match. Later, people will laugh at your motherless, fatherless
orphan. Can a girl live at her mother's forever?'

Finally the pressure had been too much for the mother and
the daughter, and the wedding was arranged. Her mother had
taken ill at the time, and the kinsman gave her away. 'An ear
lier match for the groom had broken up, and this was meant
to be my fate,' Kaki bitterly remarks. She needs no prompting
the dams hold nothing back today.

To the Given Home

Kaki talks of her discovery of her husband's affair with the
widow Sumi, on arriving at the in-laws' house after the mar
riage. Sumi had grown up as a child widow in the company of an
elder sister-in-law. These two women lived by themselves in
house nearby. They subsisted on a small tract of paddy field and
by doing farm labour on the lands Aba's father cultivated as
tenant. They began to help the men with their cooking and
household tasks also. As it turned out, the sister-in-law woul
largely do the farm work while the young widow stayed bac
in-between to perform household tasks for the two men. Tha
was the beginning of a long affair which continued even afte
Kaki's marriage to Aba.

Kaki had not attained puberty at the time of her marriag
and a strict village code in this regard ensured that the unic
could not be consummated until after she had menstruated f
the first time. In the meanwhile, Sumi had taken charge of th

ousehold, and she continued to linger there. The father-in-law
ympathized with the young bride, but was helpless before his
eadstrong son.

'Had I been smart like today's girls I would have left that
ouse long ago,' Kaki reflects sadly, wiping her eyes. The other
voman disliked her intensely, and tried to humiliate her in all
ossible ways, enjoying her hold over Kaki's husband. She
vould hide her cooking vessels and enjoy the bride's discomfort.
She would complain about Kaki's behaviour to Aba, who would
ome around and slap her. He too constantly found fault with
ier. If he found less salt in the food, that would be occasion
nough to enrage him. He took care to see that his father was
iot within earshot, and then he would beat her. She was ter-
ified, and she cried a lot. 'She really harassed me a lot. I was
ery miserable. I wept as I patted the cowdung cakes to dry for
uel; I wept as I went to fetch the water. I felt totally abandoned.
 didn't possess any artifice. I kept quiet to maintain my par-
nts' reputation. *Ami jatisathi melo*, I sacrificed myself to main-
ain my caste reputation.'

The neighbouring kinswomen were kind to her. They com-
orted her as and when the situation arose. Old Kaka's wife
advised her to return to her mother, so hopeless was her case.
But she had proudly replied, 'I am of woman caste; I'll prefer
o die where I've been given, but I won't bring shame on my
mother's head by returning to her.'

Kaki had known very little about sex or even menstruation.
When she was young she had observed that her mother acted
strangely on certain days, when she would not enter the main
portion of the house. The daughter would have to do the cooking
and all the household tasks. If she asked why, her mother would
reply that she was polluted because the crow had touched her.
She would stay polluted for three days after the beginning of
menstruation, and resume her normal tasks only after she had
washed her hair and body on the fourth day. In the meanwhile
she would not touch any kitchen or general household object,
sitting and sleeping in the back room that had a separate entrance, for fear of defiling the household with her pollution.

This is the village custom even now. Her food was passed on
to her in special vessels in the back room itself. There was no
taboo against her engaging in hard farm labour during her menstruation. Housework was often substituted by extra farm work.

Kaki was always of a very slight build. She did not begin to
menstruate until she was almost twenty, some six years after
her marriage. At that time, old Kaka's wife explained to her a
little bit of how to manage herself. Until then she had slept
alone in the inside room, while the men slept in the living room.
On the fourth day of her periods, this kinswoman had crypti-
cally remarked to her not to be afraid if her husband came to
her at night. The kinswoman also told Aba to 'go sleep in the
inner room' from then on.

Kaki was terrified at first, and hated to have him with her.
She would shake with great fear, and he would growl at her.
'Am I eating you up?' She never did care for him all her life, as
she says. Her husband would come to her for sex once a week
or so, returning to his usual place in the living room immediately after. Not a word was exchanged with him otherwise. 'Not
like these days—one bed!' Her disgust of her son and daughter-in-law's strange ways is obvious. She did gradually begin to
look forward to his visits. 'Leave butter near the fire and it
begins to boil over; if the husband is close by, the craving is but
natural,' Kaki remarks with sad wisdom. 'What use my saying
I craved for his closeness? I could never tell him, "Come, sleep
with me." I never craved for "outside food". I died for my caste.'

Aba in the meanwhile continued his affair with the widow.
Her sister-in-law was a good woman, but 'everyone is afraid of
a tiger. Poor cows have to keep quiet. I suffered my agony in
silence'. Eight or nine years after marriage she bore her first
daughter, then another. The third was a stillborn son, followed
by a miscarriage.

The widow was still around, and the affair continued. Finally
the rumours reached her mother and the kinsman who had
given her away. He visited her father-in-law and remonstrated
with him. 'If this is how you maintain your family honour by
keeping others in your house and ruining my poor child's hap-

piness, I'd prefer to take her back.' She was two months pregnant at the time. A few weeks later, the kinsman returned to
visit her father-in-law, to see if the bluff had worked. It was
Aba who insolently told him, 'Bring her back if she agrees to
live under "her" command, or else not.' The kinsman had turned
away head bowed with shame. Eventually she had insisted on
returning to her husband because she could not bear her
mother's grief and shame.

The father-in-law was getting desperate about Aba's continuing folly. He himself had married twice. The first wife bore him
two daughters and then died. The second bore him one son,
Aba, and four daughters, before she too died. The surviving
daughters had been 'given away' in time. Now the father-in-law
realized that his daughter-in-law might go the same way as his
own two wives. The family lineage had to be assured. He sent
his son to Bombay to take up a job, mainly as a ruse to get him
away from the widow.

As it so happened, Kaki was pregnant at the time, and finally
a healthy son was born to her. Aba had given up his job and
returned to the village in the meanwhile. At that juncture the
wadi elders called a meeting at the father-in-law's insistence.
They discreetly demanded that Aba give up his relationship
with the widow and set up a proper household with his own
wife. To disregard this injunction might have brought ostracism
on his head, and now that he had fathered a son, Aba was more
mindful of his obligations to his clan. That was the end of his
wild days, and he was a totally reformed man ever since.

'I was satisfied that I could now live a decent life. "She" had
to return my vessels which were still at her house. I finally
settled in my own household. He did love me a lot after that,
but I never forgave him. He was deeply ashamed before me.
Nobody would believe all that had preceded. I had suffered a
lot in silence, because I had to spend a lifetime in this house.
But the scar ran deep. I could never forget that anger, and I'm
still furious. Ever since I came to this house, I laboured and
burnt like an incense stick, but I never set the house on fire.

'There were times when I ranted at "him". He would sit there

with his head bowed, never saying anything in return, not a
word. "You set water on fire in your youth; why aren't we living
a life of comfort yet?" Or "You tortured me, didn't you? I was
brought here like a cow with a rope around her neck, and that's
how I died." He never retaliated. Finally I would grow tired of
my own ranting, and then I would say to myself, "Leave alone.
A man is like a *hando* (brass vessel). You can scrub a brass pot
and reuse it, while a woman is *madko*, merely a mud jug. Once
used and polluted, chipped and shattered, you've got to throw
it away." '

They lived a hand-to-mouth existence for most of their lives.
Aba had a weak constitution and kept indifferent health, often
falling ill. Kaki did not have that luxury, despite being emaci-
ated and having undergone eight pregnancies. There was only
one exception, when she was 'possessed' by an evil spirit for a
few days. She does not like to be reminded of this frightening
and embarrassing memory. It is old Akka who laughingly tells
me this story one day in Kaki's presence, when we are discussing village ghostlore. Enjoying her discomfort at the memory of
that escapade, all the women begin to laugh, wiping their
streaming eyes with the loose ends of their saris.

The Enchanted Forest

Kaki was quite lost to her responsibilities then, and she would
just wander around the house in a daze, lisping over and over
again a couple of lines from a bhajan. Her husband and neighbours had then consulted holy men and priests from all over the
village, and finally found an antidote to her state of possession.
They had performed some rituals, perhaps offered a rooster as a
sacrifice to pacify the evil spirit. They might have even offered
it one of the old mango trees in Aba's yard as a place of permanent dwelling, with the promise of an annual sacrifice if it let go
of Kaki. Such an offer would further ensure that the spirit, thus
pacified, might enter into a contract to provide its benevolent
protection to Aba's household from then on, against sorcery and
witchcraft by his enemies. The spirit was indeed pacified at the

end of all that cajolery and bribing, and it left Kaki in peace to resume her household tasks.

As Kaki says, she does not herself recall much of that episode, and it has merely added to her endless list of fears. It is obvious that she does not enjoy this subject, reminding her of that brief and excusable period of dereliction from her 'caste' duties. She immediately begins to speak of some other pressing concern merely to change the topic.

A Life of Struggle

Kaki describes her struggles in those days when there was no cash income and they were deeply in debt at all times in order to be able to feed such a large household. The monsoons, lasting anywhere from June to October, are always a particularly stressful period. Towards the end of the preceding hot summer, before the rains begin, the villagers have to stock up on supplies for that entire period. From dry fuel wood and cowdung, fodder for the cattle, to salt, spices and foodgrains, people have to make the most of the hot season before the rains. Once it begins to rain, there is damp everywhere in the mud houses with leaky roofs. There are days when it rains incessantly, and this is the worst time in the year to run out of any supplies, particularly when there is no money.

Kaki tells of how she managed to scrape by, particularly during Aba's frequent bouts of illness, saddled as she was with six young children. Gradually, after the father-in-law's death, they had to let go of the lands they had earlier tenanted because it was not possible for them to cultivate these anymore. When the old house was near collapse, they had to live on Divgya's mother's doorstep for a while until finally moving into the renovated manger, a glorified cattleshed, where they live to this day.

She would borrow money at the start of the rains, and return harvested rice to the lender a few months later. By the time they had given the landowner his share of the harvest, and repaid previous cash loans in rice, they would be left with only a few months' supply of rice. Following that they would start on yet another vicious cycle of borrowing.

In the summer months she would struggle with a vegetable patch, watering it with great care during the dry spell, to be able to earn a small income from selling the vegetables. Having to do this made her feel very bitter because she was a proud upper caste woman. To go trading in the market was beneath her dignity. But she had to steel herself. Covering her head like a highborn woman, she would go to the market.

Yet she could never bring herself to go trading vegetables in this village market, where everyone would recognize her as so-and so's mother or as the daughter-in-law of such-and-such household. She would instead carry the basketful of vegetables on her head over the steep hill slopes at the back of the wadi, to the market in the neighbouring village, where only a few would know who she was. Her kindly friend Akka would then on some days send her own daughter with their vegetable produce to accompany Kaki on market days.

Kaki recalls the time when Aba was ill with double pneumonia, and she had paid the doctor in vegetables—aubergines—because she had no money for his treatment. Another time, Aba was ill with typhoid. For eight days he had run a temperature of 104° F and nobody expected him to live through that. She recalls having pawned a sari for fourteen rupees to buy a bottle of glucose for him. Circumstances like that had compelled her to overcome her sense of caste modesty and go selling vegetables in the market.

At other times Aba would borrow money and send her to buy rice from the ration shop because it was beneath his dignity to be seen doing that as a farmer. She worked as a farm labourer on Nani's farm, and she would bring back her share of the produce, whether chilli peppers, lentils or other grains. 'We lived for days on just rice gruel. If we had other grains we would eat dry *bhakri*, occasionally moistened with some chutney or some such thing.' There were times when there was no rice in the shop, and on such occasions the whole family subsisted on 'butters', meaning small rounds of cheap, lightly toasted bread bought at the store, softened in milkless tea, staving off hunger before going to bed at night.

Her only brother had started working in Bombay, and during one of Aba's illnesses, she overcame her pride and wrote to him asking for money. Ever since then he regularly sent her twenty rupees at festival times twice a year until her eldest son found a job in Bombay several years later. That was her only steady source of money until then.

Her oldest son, Ramesh, left school after ninth standard and went to the regional commercial town in search of a job. One of his schoolteachers helped him to find a job there, but he could not cope for some reason. He then went to Bombay, doing odd jobs, living for a few days with one relative or the other in the big city. By then, they had found a match for their eldest daughter, and she was married off after borrowing money from all over the place. '*Dila takde mela*,' is Kaki's shocking phrase referring to her daughter's wedding, meaning 'once given away, who cares whether she lives or dies?'

It is about seventeen years since Ramesh started working at a steady job in Bombay. He is a gentle, idealistic, dutiful son. He paid off all the outstanding debts of his father and grandfather in the village. He bought a small plot of decent farm land and handed it over to his father for cultivation. He was ill at the time of Kaki's second daughter's wedding. 'He is sick, we haven't any money,' they're supposed to have asked the groom's father to wait for a while. They were distant relatives. 'He came over with two hundred rupees in his fist, asking us to return that amount to him at the wedding as dowry. Then my son got a loan and spent some five hundred rupees for her nose ring and other expenses. We felt relieved as each daughter was given away.'

Kaki's second son, Mahesh, was sent repeatedly, some six or seven times, to find employment for himself. But he had taken ill each time. He was simply unsuited to city living. He returned to the village as a farmer, a permanent drain on his older brother's resources.

Ramesh has got all the siblings married, one after another. He had arranged his own wedding and written home to inform them. They were happy because it was a good match. He is a lucky man to find a gentle, sweet-tempered, uncomplaining wife. She has shared his burdens without recriminations. They live in a single room in one of the sprawling slums of Bombay. For all the years that he worked hard to skimp and save to provide for his natal family, they could have got themselves a middle-class apartment, out of the slums. Now the prices are fast exploding beyond reach, and he is in debt once again. Kaki's heart aches for this son, for all his troubles borne with great stoicism despite frequent ill health. She continues to berate her dead husband for not having provided them well enough to begin with. Strangely, she does not blame her second son for not holding a job. Her heart bleeds for him too, for all the hard work he has to do without commensurate returns.

The Woman of Joy

On another occasion I tell Kaki of my impressions of her, before Aba's death, as a cautious, hardworking, but happy-go-lucky person. She always seemed to love participating wholeheartedly in the various wadi get-togethers, despite being in her early sixties. 'Yes, I was very *howshi*, a keen enthusiast,' she says, some of the old sparkle temporarily lighting up her eyes in fond memory. 'Once my children began to grow up and I was relatively free of their constant demands on my time, I never sat and sulked or cried.

'Once my children reared up on their own two feet, I became carefree. I would accompany my friends whenever the bug caught me. *Ilo hurup ka gele vangdak*. I really had fun then, *Khup maja karaychi*. In the afternoons we would go to the forests on the hill slopes to fetch dry fuel wood; or we gathered kokum fruit and processed sour kokum peel for seasoning the curries. We would process the seeds at home and extract precious butter from them, to use in food during the rains. We would pound our spices at home. It was hard work, but I had company as one of my friends came to help, and that was such fun.

'Once I had informed the "householder", I was free to do as

I pleased. He never stopped me from going. I was really carefree. To the temple, to hear religious scriptures, to the wandering drama company shows or to our local dhaikalas, to the women's phugadya sessions, or to any other special events. I have never said no. I was always in the forefront while singing ovya. I told myself to go out and have all the fun possible, to make up for all that I had missed while my children were very small.

'We used to turn night into day through all the revelry. "Oh, I didn't get to sleep last night," was all I'd say. I never complained that I was tired. I would have to get back to work right away. I never slept in the afternoon; there was always so much to do.'

Yes, I can see Kaki on that very cold night, all dressed up in the new sari her son had sent her from Bombay, a glowing peach colour with golden nylon thread woven into it to add a touch of brightness. Freshly washed after a tiring day's farm work and cooking, Kaki even has a thick garland of fragrant jasmine flowers in her hair, widely beaming lips stained a seductive orange colour from the betel juice.

Four or five similarly adorned elderly women follow her, sharing maybe a couple of dim hurricane lanterns amongst them. Even these latter are quite unnecessary because the voyagers are nimble-footed, adept at finding their way through the dark shadows of the forest clearing with only moonlight to mark the rocky path. Their husbands are too old, decrepit and blasé to share in their enthusiasm, so they stay behind to guard the homes. The young lads have already left immediately on eating dinner. The women have eaten and cleaned the vessels, cleared up all the housework, before dressing up for the night out with companions. Lanterns and little oil lamps cradled in careful hands, they begin to creep out of their houses, calling on each other to hurry.

These women will walk some three to four miles to get to the wadi over and beyond the top of the hill and forest at the back of our wadi, making their way past the much haunted crematorium grounds. They probably know that today even the ghosts may not afford to while away their precious time doing what they do best, spooking the travellers, particularly pretty women such as these.

A wandering cinema company is showing a much admired, albeit positively ancient devotional film, *Gora Kumbhar*. They have all seen this film several times over, through its sojourn in all the respective natal villages before they got married and subsequently in the company of their children and grand-children over the years. But the thrill of watching the mystical devotion of the potter saint to Lord Pandurang is as great as ever. We all share his wife's sorrow over their only son being trodden to death under the saint's feet, blood and flesh being kneaded into the potter's mud while he is oblivious to the world, chanting in a trance. We are as horrified as she is when he vows to abstain from touching his wife ever again, as a penance. We sob aloud at her great sacrifice in bringing her own sister to him as wife to ensure the continuation of his lineage.

The women are very excited, and they have come to invite me to join them. I have to disappoint them because while walk-ing in the night is great fun, my city-soft backbone refuses to keep up until the early hours of the morning, squatting on the sharp pebbles and red mud of the fairgrounds. The chill of the pre-dawn hours might be bearable, the clear glittering sky pure enticement, but village decorum prevents a woman from stretching out and falling asleep under the heavens once she has reached the fine limits of endurance. I decline, having un-dergone this particular torture on several occasions previously.

We sit squeezed into a sitting position in a tightly huddled group, watching the melodrama. I remember spending hours in acute agony over the faint mirage of a warm and comforting bed under a swaddle of blankets in my house, lying miles away from the fairgrounds. It is natural, then, that the sweetest of blandishments cannot drag me out into the winter night this time to see a film I have already seen twice since I first arrived at the village. It is clear to all that city women are considerably less spirited than our simple village women.

As I rightly suspected, the film show does not begin before 1 am, until a patient crowd of thousands from the surrounding villages has collected under the open sky. There is no interval, no chaiwallah. The film usually gets over around four or five in the morning, since there is always a break in-between when the old black and white film reels refuse to cooperate with the best efforts of the projectionist. The viewers are as patient as ever, using that time to renew social ties with each other. As the film ends, mothers lug sleeping children to their waists, older ones being rudely shaken out of a blessed slumber. The women shake the dust out of crumpled saris, and so begins the long trek homewards, to another day's mundane labours. The sky is already lightening in the east, and the first rooster begins to crow as weary bodies approach the wadi in the early morning mist, signalling that it is time to light the fires to the start of a new day.

'Fetch My Shards from Oblivion'

Kaki remembers her days with her *jodidarni* or companions, with sad nostalgia. As a widow, all such childlike enjoyment is beyond her reach. Now there is only the realization that her days are numbered in this life. She tries not to intrude on the living space of others, drawing her limbs inwards, symbolically letting go of all extra space that she might have occupied, already a half-ghost.

There is an insurmountable wall between Kaki and her old companions of the fortunate marital status, the *saubhagyavati* women. Every year the *gosavi*, the priest, at the *math* or ashram in the forest behind the wadi holds a special feast to honour these women of the fortunate marital status. She sees them laughing and going about their carefree ways, and she draws back instinctively lest her stigma mar their happiness. They still have a kind word for her as they pass her on their way to the fields. They come to see her to ask about her distant son's well-being, or to find out about the new proposal for her youngest daughter's marriage. She replies to them eagerly enough, but the heaviness does not lift from her heart. She envisions her place as being beyond the pale of normal womanly interaction, and the dark shadow veiling her eyes from the moment of her husband's death does not dissipate.

A Change of Seasons

'My daughter-in-law is all right. I don't blame Mahesh. He has to work so hard, my heart bleeds for him. He doesn't talk very much with me. He is always grumbling about something or the other. He's fine with "her". She can order him about directly, "Bring this," or "we've run out of such-and such-thing, you've got to go buy some."

'He listens to her. I could never speak directly to anyone. But if he had not cared about me, we would have quarrelled each day.

'You can never tell what a new person is like while she is new,' Kaki continues, referring to her daughter-in-law. 'It is only after you've interacted sufficiently in the house that you can understand what she is really like. If my householder had been alive, I would have stayed in control. Now that he's gone, she's taken over from me. But I can't cope any longer, and who wants unnecessary quarrels?

'I'm content with this life. What can I ask for? But my timidity is the bane of this existence. I can't stop worrying. I'm so anxious all the time. My older daughter-in-law, who lives in Bombay, is very kind to me, just like a daughter. She calls me mother. When I visited them, she would serve me meals even before her husband returned from work, insisting that I should eat before anyone else. She never let me do a single chore in the house. "You are old now, you ought to rest," she would insist. I was very happy at their house. But then I would worry about how my younger son and his wife were coping with all the work back home in the village. I'd feel very guilty about enjoying myself in Bombay leaving these people with all the heavy work, and then I'd want to return immediately,' Kaki reminisces in a sad voice.

'My younger daughter-in-law does not talk much to me. I didn't need to show her how to do anything. She's learnt all the work by herself. I keep saying to her, "Say something. People should talk to people." But she keeps quiet, does not talk back. She's frequently ill. What with her father-in-law dying so soon after the wedding, someone might have blamed her for the misfortune. I don't hear anything. But then her mother died. She lost weight, and was constantly ill. Then she bore this sweet daughter who is the joy of my existence. Two months ago she had that miscarriage, almost in the seventh month of her pregnancy. It was a boy, stillborn. I can't stop worrying. Someone must be working witchcraft against us,' Kaki speaks in hushed tones now. 'He's making enquiries as to what this might be; we'll soon find out.'

Kaki has little ever to speak about her old sister-in-law, 'his' sister, the child widow. She is annoyed that her younger daughter-in-law gets along so well with Aba's sister. They have no problem chatting with each other, as she bitterly observes. Old Malti is almost seventy, nearly blind with cataracts in both her eyes. She has slaved away almost her entire life in her brother's household, grateful for work in order to earn her keep. To this day she has never missed a single day's farm work, and Kaki hates her more for all the sympathy she gets for her plight from outsiders. Their concern for Malti is perceived by her to contain hidden reproach for exploiting the older widow, as indeed may be the case.

Malti was married off just a few months before Kaki's wedding. Her husband was soon discovered to suffer from tuberculosis, an incurable disease in those days. He died without the marriage ever being consummated. There was a single relative, a widowed sister-in-law. She was afraid to take charge of Malti. 'I can't look after such a grown up wench,' she is reported to have said. 'I dare not show my face to anybody should she go astray. There's nobody to support me as it is, so how can I afford to keep her here?' At that point her father, Kaki's father-in-law, had brought his daughter back home. 'A broken twig returns to the roots,' he said. 'Let her stay here, she can eat so long as she works.' She has never stopped working since then.

Kaki had a large brood of little kids, and over the years she certainly welcomed Malti's help in all the work. 'She never knew the pleasures of married life. But all these years she's lived with honour. All her ancestors must be very fortunate to have such a daughter of the house. She never did anything to bring dishonour to the family,' Kaki remarks with pity. At the same time she resents the amount of warmth people show towards Malti, both in the house and outside. For truly, a sweeter tempered woman than Malti was never known. She always has a kind word for everybody, and not a word of complaint has left her mouth for all these years that she has slogged away for her brother's family, ostensibly only to earn her keep.

Kaki spends her days looking after her three-year-old granddaughter, while the rest are away working on the farm. She potters around the house, lighting fires in the hearth and outside to warm their bath water when they are due back. She feeds hay to the cattle that are tied up in the shed outside. She occasionally does the washing and helps prepare the cooked cattlefeed or rice gruel. But mostly it is a life of quiet retirement, a rare luxury for an able-bodied woman in the village. She is largely her own boss, and they leave her alone to her sad ways.

CHAPTER IV

Woman of Work, Akka

AKKA WALKS UP the path to my house, calling out my name from a distance. She has a wild air about her frail old body, her faded rag of a nine-yard sari tucked up to the knees, dry rice straw sticking out of her hair, and no trace of the usual red dot on her forehead. She visits my house to catch her breath from all the morning's threshing of paddy. The bullocks are tied to a central post while the paddy straw is pulled out and spread under their feet to separate the grain, and they go round and round in circles. All morning she has been gathering the grain, which will be winnowed in the breeze before storage. She will later have to pile up huge bales of hay over her daughter-in-law's head who will carry it indoors into the storehouse, a task of some urgency because the monsoons are drawing nearer. She sits there and curses that good-for-nothing son of hers who has vanished after bringing over his bullocks and tying them to the post for the threshing early in the morning.

She must have been quite a beauty in her youth. I tease her old husband about this once, when he is apparently in a good mood. He draws in a dramatic gasp with a palm laid flat across his chest, saying that he had lost sleep for an entire month after he first laid eyes on her. His sister had been married into her uncle's family in the ancestral village. He would visit under the pretext of seeing his sister. 'He sat under the jackfruit tree and stared for hours.' Akka laughs at another time of gajali-making, wiping her streaming eyes at the memory of that strange courtship.

'At my father's in Bombay, I was the second daughter in a brood of eight children. The ninth sibling, a female child, was born at the same time as my first son, Vijay. My father worked in a supervisory capacity in a textile mill in Bombay, earning a monthly salary of Rs. 250, which was a lot of money in those days. So we were comfortably off. I was born in Bombay, as were all my siblings. My elder sister used to help my mother with all the housework. I would escape, ostensibly to care for a younger sibling amidst all the kids. I was responsible for most of the shopping, particularly doing errands at the bustling wholesale vegetable market in Byculla, in the heart of Bombay city. I loved to haggle over the merchandise, and it gave me excellent business skills.

'I was the darling daughter, and my father particularly indulged all my whims and fancies. He often worried that his darling child might invite adverse comments after marriage because she was so pampered at home. I was never asked to do any housework, and they never tried overtly to socialize me to the burdens of a woman's existence. Even more than my mother, I was the love of my father's life.'

Another time Akka tells about how her father was insistent about sending her to school, dreaming about her acquiring a higher education. Nobody ever doubted her intelligence. But the headstrong child had better diversions than attending school, which she simply refused to do. To this day she has remained totally unlettered, like other village women of her day and age, and very proud of her early defiance.

As she was growing up, her father's brother brought her to the village to look for a groom for her. They all doted on her, and in the village, she was one of the only two daughters in a household of twenty-three people. A sister of Akka's future husband, Baba, was married to an uncle's son. Baba was besotted by the young Akka during his visits to his sister, and finally one day the proposal was put forth.

'I'm sure he bribed his sister's husband with a fowl dinner,' Akka remarks caustically. This worthy relative then probably did all to smooth love's path from within her family, and the match was indeed arranged without much delay. Tales of the prospective groom's caste eminence and landholdings in his own village undoubtedly helped to that end.

Her father raved and ranted in fury over the obvious mismatch, when he was summoned by his brother before the wedding. 'Give my fair, delicate city doll to that ugly, uncouth giant? And those huge farm lands! My child will be worked to the bone. How could anybody bring about such a perfidious alliance for my princess?' He fumed, but it was of no use, since a match once set could not be backed out of for such 'frivolous' reasons without dire consequences for the bride's family's reputation, ruling out all chances for a second alliance. Ultimately he consented with bad grace, departing for Bombay a day after her wedding.

To My New Home

Akka was fourteen years old at the time of the marriage, not having attained puberty at the time. The marriage was not consummated then, and her husband left on military service soon after. Her father-in-law had died early. He had reportedly been a simpleton. The kin had taken advantage of this fact and done the widow out of considerable land, until Akka's husband grew up into a tyrant in his own right. He had then paid the kin back in full, to marshall back all his ancestral property, even resorting to machiavellian tactics. This had left its mark on him early on, and he only grew more and more bitter and manipulative with each passing year. Thankfully, since he was away from home that crucial first year after marriage, Akka had enough time and space to come into her own in this household and wadi under the indulgent eyes of her mother and brother-in-law.

'There was plenty of work. Sometimes I would quietly steal into a corner and cry my heart out. But I obeyed my father's injunctions at the time of my marriage. "You only have to send me word of it, should you hanker after anything at your in-laws' house. I will discreetly take care of all your needs, but don't let these strangers call you names. You must bear all in silence, without complaining. Be patient and obedient. Do your duty, and don't give anyone cause for complaint. My reputation is in your hands." ' These were the time honoured words of Akka's doting parent, and she was very mindful of that advice.

Akka was lucky to find a kind and gentle mentor in her brother-in-law. Other city daughters tell sad tales of quietly weeping tears of shame over the ridicule and contempt heaped on their heads by uncaring in-laws until they learnt all the farm and household tasks. Even the slightest disparagement by the father-in-law patriarch would be enough to bring a deep sense of guilt and shame on the errant bride.

'I didn't know any festival tasks. I would quietly watch others and learn to do as they did. My brother-in-law would then shower praise on my head.' That first year after her marriage was a tough life away from her loving father's home, but city-bred Akka soon surpassed other village women in all that she did, until she became altogether indispensable not only to her own family, but also to the entire wadi.

Her husband, Baba, had returned following a break in military service about two years after her marriage. She had begun menstruating by then, so sexual relations were initiated at that point. She had some awareness of what this entailed, though she received the sketchiest of preparation from her mother-in-law in the injunction that 'don't worry, he won't eat you up, he won't do anything drastic'. Whenever Baba was visiting, the couple would spend the nights in the vacant manger at the back of their house. After she had children, her brother-in-law and his wife would use the manger, leaving the main house for Akka and her husband, while the mother-in-law slept in the outer room.

Earlier, Baba treated her with great love and affection, and she too responded in kind, looking forward to his attentions. For a brief period of about a year and a half Akka accompanied her husband to another city in the state where he was posted on duty. Akka has faint memories of matrimonial bliss in that period spent alone in her husband's company. Her father continued to provide her discreet financial support, but she tried to maintain her dignity despite Baba's expectations of his father-in-law's munificence.

Akka remarks with asperity how this had simply served to emphasize her independence in the face of her husband. Having eaten crow in front of his father-in-law, he could hardly dare to use a word of reproach against that devoted man. He was materially beholden to his father-in-law, and Akka was clever enough to turn that to her own advantage whenever the need arose. She learnt to cut off this proud tyrant's abuses midair by publicly flinging in his face these deprecable facts. But that was later. Baba was terrified of his stern father-in-law. That her father could even use stern language against her husband pleased Akka no end, since she herself was mortally afraid of Baba's terrible wrath in those initial years. But Baba put up with it since he could ask him to provide for all his needs from time to time.

In the first year that she lived with Baba in the other city, Akka had a miscarriage in the fourth month of pregnancy. She was barely around sixteen or seventeen years of age at the time. Her eldest son was born about nine years after the marriage, and her husband was on active war duty at the time. Her brother-in-law had also followed his brother into military service, and they both returned to the village within a short span of each other at the end of World War II.

The birth of her first child coincided with victory on the war front and it was her brother-in-law who had jubilantly telegrammed that the son be named 'Vijay', meaning victory. The boy was always referred to as Vijgya, in village fashion, and his uncle made much of him, adoring him much more than his own offspring. A couple of years later Akka gave birth to a second son. This child had been very sickly, and had a strange abnormality so that his stomach distended like a balloon at the time of each nursing. She recalls that the local quack doctor had given her some medicine for the infant. On the fourth day of giving that medicine, the infant did not stop crying for about half an hour, and then he died all of a sudden.

Her only daughter was born two years later, and another

son, Govinda, a couple of years after that, bringing the total of Akka's offspring to three. In the meanwhile, her husband had been fully discharged from the military, and had begun farming in earnest. His behaviour was increasingly cantankerous, not to be borne by Akka in silence for very long.

By then, she had created a very special place for herself in the affairs of that household. Her husband could not afford to antagonize her very much since the pre-eminent status of that household in wadi affairs depended almost entirely on her. As a farmer too he needed her full cooperation. Her mother-in-law had grown old by then, and her sister-in-law was too indifferent about work. The brothers had a falling out, each setting up separate households close to each other. Akka, then, made very skilful use of her work roles and her indispensability to the household and wadi affairs to negotiate a better status for herself vis-à-vis her husband.

Of Sexual Bonds

I ask Akka about her views on sexuality. She looks on sex as a natural urge for both men and women, unavoidably strong in youth, gradually tapering off for a woman by menopause. It is unthinkable that a woman may continue to be sexually active beyond menopause, say about forty years of age. Her children may be grown up by then, and it is not seemly for a couple past its youth to engage in sex, particularly considering the lack of privacy in a growing household. Sex is intiated by the husband, and often by the wife herself in a tactful manner, Akka admits. On occasion a mother-in-law or some elderly woman may deem it necessary to nudge a laggardly couple along, hinting that it is time, particularly if the birth of a child is at stake.

Speaking for herself, Akka mentions that initially she had looked forward to sex with her husband. As he began fault-finding at work, nit-picking all the time, she realized it was better when he was away on military service. Within a few years she was thoroughly disenchanted with him. She stopped relating to him in terms of any romantic attachment by the time her third child, the youngest son, was born. She ceased to make any special efforts towards his welfare, apart from what was customarily expected of her in the community culture. Being overburdened with work proved a handy excuse. On a few occasions when her husband approached her for sex, she repulsed his advances by abruptly saying, 'My children are growing up now, and I don't have enough stamina for it.' He had to accept that in silence. She never engaged in a sexual alliance outside her marriage, and she is pretty certain that her husband did not either. She was in her early thirties when she reached menopause, a fact that had caused quite a bit of comment among her companions and female kin. Akka herself was greatly relieved, since it meant a definite elevation in her household status.

Menopause was an important station that distinctly put her beyond her husband's sexual control. Not being subject to the hormonal surges that justified her biological, and hence, in the eyes of the community, her total dependence on her man, was definitely perceived by Akka as a liberating influence in her life. It brought her more on par with her husband within the household authority structure, in a very subtle psychological sense. At last it enabled her to surmount the gender division in a very immediate fashion in terms of exercising her control over domestic matters, particularly since her mother-in-law was dead by then.

It is true that people in the village society, as elsewhere, value the affectional bond between a married couple, although it is certainly de-emphasized in contrast to the western, commercially touted romantic myth. Also, it is easier for village men and women to accept the lack of such a bond for whatever reasons, without having to internalize the blame.

Following an abrupt rejection of conjugal relations by an insubordinate wife, it may be possible for a man to overpower her physically for sex, but it reflects badly on his manhood if it is known that she no longer sees him as desirable. Also, since there is a high premium on privacy, it is not easy for a man to use force against his wife. Akka was intelligent enough to use this knowledge to her fullest advantage in negotiating her de facto autonomy from her husband. The sexual battle was the most fundamental one in that context.

Her husband had no longer any 'real' business inside the house, beyond occasional forays to the kitchen. Village men sleep or entertain visitors on cots in the verandas outside, through all seasons, leaving the inside of the houses for women and children. The veranda houses the male domain. Few visitors get past the veranda into the main house. Akka's husband even insisted on being served his tea and meals on the wooden cot outside, and there was little protest on her part against this strange custom. More important, his symbolic exile from his own home was complete. There was constant bickering and minor skirmishes between the two, but all understood that the war went Akka's way long ago, the very day she spurned his sexual advances one last time and became independent of him in a personal sense.

I ask Akka about the noticeable premarital alliances between some of the boys and girls on the wadi. Most people are aware of the strong attraction between young couples in and outside the wadi, from age fourteen onwards. Rigid rules of village exogamy entail that these couples will never be permitted to marry each other. Almost all families on this wadi are connected by kinship ties, implying a fraternal relationship between entire families and individuals, even among those with different surnames. While spontaneous romantic alliances between young boys and girls as they grow up together in the wadi are looked on with indulgence, without harsh reprimands, and viewed as well within the natural order of things, all parties involved are very much aware that marriage is beyond contemplation. Onlookers shrug with indifference, with perhaps occasional backbiting, or may be even with a rare malicious letter to more influential and prudish Bombay relatives, the final arbiters in matters of dispute. Open confrontations are very rare and looked upon as indecorous.

Young couples have many occasions for private assignations, particularly under cover of lone tasks such as grazing cattle in the mountains, or fetching fuel wood or grass to feed the cattle. Unfortunately, should pregnancy result from such trysts, the matter can no longer be kept secret. Considerable loss of face for both families, particularly the girl's, may result from such contretemps. Akka remembers old Nandya's sister's affair with Malgya's son, lasting several years. She ultimately got pregnant, and was packed off to Malgya's house in the neighbouring wadi for eight days when the pregnancy was full term. This was in the days before abortions became legal and easily available in India. They might have resorted to quack medicine fruitlessly, until it simply got too late. In any case, it was a very badly managed business, as Akka remarks in hushed tones. After birth, and it was a bonny boy, the baby was trussed up and drowned in a well. The dead baby in its bundle was discovered by cowherds the very next day. The news was all over the place. The girl was later hurriedly married off to some 'piddling farmer' in Akka's language, a man with very little land or wherewithal to support a wife and family.

Another woman, old Madhgya's sister-in-law, had the temerity to get pregnant despite her husband's being stuck solid in Bombay over several years. Everybody knew who the father was, but that was of little consequence. She was cast off by her husband's clan, and went off to deliver the baby in an orphanage in a distant town in the region. These days, of course, besides the pill peddlers, there are certified abortion clinics to which families discreetly take their daughters, before getting them married off out of the village in a great hurry.

According to Akka, then, people generally have a matter of fact attitude towards premarital liaisons, and a considerably more humane attitude than is generally believed to exist in such hopeless situations, since marriage is forbidden. Parents, if aware of the situation, may of course resort to repressive measures in secret. They may simply resort to denial, by insisting that 'my child will never do such a thing', or by blaming the informant of malicious intent. Wise parents, of course, often seek to arrange a suitable marriage before the situation gets out of hand.

Akka's Own

Akka's only daughter was never sent to school, but was kept back to look after her infant brother while the mother was busy with all the heavy work on the farm and at home. She was a very gentle and obedient daughter, and was married to a decent boy with a job in Bombay. In time, the decent boy turned alcoholic, and the young wife was in dire straits with a couple of little children to feed besides herself. She had once appealed to her father for help, during one of his infrequent sojourns in Bombay. 'Why don't you sell off those brats if you can't afford to keep them,' the old curmudgeon had replied in a flash before walking out of her dwelling.

The proud daughter had kept quiet for a long time, and had managed to scrape along finally by seeking a hard packaging job that entailed commuting for hours every day to the centre of the city. It was much later, after several years in fact, that she had broken down in front of her eldest brother during one of his visits, to relate that humiliating snub from an uncaring father, in between sobs. That, of course, had led to a rare to-do between the father and the rest of the family members after the son had returned to the village in high dungeon.

The daughter's husband was eventually cured of alcoholism, and her family reverted to better times. She continued working outside simply because her income was indispensable to the family. She was proud of having contributed a great deal to her children's upbringing. She was determined to educate them to a better life. But Akka neither forgot nor forgave her husband for his callousness. She never ceases to shed tears of sadness at her only daughter's life of misery and toil.

Akka's two sons, particularly the eldest, were much pampered. The eldest was always very naughty. He was the target of his father's wrath throughout his childhood, but Akka indulged him. If her husband tried to use enforced starvation as a disciplinary measure, she would bring him into the kitchen surreptitiously by the back door to feed him with extra fondness. It did not take her very long to understand the true worth of forging a political alliance with this gem of a son in the ongoing skirmishes with her husband.

As he was growing up, Vijgya's pranks became legendary. His amorous dalliances were equally well known all over the village. Govinda, in comparison, was very docile, obedient and even sickly as a lad. He did not possess his brother's impudence, displaying a more sombre, brooding mien. Both brothers played truant at school, and never finished high school. They both found reasonable jobs in Bombay, through the good offices of kind kinspeople. At this point their career paths diverged sharply. The younger son worked steadily for a while. He got married at the right time, with his older brother's permission, to a nice, pleasant-mannered, intelligent girl of his own choosing, out of his own resources. Baba had of course refused to part with any of his long-standing pension funds, as his own way of getting his back at the rebellious wife and sons.

Govinda lived in a tenement room in Bombay with his wife and an increasing brood of children. He had refused to turn his wife over to his mother in the village to help her in her drudgery, as more devoted proletarian sons did. Vijgya also worked at a steady job for a while. However, he quit this job in a fit of caprice and returned home to tend the ancestral lands. Akka blames him for this waywardness, particularly since the life of a farmer has very insubstantial compensations. The son developed other diversions in the meanwhile, in the form of new romantic alliances.

At one time, he was suffering from heartbreak over the sudden death from typhoid of his current beloved. His younger brother had been urging his marriage for a long time, and had even offered to bear the financial burden. Finally, he agreed to his father finding a match for him. The wife that his father found for him was the opposite of everything that Akka represented. She was as dark as Akka and her son were fair. She was evil-tempered, without the abilities that could make that temper bearable. Her father was exceedingly poor and without any resources to feed his large motherless brood of six children. He was unable to give her the barest of jewellery at the time of her marriage.

To start with, she insulted her mother-in-law within the first week of her marriage, deluded enough to imagine that her own position vis-à-vis the older woman could be worked out in her own favour through the exercise of sexual control over her husband. She even dared to gossip boastfully about this to a newly acquainted neighbour, who was sufficiently scandalized by the new bride's unseemly talk to report the matter to Akka without delay.

In those early days after his marriage, Vijgya was besotted enough to take up cudgels against his mother on his bride's behalf without bothering to ascertain the reasons for that conflict. This was simply unacceptable by village standards, particularly since the daughter-in-law had been guilty of a serious transgression in the eyes of the community. Her son's perfidy was a shock to Akka, and she never did forgive him for that act of betrayal. She had been deeply humiliated in front of outsiders by the daughter-in-law. It was particularly sad, considering that her younger son had already reneged on his duty towards her by refusing to send his wife to serve Akka as she grew older. It hurt her to sense her husband's satisfaction over the way his chosen daughter-in-law had made short work of his tormentor in no time, particularly since the powerful mother-son alliance had been effectively dissolved. His joy was short-lived.

By-and-by the new bride also insulted the hapless father-in-law for fetching her a cheap rag of a sari as a gift rather than something more presentable. Her biggest mistake was in cursing her husband—her only potential ally in the new family—before the entire household, for being a wastrel, a choice fact she had garnered over gossip with some new-found friends. It was her misfortune that he had just then returned from his errands and stood within earshot, listening to that ungoverned diatribe. After he had heard enough, he came forward to inform her in rage that she could consider herself a free agent if she so desired, to return to her father's house since he was not a worthy husband for 'Her Highness'. She however never had that option, since her father was well rid of her. But that was the end of her high and mighty ways, and she had herself to blame for it. In all his repressed rage and frustration, Vijgya was not very wise in the exercise of his judgement, and his by now angry and bitter mother made much of the fact, using her weaponry as much against the son as against the husband. None in the house was very wise any longer.

That was the end of any semblance of peace and harmony in Akka's household. Earlier cleavages splintered irrevocably, so that mother turned against son, husband against wife, brother against brother, and Akka's carefully nurtured world crumbled against the onslaught. They were all individuals staking out winnings from then on, with never a sign of unity, and the family became the laughing stock of the village.

No wadi resident has any doubts about the meanness of Akka's husband, Baba. He would have long ago driven a lesser woman than Akka into the burning grounds with his constant foul-mouthed abuse, if not physical maltreatment. There is a bitter sense of mistrust and misanthropy in his mind, and an uncontrollable desire to get even with the world. There are no limits to his furious tantrums when aroused, and the frequency of these are high enough for the neighbourhood to be altogether sick of him.

It was the weight of traditional patriarchy, again, that has held behind the curious mismatch between Baba and Akka. She has gradually learnt over the years not to waste precious tears over his hurtful behaviour. Even later she was determined to neutralize all that destructive energy her own way, so that she could get on with her work and keep away from total disintegration. She has succeeded admirably.

Yet the wages of patriarchy are formidable, and she has no peace now in her old age. They judge her harshly for her shrewd, and at times shrewish, calculating ways, not understanding the battle she has waged all her life to maintain a good amount of sanity and goodwill in her world gone mad. Divorce was no option, of course. She was grateful, despite herself, that Baba had not taken another wife, as is village custom even though bigamy is outlawed by the courts.

Through sheer dint of hard work and self-denial, Akka has made herself indispensable to her household and to the wadi. Thus the possibility of casting her off, abandoning her to a life of destitution and worse in sheer revenge, was not a strategic option for Baba. He is intelligent enough to perceive advantage through all his infuriating bluster, and that is one of the few saving graces of Akka's life. Maybe the old man even loved her in his own cruel way, his inability to control her spirit simply adding fuel to his bitterness. When she was seriously ill a few years ago, wasting away from fever, it was he as much as her son, who had bustled around her from time to time in great worry. The dropping of his mask of indifferent contempt was possible only while she was unconscious, of course. He had even unstintingly dipped into his pension chest for all the medical treatment that she needed. This was only until the danger to her life passed. Then it was back to business as usual.

Mother's Revenge

As he approaches middle age Vijgya's own lot is fairly sad, since his father controls the pension while his mother rules the air waves at work, both undermining his status in the family. The slightest of transgressions or omissions on his part are magnified several times over by a resentful family. There are times when he is mortally tired of being a pariah in his own house. This is despite his status of being very much a man of the house, which he has wrested from an aging father, only to realize the hollowness of this victory.

Akka's second son, Govinda, is of little comfort either, since he has become mentally unstable under the high pressure of city life and a growing family. He has had a frequent turnover of jobs because of increasing irritability, being unable to work steadily at a job for too long. He refuses to let his wife seek outside employment, nor does he permit her to undergo sterilization, though the growing number of children is definitely a serious strain on his role as the breadwinner. It is a separate matter that his wife, an intelligent and self-willed woman, has gone ahead with a secret sterilization operation after the birth of their fifth child. She belongs to a proud, well-off farming family, and is resigned to the insecurity of increasing poverty due to his instability. Following a bitter fight with Baba, Govinda returned to Bombay.

The major consoling factor in Akka's life then, is her work, and that is quite a lot for a woman of her stature. It is her life. Work to Akka, is like the tumultuous ocean, clamorous, rushing in to flood all the nooks and crannies of her mind. It threatens her with drowning, with total submergence. She has lived many seasons, and knows that the waves will recede to offer brief respite. It allows her to fill up her lungs with the sparkling air of creative satisfaction, before reaching out to touch her life with ever new demands on her limited time. The work ocean is unbounded, but she is the leviathan. No matter what the current trauma of her shattered household, Akka fills her life with the joy of being at work, particularly farm work in the clear village air. She radiates that happiness to her favoured ones, to her grandchildren, and often to me.

She introduces me to forgotten ways of food processing, joyously teaching me the art of vegetable gardening. She brings me the choicest of vegetable seeds, carefully garnered over the dry months from distant villages and even from acquaintances in Bombay. She teaches me the joy of nurturing plants from seeds to sprouts, to the first riot of delicate flowers, and then to little baby vegetables. She comes shouting my name from a distance, making a quick detour on her way back home from the fields. There is little knowledge that Akka does not have, or cannot put to practical use right away. So she was an apt mentor, as she introduced me to the fading ways of artistic living in the village. She cherishes those ways, and is sad that hers is the last generation to understand and value them.

The Woman of Work

During the heavy paddy transplanting season at the start of the monsoon each year, Akka has the air of a possessed woman. I have no doubt that she does enter a trance-like state throughout that month-long period, to be able to do all that only she manages to do. She scrapes up labourers needed for the tasks from the bottom of the village barrel, courting them with food and chai, supervising all the work with an eagle eye even as her hands are busy with the rhythm of work. She rushes from farm to home and back again several times, because she is needed at both places at one and the same time.

The daughter-in-law cannot be trusted to cook even one proper meal, as she tartly remarks, and all the family and the labourers have to be fed good meals after their heavy work. If she leaves the daughter-in-law to cook lunch for one day, or even just the rice gruel, she undoubtedly makes it overly salty. If the woman is left to the farm work, she invariably dawdles. That is simply not permissible. If the woman of the household herself falls back, the rest of the labourers are going to take it easy too. Not only will that increase labour costs, whether in cash or grain, but also the time taken for paddy transplanting will be lengthened beyond endurance. The family will then become the laughing stock of the village, for all their vast lands. Good management implies that the faster this task is accomplished, the better utilization of good wet weather will be achieved, along with an earlier harvest. Also, no family can live with that maniacal momentum forever.

'You've got to pull all the labourers along with you,' Akka explains to me one day on our way to transplanting in her farm. She appreciates my volunteering to help her for free, and pampers me with extra paan, chai and food from her house since I will be too tired to cook by the time I return. Of course, she has to pamper all the workers to a reasonable extent, to get them to work wholeheartedly for her.

For example, she has to ensure that they have proper covering in case of rain, in the form of woven bamboo sheaths, called *irla*. These extend from the head, down the back, and make the wearers look like giant oversize snails at work in the rain. She may buy one for someone like poor, near-destitute Mali, Tato's wife, out of her own meagre earnings from the kokum sale. She may patch her own old irla with scraps of plastic sheets to prevent it from leaking. She will have to nag her son to get all the little wooden stools, which have one thick central column supporting the flat base, repaired in time. The workers sit on these little stools in all the muck, moving them as they move up row after row of transplanting paddy.

Akka leaves the farm an hour or so before the other workers to return home to cook a fresh meal for all of them, often fifteen to twenty people, including her family and the children. She will stone-grind huge quantities of coconut and spice paste to add to the curry. The rice gruel was sent around ten o'clock to the fields, but they will all return to her house for lunch, and for a brief rest after helping her to wash the vessels. They have started with chai at her house in the morning, and there will be one more chai and bhakri in the afternoon. After the day's farm work is done, around six or later in the evening, some women will prefer to go home and be with their families for dinner, while those who are single and living nearby may prefer to eat at Akka's home. Akka will have already started the fire under the huge pot at the back door to warm their bath water. The women get busy cooking after a quick wash.

Nursing mothers hug their infants for a while. Despite all the bustle dinners are always late. By the time all the men, the children, and they themselves are fed, the vessels washed, and tired bodies drop on the floor for a night's rest, it is already past eleven in the night. They will have to wake up before six in the morning, in the cold damp of the monsoon, to start another heavy day at transplanting.

Often in the day, Akka's granddaughter has returned early from school, since the teachers need to farm too. Schools are run only part of the time in that season. She obliges by fetching the rice gruel that Akka had left cooking on a low fire or the chai. For most children of farmers, this is a happy season of hard work, to be out in the heady open air of the fields, under cloudy skies or in rain, and to share in the togetherness of all the busy workers, singing and chatting under the heavens.

Akka also has to ensure a congenial work environment

amidst all the hard labour, so she begins to sing ovya, the songs
of the grinding stone. Through rain and cold, fast-numbing
hands move rhythmically at the seemingly unending tasks. She
keeps up a flow of interesting gajali, occasionally yelling at her
daughter-in-law not to lag behind so, to hurry up.

Akka's Exile

Akka was sniping at her son over some task. Those were tense
days. Her younger son had brought over his family of wife and
five kids. He was currently out of work, and it was impossible to
continue with all of them in the city. There were daily spats in
the house. He did not know farm work, and also did not allow
his wife to do her share despite her entreaties. It was an embarrassment for all, since without their doing their share of the
work, it was an unbearable burden on the other family members
to feed seven extra mouths for very long. Finally Govinda returned to Bombay following a major brawl with his father, but
the rest stayed behind. Vijgya had deeply resented his younger
brother's unfair treatment of his three children, while pamper-
ing his own. Now the same Govinda had left his family presumably in Vijgya's care, dependent on his labours, without so much
as a courteous word to him. He was furious, but it would not be
seemly to say anything to his sister-in-law.

When Akka continued sniping at him for some paltry reason,
he exploded in rage, all his frustrations directed at his mother's
head. 'If you disapprove of the way I conduct my farming, you
should not step into my farm lands from tomorrow,' he had
yelled at her in fury. They had lived with frayed nerves, while
still carrying on with tough farm work and dwindling supplies.
Now that his brother had left, it was safe for him to explode
without the additional charge of violence on his hands.

Akka was stunned by those words. All her life, except for
the brief initial apprenticeship years under the supervision of
her mother-in-law and brother-in-law, she had been the
malkin, the mistress of the farm and the household. For him
to speak so, to banish her from 'his' farms? Akka's world

turned dim, the very light seemed to go out of her life.

It was sad. She saw the gleam of satisfaction in her husband's eyes. He had lived for this day, ever since she had taken up against him over that terrible act of being thrashed by his own son. It had been almost twenty years ago, but now he had his revenge against her, and he perversely spoke out in support of that same son at this point. She saw the gleam of satisfaction in the eyes of her daughter-in-law, Tara. She too had waited her chance, it seemed. The wheel of fortune turns: what goes up, must come down. Four days belong to mother-in-law, four to the daughter-in-law, as the saying goes. Now Tara's days were not far off, or so she thought.

Akka was deeply wounded, stung by her son's barring her entry to his farms. He had decreed that she was an old woman. What business did she have doing all the farm work at that age? She could stay at home, and cook for all those thirteen mouths, Govinda's brood included. Tara, suddenly elevated, would tend to the farms. Akka sent a message to her nephew in Bombay, to come to the village and take her away to the city with him. He came to fetch her immediately. But the worst point came when Akka wanted to take some rice from her stores for the nephew's family in Bombay.

Vijgya would never have said anything, but taking advantage of the fact that he was away, Tara came forward like lightning, and told Akka not to dare touch any of 'her' rice! The gentle nephew looked up in shock, asking if she had lost her senses to speak to Akka in that manner. 'You keep out of this, brother-in-law,' she spoke with biting sarcasm. He bowed his head in shame, and urged Akka to forget about the rice. She left the village in deep disgrace, with a leaden heart and head bent low, following in the nephew's footsteps to the bus stop.

Four Days, Daughter-in-Law

So Vijgya, his wife, Tara, and his brother Govinda's wife, Sumati, were left to farm the lands, tend the household, and to feed the family of twelve, including eight little children. The fact that neither woman was very clever at any of the tasks did not help. Vijgya had to show the world that they would not starve. He worked like a man possessed. He supervised mealtimes to see that the women took proper care to feed the children, the old man, and the retarded cousin. He could never trust them to do this on their own.

He took care of the cattle feeding times himself. He even made it a point to redeem old debts to lone women by getting them to lend a helping hand in farm work, for a payment, of course. They passed that season without anything untoward happening. Except that meal-times, particularly at nights, were considerably delayed. Tara constantly bickered with the old man, now that there was no mother-in-law in the house to check her. She even cursed her companion Sumati and her children, accusing them of sponging on her and her husband. All this was behind her husband's back. Who would have dared to complain to him?

She tried to be insolent to him, but a tight slap from the goaded man was enough to win her silent obedience. She knew her limits with him. When the monsoon arrived, Vijgya's farms lagged way behind all village farms in transplanting. Finally it was the carpenters' wives from the neighbouring community who took pity on him, and gave priority to working on his farms after their own were done. As old Kaki told me, had the farms been left to Vijgya's women, the paddy would never have been transplanted while the rains lasted.

Following that, the all-important Ganpati festival was near-at-hand. It was with deep shame that Vijgya realized that his wife had run through their entire grain reserves. It was only August, and the new crops would not be ready for harvesting until almost November. The family would have to buy inferior grain from the market to celebrate the festival. Such a thing had been unheard of. This was the first time that a family as prosperous in grain such as this one ran out of rice stocks on the eve of the most important annual festival. If people came to know, would they not fill his mouth with dung? But he had to keep silent and fetch the rice from the *bajar*, reasoning that perhaps it was because of all the extra mouths to feed that they had run out of grain.

It was at that very juncture that Akka returned unasked to the village. It was her duty to eat crow if necessary, but for a woman to stay away from her 'given' house during the Ganpati festival was a serious dereliction of duty. It might not matter to her ungrateful family, but it would certainly rankle with the Gods and ancestors. So she returned, weak in health. For the nearly six odd months that she had lived in Bombay, she had been ill and homesick most of the time. Neither the son nor the husband had written to inquire about her well-being, particularly since she had left without saying a word to either. Nor had she written, on her own part, having once reached Bombay. The city migrants from the wadi and even from the village made much of her visit. Many felt as if their own mother had come on a visit. But she was heart-sick for her village home and hearth, and finally decided to return on her own, in time for the festival.

For several days upon her return, she did not speak with anyone in the house. She was happy to be back, of course. They were all happy that she was back. The wadi residents gave her a very warm welcome, but the old women never failed to ask why she had left in such a dungeon in the first place. Could she not have forgiven that son a little bit, understanding how goaded he was at that point, rather than hurting herself to the extent that she had returned more frail than ever before? She had no reply to that as she had little strength to argue any more.

Indeed, they were happy to have her back. The festival of the Lord of Auspiciousness, Harmony, and Good Fortune came and went, and all the remaining bitterness was swept away. Akka became radiant again. Her husband was grateful for her return. He had silently worried about the havoc the departed ancestors and Lord Ganpati might have wrought in anger at not having her there to worship them at this important time of the year. She was, they all knew, the unquestioned mistress of the house. Imagine then, the affront those all-important Guests might have felt had she not been present to greet them into her house! He was also thoroughly sick of Tara's foul mouth by then. She matched him word for word, and then some, and he did grieve over this insubordination by the daughter-in-law of his own choosing.

The grandchildren of course, cried to see her, for they had missed her terribly, particularly at meal times. Tara was relieved, because she obviously could not cope. So was Sumati, the other daughter-in-law, because she was tired of Tara's constant sniping at her for encroaching on 'their' rights.

Both Akka and her son had missed each other, in that strange love-hate syndrome that bound them together. Each had felt betrayed by the other, but both had mellowed in that terrible interregnum. They knew that they could not really carry on without each other. At that point they had learnt to forgive one another, and peace was upon them, for a while.

Akka did have her moment of sweet triumph the following year when, with one additional mouth to feed, she had managed to save an extra bag of precious old home-grown rice until the new crop was harvested. When she called her son into the storage room to show him, he had asked with great respect as to how she had managed to do that. 'Nobody starved,' she replied. 'I take care to see that all are fed as much as their stomachs can hold . . . even the cattle, but I don't waste any grain,' she had added with a sweet smile.

Better still, she had turned to Tara one day to remark, 'Those four days are a difficult test, daughter-in-law. It is important not to fail. You can be mistress only if you graduate beyond that. Remember how you forbade me to take "your" rice to Bombay? My needs are very little, daughter-in-law, be careful to provide well for your own.'

CHAPTER V

Earth Woman, Parvati

TAI, O TAI, she comes calling to me from afar, in the time-honoured way of the wadi residents. She is looking for *vak-handi*, a wild herb she bathes her young girl with routinely, as a preventive measure against illness. She asks my permission to look around my backyard amidst all the wild underbush for the medicinal vine. Parvati is a special friend, amidst all those curious friendships spanning across our vastly divergent backgrounds. Yet not so curious, considering all the common ground between us, including geography, gender, caste, kinship and even living conditions.

Parvati always takes care to tear the paan I offer her into two equal halves, never transgressing her womanly economy in that matter. This gendered sense of modesty and economy is a curious trait that I have observed in the village. Offer a paan to a man past his initial awe of city folk, and he will take two leaves instead of one, in the cultured mode. Offer the tray to a woman, and no matter how well she knows you, she will make it a virtue of tearing up a single leaf into two to emphasize her limited needs.

Gathering Adventures

The wadi women are grateful to me for reviving with fresh enthusiasm their neglected customs of mussel-gathering. It is through Parvati's gajali that I learn of that favourite sport, when wadi women used to go in groups of jodidarni in their youthful days to the four-odd kilometres distant river creek at the end of the village, as the tide dried out on the *Ekadashi* afternoons.

With great excitement we all set out one day, young and old householders, schoolgirls in tow, walking across the cultivated fields, fording through two narrow branches of the Ramai River on our way to the mouth of the big Gad River as it flowed out on its way to the Arabian Sea. At first we cautiously wade into the thigh-deep waters, saris tucked to crotch-level, peering through the murky waters and blindly scratching around the sandy river bed with bare toes for the tell-tale lumps of mussel shells. In no time the tide begins to run out, the water gradually receding to knee-level, then to mid-calves, and finally to bare ankle-level as the sun is close to setting. By then we have gleefully gathered our precious, mouth-watering treasures in little cloth shoulder bags.

There is a great sense of liberation for all of us, searching for mussels in the sand. At first we group in twos and threes, until finally the fascination of the hunt separates us as individuals staking out our own territories in the fast drying river bed. Silhouettes of women stand out starkly against the open sky, with the beautiful palm-fringed river widening out to the sea at the distant horizon. I learn precious village lore during those ventures. The mussels taste altogether different before January when the river contains sweet water from the rains. Once the excess rain water has washed away into the sea, it is sea water that gains precedence, the river turning salty for a long distance inland. So the mussels taste very different then, until the next monsoon off-loads extra amounts of salt-free water into the river all along its course, from the distant Sahyadri ranges to the Arabian Sea just off the village.

Nobody wants to leave the shores until almost sunset, and leg muscles ache from the constant bending to gather mussels. The journey back home is truly wearisome, trudging back the great distance all the way home with a heavy load of mussels. The mussels are cooked in spicy hot and sour curries with coconut paste, or put in salad dishes with grated coconut. The women are ready to go on another such adventure in a fortnight or month's time. Women who lived near the river had always gone mussel hunting, but those on our side of the village had stopped doing so for over a decade. When I pointed out that the effort expended in gathering all that free seafood was much less than what they would usually spend on farm work or wage labour, and much fun besides, they agreed to resume this activity on a regular basis each month. Their families, of course, greatly appreciated the addition of tasty mussels to their diet, and there was little resistance to the venture.

The Stigma of Careless Womanhood

Besides introducing me to the joys of mussel-gathering, an adventure so happily taken up by other kinswomen, Parvati has also taught me many mundane operations necessary for survival in the village. These include tasks such as fetching well-water, lighting a kerosene lamp, and also the kerosene stove, for example, without failing to impress on me the importance of not wasting precious matches, since they cost money. That I could afford to waste a few matches here and there in typical city-bred carelessness was a point beyond consideration. It would have tarnished my image in the eyes of other villagers, and the stigma of careless womanhood is not lightly tolerated thereabouts.

I learn from her the art of plastering my floors with cowdung paste, and understand the pride that every village woman feels in keeping her floors beautifully decorated, particularly on the many festival days. Since my house has mud floors too, the matter of using cowdung on the floors has been perhaps the greatest leveller in terms of my gradually kicking off the supposedly superior city airs, and taking over the persona of a village woman until it grows into the most natural way to live.

We have become friends, of course, by the time Parvati teaches me how to use dry coconut fronds to light a fire swiftly using well-chopped dry wood. This is some six months after my arrival in the village, piteously managing to cook and eat by the labours of a single kerosene stove until then. Parvati instructs me so well that I deprive other village women of their usual sadistic pleasure over an expected failure. These are the unexpected wages of participant observation, not so easy to shrug off if you seek acceptance as a community woman.

They have gathered to witness the common enough sight of some poor victim of a visiting city woman sweating, fuming and coughing over a fire that belches more smoke than flame. This is one of the earliest opportunities they have of witnessing me light a woodfire on my own. At that juncture, most probably, I have passed the crucial test of village living, joining the ranks of beaming village women so proud of their several accomplishments.

It has been tough for Parvati too, since she did not always live in this village. May be that is the reason for her deep empathy with my plight, trying to understand village India for the first time from a worm's eye view, my very own. Parvati is a literate woman. She attended all the years of primary school and has continued to read and write ever since, so that she does not need help in these matters at a simple level.

House of Gold, My Mother's House

Parvati's father owned extensive lands, and they grew rice, nachni —a variety of millet—lentils, groundnuts, beans and so on. A description of this wealth is never complete without a reverent enumeration of *maad-pophli*, which are coconut and betel nut palms. To top it all, her father was a literate man, educated up to the third class in school. He had a permanent job in Bombay with a Government of India undertaking, which meant that their status was fairly high in the village. She recalls that her mother was an able woman, 'always striving in the cause of justice'. She had even gone to court to win back disputed parcels of land while her husband was away in the city. It was her mother alone who tended the farm lands with the help of labourers, and also looked after the household and her three children.

Parvati was the oldest of the three, followed by a sister, and then a brother. She remembers taking on the responsibility for the younger siblings and the household fairly early, since her mother had to keep busy with farm work. Her parents sent her to school with the hope that their daughter would at least be able to write letters. She was very intelligent and enthusiastic about her studies, and remembers being very upset at having to give up going to school because of the pressing need to help with the household workload.

More specifically, she had to stay home to cook for all of them. She must have been about eleven years old then. Her mother had delivered her third child, a son, and according to village custom, suffering from birth pollution, which meant that she could not enter the kitchen for a month. So, with only vague instructions from her mother, Parvati began to cook for all of them. Later, both her younger siblings studied only as far as the third standard because of lack of interest.

She did not have any specific expectations regarding marriage. Her parents used to talk about 'setting her up with clothing and linen' as marriage may be referred to, 'with honour intact', or 'given into some stranger's custody'. She acknowledges that the parents were ever worried in case 'a daughter goes astray and does something forbidden, by which she would grind the parents' honour into dust'. They had saved early enough to invest in a nose ring, ear studs and other small items of jewellery for her. She was then prepared to be married.

Why Did You Drown My Daughter?

Her marriage was arranged by her father in Bombay around the time she was fifteen years old. As she tells the tale, her husband's kinsman Baba, the Egypt veteran and Akka's husband, was in Bombay at the time, and took the initiative to negotiate the match. Her father-in-law was dead by then, having bequeathed his own tenement room in the crowded heart of the city to his two sons, along with jobs in the textile mill that he himself worked in. The prospective groom was visiting his own

native village at the time, and it was Baba's devious talk of vast
landholdings and a good match that probably induced her father
to agree to the match without even setting his eyes on his future
son-in-law. This was common enough in those days.

Parvati recalls the consternation of her father's guests at the
time of the marriage when a much older, half-blind groom was
escorted to the canopy. Her mother remonstrated with her father later, for having 'drowned their daughter' by giving her
away in such an alliance. 'He was destined to be my husband,
so what was the point in blaming anybody for the mismatch,'
Parvati says in a matter-of-fact manner. Worse was to follow,
for it did not take her long to discover that her husband's family
was almost landless, with just three to four small plots of rice
land, totalling to less than an acre.

They did not even have a decent dwelling of their own in the
village, simply being put up in an upgraded cattle manger from
more prosperous times. When Baba had talked of vast lands of
the family, he had not clarified that the groom belonged to a
much impoverished branch of the family, which had sold off
most of the lands. In any case, Parvati was happy enough living
in two tiny rooms in the midst of all the city bustle. She had
no knowledge about sex, no preparation whatsoever. But the
powerful wedding rituals readied her to give herself up to her
husband, for his own pleasure, as she puts it. She remembers
happy times of sexual fulfilment together with her husband in
the city, particularly till her first two children were born.

Her mother died a few months after Parvati's wedding. She
had been pregnant a fourth time. She had a very difficult delivery, having had to be carried in a *doli* to Malvan town several
miles away in those days before roads and buses existed. This
was at the point when the neighbours realized that she was not
going to deliver normally, and that medical assistance was unavoidable. She died of tetanus following childbirth, along with
her infant son. At that point the new bride, escorted by her
young brother-in-law, returned to her mother's house, to take
care of the household until her father made other arrangements. Her youngest sibling, a boy, was only four years old

then. She took charge of all the farming that season. She lived
there for eight months before returning to her husband in the
city. Her younger sister was married off. They had a live-in
labourer who was treated like a brother, and her father had
also got him married. She then took the young brother to live
with her in Bombay for a year.

Her father later got married a second time, to a girl from a
poor family, since he needed someone to keep the land and
family together. By the time her father retired, this woman had
allegedly engaged in an affair with a local landowner who was
helping her out in the farming. She did not have children of
her own, but had always ill-treated her step-son, trying to do
him out of his rightful share in his ancestral home and family.
Parvati's father had become an invalid following an attack of
paralysis, and the stepmother did care for his needs. According
to Parvati, since the old man was so completely dependent on
his wife, he hardly ever intervened to prevent her scheming
against his son.

Parvati's brother is now in his late twenties, meek by temperament, and already bent and aging because of all the worries. He worked for a good many years in Bombay, but poor
health had made him give up his job after marriage and return
to his village to claim his inheritance. His father-in-law who
was a man of substance in a neighbouring village, encouraged
him in this, although the going was obviously tough.

In any case, Parvati could not overly concern herself with
her brother's plight, beyond the dictates of mutual cooperation
entailed by their survival needs. For example, when her husband lost his job in the strike seven years ago, it was her brother
who helped her out by regularly sending small sums of money.
She lent him a good amount in return at the time of his wedding,
but it was not so bad because one of her sons had taken to doing
odd jobs around the village as a carpenter's assistant. She also
visited this brother's house when his wife gave birth to their
first child, simply to officiate in place of a regular mother-in-law,
to help the young mother after she had returned from
her parents' home.

Parvati recalls yearning for her dead mother and grieving over her loss those first couple of years after her marriage. She would go over her carefree childhood memories, recreating her mother's happy world as a householder. She remembers that her father had regularly sent home money for all their needs, and that her mother was a very happy woman indeed.

Parvati's mother-in-law had attended her wedding in Bombay, then returned to look after their manger in the village. About a year after her marriage, Parvati was pregnant. She visited the village for the annual Ganpati festival, to set up the ancestral home in a better way, before returning to her husband. A few years later her brother-in-law also got married in the city and brought his wife to the same small tenement dwelling. He had been quite a rogue, with an unsavoury reputation. Until his marriage Parvati had dutifully fed and cared for her brother-in-law along with her husband, Gangaram. But conflicts arose over his expectation that they continue to feed and look after both him and his wife without his making any financial contribution to the household. After a few years of putting up with all the quarrels, Parvati gathered her three children, the eldest daughter barely seven years old, and the youngest son, a nursing infant, to come to Gangaram's ancestral home in the village to live with her mother-in-law. That was some seventeen years ago, and she has lived in the village ever since.

She says that once she came as the wife of a migrant in the village she never missed her husband, even after all those years of togetherness. 'I accepted my lot with stoicism. I never cried over his absence. I did not yearn to go visit him, nor did I wish for his return,' she says with disarming frankness. The reason for this is that Parvati's emotions were primarily invested in her three children. An archetypal protective mother hen, as she likes to think of herself, she saw little reason to be miserable over the separation from her husband. Besides, all the stress of learning the ways of her 'given' village, and of looking after three little children hardly left her with any leisure to be sorry for herself.

Her mother-in-law was about sixty years old then, managing to live on what little money her sons could send for her welfare. When Parvati returned to the village her husband was already running a large debt. All he could send for his wife and children at that point was an occasional money order of Rs. 50 to Rs. 100, and small gifts from the city during major festivals. Their living conditions deteriorated considerably compared to what they were used to in the city, and she remembers being constantly indebted to the shopkeeper for their monthly groceries. Even then they lived several days a month on plain rice gruel for food.

She learnt to hire out as a wage labourer, and neighbouring kin would help her with foodgrains only in exchange of labour. Her mother-in-law began to grumble about being crowded out of their home by Parvati and her children. For a while the older woman did take herself off to Bombay. She had never got used to living in the village, having spent a major part of her life in the city. She had first come to the village only after her eldest son's marriage. Now she could not get along with the younger daughter-in-law in the city tenement, so she returned to the village and died in a few years' time.

Parvati, Head of the Household

Parvati remembers her sense of desolation, of being alone with three little children as the old woman drew her last breath. Thankfully, a few kind women from among her kin came to spend the night with them even while the corpse lay in the outside room. Her husband returned to the village for a few days to carry out all the mourning rituals.

There were skirmishes with the kinspeople now and then, but Parvati never could bear a grudge towards anyone. It was also wise not to do so, since she could hardly afford to antagonize people in her straitened circumstances, burdened with a brood of young children. Cooperation was a matter of survival for her, particularly since she was without the day-to-day protection of a man. 'I always instilled in my children that we needed to stay humble and uncomplaining even in the face of provocation.'

Earlier, her in-laws had claimed the tiny piece of land housing the manger as their dwelling. Akka's husband, Baba, a young lad then, had purposely planted and nurtured a prize graft variety mango sapling, along with a jackfruit tree and sundry other saplings in his own piece of vacant land right next to the walls of the manger. He had taken great care to see that all these trees grew lush into their prime. What it meant for Parvati was that the dry or rotting branches were a permanent threat to her roof. The tree unerringly invited hordes of marauding monkeys whenever they passed through the wadi, in the process jumping over Parvati's roof and adding to her difficulties.

The trees also obliterated sunlight from her dwelling, forcing them to grope around in the dark indoors, besides making her dependent on sundry kinswomen for sharing their sunny yards to dry her summer produce. Once her young son chopped off an overhanging limb from the jackfruit tree, only to invite a stinging rebuke from old Baba. She could rightfully approach the village panchayat to have these trees cut down. But the panchayat would not be able to protect her and her family from any nasty retaliation by the kinsman.

Her situation began to ease a little as her children grew up to become young companions. Her eldest son, Mano, began to hire out as a farm labourer, mostly in exchange for rice grain. This was the year after he failed at the high school leaving examinations. He was a gentle lad, much appreciated by women around the wadi. He never talked back to his mother, sitting with head bent, a half smile always playing around his mouth. He even helped around the house, fetching water for his mother, as kinswomen looked on jealously at the well or from their secure perches on their verandas.

Travails of the Migrant Son

He left for a hardworking job at a glass factory in the city suburbs, sending a small sum of Rs. 50 to his mother every month

if he could manage it. This was after the textile strike, and his
aging father had been out of work for four years already. Mano
was employed as a temporary hand, and there was no job security or protection of any kind. He earned around Rs. 300 a
month at the beginning. He was lucky to find a job in the first
place, through the good offices of a distant cousin. It was a harsh
world that he found.

He commuted long distances to work, and the railway pass
also took a chunk out of his salary. He lived with his uncle's
family in the tenement rooms that his grandfather had bequeathed to his two sons before dying. He paid *khanawal* to his
uncle, amounting to Rs. 200 each month for a spartan fare consisting of rice and curry, also tea. He sat with his head bent,
allowing his uncle's diatribes against his parents to slide off his
back without talking back. He did reclaim his parents' cot to
sleep on in one of the two rooms. His uncle had five daughters
and no son. His wife did not work outside. He was frequently
in and out of jobs. The eldest daughter, an intelligent girl in
her last year at school, would soon be sent for work outside to
support the family until she got married.

There were two other kinsmen sharing the living space, sleeping on the floor in a curtain-partitioned portion of the outer one
of the two rooms. They too paid Rs. 200 a month for meals, and
were grateful to have a place to rest their heads while working
at their low paying blue-collar jobs in the city. Mano spoke of
how they would have to wake up at 5 a.m. to join the long line
at the communal water tap, braving the frequent brawls, to fetch
their quota of water to hand over to the woman of the house. In
slum communities, particularly, where water is scarce, the migrants even have to pay the householders for a couple of jealously
guarded pots of water, along with their keep.

When he returned home to the village on a brief vacation
after about three years since he took up the job, his mother
wept to see how thin and gaunt he had become. He had to keep
long hours at the glass factory, working docilely at a
particularly strenuous job that few workers opted for. He was
constantly near the hot furnace, working over glass without any

covering for his eyes. He had begun to have passing spells
of dizziness.

Yet leaving the job was no option. It was a small privately
owned unit, and most workers, specially those with families to
feed, were ever-insecure and worried in case the owner shut
the factory to reopen elsewhere. Such a stratagem is regularly
resorted to by thousands of small-scale industrialists all over
the city, simply to bypass the Factory Act regulations, so that
workers who have worked longer than the fixed probation period are cheated out of job security and all the benefits it entitle
them. Mano was lucky to find a job at all at that critical time
out of the teeming multitudes of unskilled, unemployed job
seekers in the city.

His cousin who had got him the job was in the good book
of Mano's uncle. They both had worked out a strategy to keep
Parvati's elder son beholden to them, so that he lived like a
orphan, dependent, head bent, sitting in a corner, in the tenement rooms of shared ownership. The cousin was afraid of losing his own space in that room, and he certainly could not afford
to find another room in that expensive city where every squar
inch of space was worth the value of gold.

Mano was gentle by temperament, but he was not a fool. H
related all the ill-usage at the hands of his conniving kin to h
mother when he visited the village. Parvati and her fami
smouldered for days over his humiliation. At another time, c
course, Mano would have landed a relatively stable job at tl
textile mill where his father had worked, following the latter
retirement. The textile strike dashed all their hopes. His fath-
lost the job very close to retirement, even as he was going blir
for all practical purposes, no longer job worthy.

Private Agonies

In the village when Parvati and her brood first got news of t
strike, they were very sympathetic towards Gangaram, even
the flow of remittances immediately dried out. Gangaram r
turned to the village at the very beginning of the strike, stayi

over for several months before going back so as not to miss out on recruitment. He nurtured a fond hope that a resolution was not far away considering the length of time already spend over the impasse between the strikers' representatives, millowners and the state government.

During that relatively prolonged visit of six months to his native village, he got his wife pregnant for a fourth time, after a gap of over twelve years since Raju's birth. Parvati had given birth to Raju, till then the youngest of three offspring, in a hospital in Bombay. This was before her long-term return to the village. She wished to undergo a sterilization at that time to prevent further conceptions, but Gangaram had refused permission fearing that such an operation might affect her health. The couple then started using condoms regularly as a method of contraception. Gangaram had been introduced to condoms by way of birth control propaganda while he was at the mill, but his supply of city condoms was over within a few months after visiting the village. He did not wish to approach the village dispensary out of fear of ridicule. Some four months after his return Parvati had become pregnant once again, to their mutual shame and horror.

She asked herself if she should get an 'injection' from some local quack doctor to abort the foetus, as she had heard many women mention in hushed undertones. She wondered if she should go to the government clinic in the small town for a legal abortion. She was upset about what the neighbours and kin would say when they realized that she was pregnant once again at that late age, turning forty, with grown children besides. With her husband on strike, moreover, they had no source of income whatsoever. Feeding existing mouths was a strain in itself, without the addition of another child. She agonized over all the possibilities, but eventually felt that it was sinful to abort a living foetus, so vetoed that option. At that stage she made a pact with herself that she would work hard, no matter what, to feed the family.

They would manage one way or the other, she reasoned, but she would look after this yet to be born child with love, care

and affection, just the way she had brought up the rest of he
children in better times. Her husband was personally agains
her getting an abortion, but he left the final choice to her, par
ticularly since he was jobless and could hardly assure suppor
to the child. He left for the city after a while, hoping to b
recruited in the mill once again, a sad man bent in the knees
and almost blind in the eyes.

It was during her advanced pregnancy that Parvati's childrer
began to help out in the house and outside out of deep sympath
for her plight. They were all overjoyed when a bonny baby gir
was soon delivered into their midst by a loving and beamin;
mother. This daughter was the delight of the family. Fair anc
chubby in appearance, she was pampered and encouraged jus
like any longed for upper class child. They would deny her noth
ing, and they all worked hard to return to her hugs and kisse:
and cheerful lisping of questions full of naive curiousity abou
the happy world she found in that humble manger of a dwelling
For Parvati, she became a secret blessing at that stage in her
life, filling her nest with joy and exuberance even as other fledg
lings were learning to spread their wings and would soon take
off on their own. She could hardly contain her breathless anxiety to return to the child at the end of a long work day as a
farm labourer. She would spare no effort to cosset the girl withir
her meagre resources.

Breadwinner, Patriarch

In the meanwhile, Mano, her first son, had left for work in
Bombay. It had become painfully clear that Gangaram could
never hope to be employed once again at that age and stage of
physical decrepitude. Worse, through that very difficult period
of deprivation, when they would spend days on end on rice gruel
alone, they could not even hope for the early refund of his
provident fund and cooperative contributions locked up by
the millowners.

Gangaram kept up his sad flitting to and from the village,
leaving each place as the support systems at either end began

to groan and kick under the burden of feeding his now useless body for prolonged periods. The earlier sympathy and commiseration of wife, children, neighbours and kin giving way to a sullen rage and contempt over his meddlesome, nosy ways, the situations being worse by several degrees in Bombay where he lived on his brother's charity while awaiting some resolution to the strike imbroglio.

He was a devout man, doing puja for a couple of hours after his bath each morning. In the evenings he would sing aloud bhajans on the veranda. He fasted on two days every week, and had turned a full vegetarian to the derision of his kinsmen. Needless to add, he was also a teetotaller, abstaining from paans and bidis even, and his wife was deeply grateful for that.

Yet when he tried to educate his children to better ways of the city they were outright impatient with him. As he bumbled around the wadi in a seemingly artless way, irritating people and earning well-chosen epithets from his victims, that impatience turned to scorn. Parvati and the children learnt to ignore him even as they busied themselves with all manner of tasks to keep body and soul together. If he was too intrusive they asked him to shut up and quietly eat what they fed him. She did not hesitate to tell even casual visitors from outside how he was a burden on her since she had to support him for all he was worth.

So they bore his name. They were acknowledged to be his property in the culturally sanctioned way. People were even expected to provide well for their cattle, if they owned any, so why had they worked so hard all their lives to feed themselves, subsisting on rice gruel more often than not? Their sorrow was borne on deep waves of anger against his stupidity in supporting the strike to the point of losing that one job without which he was a worthless man. Their feelings were not assuaged by the thought that he had done the right honourable thing in standing by his co-workers. In any case, there had always been the danger of being attacked by his own furious colleagues if he had reported for work during the strike. But they had heard those explanations for a long time, and now they too, as his dependents, had become the laughing stock of a cynical world.

Like most other men, he had enjoyed being on the cutting edge of a harsh patriarchal system, ruling his family with the metaphorical iron fist. He had laid down the law for them to obey. But that had been when he was regularly employed, able to send some money for their upkeep, however irregular the remittances were. Now he was not even a respectable member of the same patriarchal system. His children were all strangers to him, and they were ashamed of him. He was unfit for any kind of farm work since his long sojourn in the city. He depended on his wife and children for sustenance, the long-drawn strike having totally emasculated him in the eyes of the villagers and his family.

Better Days, Mother

By and by Parvati's second son, Raju, was in his last year at high school, only to fail in the school leaving examinations. Then he began to hire out as a village carpenter's apprentice, transgressing the caste barrier. The carpenters were somewhat lower in the caste hierarchy in the village, and it was not permitted for people from Raju's caste to eat with the carpenters. The kinfolk looked askance, but they could hardly intervene in case they were asked to provide financial support by the insolent children. Raju already knew farming very well, and had often been helped out by grateful kinsmen with seasonal use of stray bits of land to grow his own crops with the help of his mother and sister. He earned more working on house construction with the carpenters, and it immediately relieved the considerable strain that the family had worked under for the past five years.

The united front that this family presented to outsiders, despite severe stress, was certainly a creditable achievement for Parvati. Her primary attachment was to her four children, with some ambivalence in her relationship with her husband. At one point through a lucky contact in Bombay, I helped to obtain a job placement for her elder son, Mano, in a modernized textile plant. His health had begun to flag in the face of the exacting work in the glass factory. Parvati had applied to me for help, and things somehow worked out well in his favour. With another lucky break, her second son also got a job in a bank in Bombay as a peon or messenger, the acme of success and achievement for most villagers stuck with failure at the school leaving examinations.

Parvati's heart swelled to the point of bursting. Her sons were also full of excitement, for now they had truly reached manhood. They had seen all the sacrifices their mother had made on their account, even braving community wrath to shield them from injustice. They vowed to keep her out of hardship, and also to work hard so as to educate their little sister 'to the limits of her intelligence'. Their mother did not fail to see them off with the usual homilies to keep out of trouble, to live a chaste life, not to let their uncle harass them overmuch in their tenement room in the city, and to stay away from drink and addiction of any kind. 'Don't worry about us,' she had warned them.

In the end, as she saw them off at the bus stop near the temple, she had broken down and cried to see them leave together. They had all cried, for it was the end of a complete chapter for all of them. They were leaving their days of childhood innocence behind forever. For those left behind, and for their mother, the nest was going to feel very empty for a long time.

Fortunately, Gangaram's provident fund and savings money had also come through a little while earlier, so the family was well set on the road to financial recovery and happier times. She was very wise in her management of that money. They had never seen such a large sum of money before: his savings from an entire lifetime's hard work. They wisely decided not to use up any of that money in their day-to-day existence. They would all continue to work as hard as before. There would be expenses enough later. The roof needed urgent repairs, an expensive proposition. The daughter, Neela, was to be married off. They would have to make a choice at that point, rather than splurging it all away in one spectacular burst.

Her daughter intervened then to remind them that she would go to a 'strangers' house' after marriage, but what would her

natal family do if the roof collapsed on their heads? She insisted
that they make the roof repairs their first priority, and they
had to agree with that sensible argument. So they put
Gangaram's funds in a fixed deposit in a joint account, and took
a bank loan to repair the roof. Their kinsmen neighbours were
very envious of the sudden elevation in the status of this family,
in their even being able to afford expensive roof repairs
while they on their part had to patch their roofs with
makeshift material.

Of Houses and Mangers

Since the bottom dropped out of the once thriving village economy, the skilled Christian potters who used to manufacture roof
tiles for decades, have taken en masse to distillation of illicit
liquor. The Christawadi, or Christian hamlet, has become syn-
onymous with hooch dens, and their clientele is derived from far
and wide.

Pollution barriers and religious injunctions have ceased to
exist in this important matter for Hindus and Muslims. There
are frequent police raids too, and this has rendered them vulnerable to open blackmail. Yet it is a more profitable trade than
making pots and roof tiles to serve the needs of the villagers.

The tiles they manufactured had been much cheaper than
the Mangalore tiles imported into the region, and suddenly the
costs of roof repairs have escalated beyond the reach of most
farmers. Also, the old mud houses lasted in this termite terri-
tory because they had only used superior teak and jackfruit
trees. Traditional ecologically oriented wisdom has now given
way to a rapacious monetary consciousness, particularly as a
result of illegal commercial exploitation of the forests by private
contractors in league with the authorities. So even the villagers
have learnt to assess the monetary worth of each standing tree
right from its infancy, contributing in their part to the loot of
the forest wealth, and being ripped off in the bargain. Now they
themselves cannot find good, solid timber for their paltry construction needs. Very often, old houses cannot withstand the

onslaught of the torrential rains during the monsoons, particularly without good roofs. Top quality indigenous material, local laterite pillars, timber, or fortress-like mud walls all eventually collapse into the mud.

The residents usually move their belongings to more humble mangers of the olden days, often with patchwork bamboo repairs overhead. The old abandoned houses bear testimony to the earlier times of real material prosperity, intricately carved rosewood and teak ornamentation providing proof of a cultured way of living that the villagers have descended from within a few years of 'development'.

Parvati and Gangaram were very proud of their renovated, restored house. Once again, there were conflicts with the brother in Bombay, who also had a share in the dwelling. He refused to contribute to the repairs, but this served to their benefit in the long run since it gave them the upper hand in terms of ownership.

A Gentle Man, My Husband

Parvati continued to be the de facto head of the household in all concerns, particularly economic decision making. Yet the family softened considerably in their attitude towards Gangaram, a little ashamed of themselves since he had borne all that ill usage without flinching and without retaliating. He continued to be proud of his wife and children, openly expressing his love for them whenever the opportunity arose.

When they lived in the big city after their marriage, Gangaram had full charge of the finances and budgetary affairs, including shopping for all their needs. Parvati took over this responsibility after she came to live in the village with her children. Her experience in this regard at her mother's house before marriage was an asset. Their daily situation eased up after her sons started working, giving them access to a regular cash income.

She continues to hand over all the money to her husband, secure in the knowledge that his own needs are very few, and that he would not spend a single paisa without consulting her. 'It is important to acknowledge his control as the *malak*, or master,' as she says seriously. 'I never gave him occasion to complain on that score,' she adds, 'or to say that nobody showed him money now that he did not earn any himself.'

Her relationship with her husband also improved. At one stage some six years ago, Gangaram agreed to undergo a vasectomy, when I broached the topic with him at Parvati's request. He consented with alacrity, out of deference to my status in his eyes as a woman of learning. His wife had been at him for years, but he had refused to consider it. When I communicated his consent to her, she covered her mouth and began to giggle, asking me what life-threatening measures I had used against him to help her in this matter. It provided hilarious relief to her for quite a while.

She does not need much encouragement to talk about her sex life. She had a very happy experience in that regard for all the years they lived together in Bombay, her urge tapering off a little after the birth of two children. Yet they had derived mutual satisfaction in their intimacy. As she described it, the children would sleep on the floor, while husband, wife and the youngest child slept together on the cot. The infant stayed with them until it was five or six months old, later to join its siblings on the floor.

They would have sex around once a week, in a hasty fifteen minutes or so, without taking off their clothes. There was no possibility of talking, of being demonstrative in love. She began to lose interest gradually, but meekly submitted to her husband. 'Can a male understand the pains of childbirth?' is her inimitable way of explaining this.

In their village dwelling in the manger, all of them sleep in the same room, on the floor, since there is no cot. There the husband and wife sleep at one end of the room. She admits to waking the husband for a second time in case she has not experienced orgasm. Parvati candidly adds the rider that sex is very important to keep her husband bonded to herself,'*muthit thevla tar aiknyat rhail*', 'for that is the way to keep him under control'. Then she talks about their beautiful sense of togetherness, particularly in the last two years since their financial situation improved. He is very devout, never missing on his puja or worship. He also follows the discipline of regular bi-weekly fasts, besides eschewing the fish and meat so dear to all non-Bramhan villagers.

He has never insisted that they follow his example; nor have any of them done so. Each evening before going to bed she reads out to him an entire chapter from the religious texts. He discusses important sections with her and answers her questions patiently, and they go on past ten or eleven in the night. They keep up this routine every day, reading from the *Ramayan, Kashi Khand,* and occasionally adding the secular *Chandoba,* a popular illustrated children's magazine, for variety.

It is only during peak agricultural seasons, such as paddy transplanting in the monsoons, that it becomes too difficult for her to keep up this routine. They then limit the readings to Mondays and Ekadashi holidays. 'Otherwise,' she says, 'I read, he listens. I'm the only person of whom he can ask anything by right,' she proudly explains. At other times they work in the deep satisfaction of togetherness. They tend to their little backyard garden of growing maad-pophli and plantain trees. He mends the fence, helps her clear the leaves. He lights the kitchen and bath fires, and fetches groceries from the store for her. Some days he even helps her cook.

She has lived a life of struggle, amidst shifting cliques and alliances. Earlier it was the mother and children bond that had prevailed. As the children are growing up, learning to become independent, a new appreciation of her husband is beginning to dawn upon her. She now admits to an increasing awareness that they will have only each other to depend on for companionship and love in their mundane daily lives. For the first time in their lives, a close bond has begun to develop between Parvati and her husband as they face a common future together with contentment and hope.

CHAPTER VI

Woman of Faith, Savitri

THERE ARE MANY women living in these parts who claim to have a direct link with God. There are some who channel obscure deities on specific weekdays at the mere whiff of an incense stick. They answer questions of the humble and the harried, to tell who must have cast a hex, and how to put it to rest with offerings to the Lord, with special kinds of penance, or with ritual and worship. They even manage to earn their humble keep this way. Then there are those like the despised Nalini in my hamlet, who claims to be an evolved *santin*, that is, a she-saint. When she first manifested in the village in her white robes, face smeared with ashes and hair in wild tangles, she is said to have caused a mini riot at the bus stop. Gullible believers, who hoped for saintly benediction, vied with each other to touch her hallowed, albeit muddy feet.

Some Normative Models: The She-Saints

She is Ganpya's wife, still in her thirties, with three kids to boot. She arrived just a couple of months before my own first visit for research. She had returned after a lengthy sojourn in tenement quarters in a distant suburb of Bombay. Her husband was a hard-working millhand, who commuted long hours by train every day to the dusty and choked heart of the city to earn a living for himself and his family. This was her first visit to the village after donning saintly robes.

A couple of years later, the robes changed colour to a bright saffron, to add further drama to her assertion of possessing a high level of saintliness. By then, of course, she had changed from a superior being commanding veneration to an object of ridicule, the butt of sarcastic jokes around the wadi. They had to be careful not to catch her ear at it, though. Her saintly pilgrimages to the holy places had helped her to develop an enriched vocabulary with the most colourful repertoire of foul language. This she uttered with great gusto for hours while raging up and down the length of the wadi walkways in order to cover as wide a range of broadcast as possible.

But the farm women did not approve of a mother reneging on her duties and responsibilities towards young children, to wander around irresponsibly in the name of God. Her thrashing the little children during her frequent fits of rage were even more difficult to bear. Everyone heaved a sigh of relief when she returned to Bombay following an aborted mission to saint-hood. Her long-suffering husband, who had returned for a brief vacation, was very angry at her gross neglect of their children, which included starvation despite his sending her a regular money order. One day he soundly beat her until her haranguing voice was stilled for many days. The wadi residents were sorry that he had not returned much earlier.

There is yet another 'normative saint' in this region that so graciously permits its independent and eccentric women to drop out of the rigours of housewifely existence. They may excuse themselves from the drudgery of daily toil that poor women are subject to either by donning saintly robes, a string of holy beads around the neck, or by taking refuge under the cover of spirit possession and temporary insanity. This other is a truly saintly old woman, although not averse to using street-level Malvani profanity, or to discussing Indira Gandhi's charisma during her special *pravachan*. She is occasionally invited to give discourses in distant temples in the region. She travels on her own, and has a fairly liberated life style for her middle-class, rural origins. The saint woman wears white saris, with the standard rosary of protective holy beads around her neck, and she does not hesitate to deliver godly discourses to hapless captives on

crowded buses and in marketplaces. She has an aura of peace
around her, and is happy to travel far and wide as a part of
her journey in search of God. She has done her duty to her
family, and has now turned to Him, although there are days
when she is happy just to cook for her now wealthy family during their infrequent visits to their posh house, newly constructed in the village. The light shines out of her eyes, and it
is no trouble to heed her words, even though she seems slightly
unhinged in the manner of Godwomen.

Women Organized in the Name of God

There are many other women like that in the district, but none
are a patch on the ordinary, humble woman of faith, Savitri,
with her deeply philosophical approach to work and to living
itself. Today, as I approach the temple grounds, I begin to hear
female bhajan-singers' voices rising sonorously towards the
beautiful temple roof just round the bend. My feet quicken to an
increased pace, as I walk towards the gathering.

It is no small matter for a group of village women to organize
a bhajan mandal to sing devotional songs in the temple. Then
again, it is well within the tradition of Maharashtra, with its
artisan saints from different castes, including a potter, an untouchable, a weaver, and also ordinary women mystics whose
devotional poetry is a live and treasured part of the common
culture to this day. I hear of the bhajan singers from the carpenters working on my roof repairs. The women belong to the
Mestry caste, which is the occupational group of carpenters. They live in the neighbouring hamlet surrounding the
Bharateshwar temple, in a mixed grouping of various castes,
unlike the more homogeneous hamlet that I live in.

Every single day throughout the year, they gather in the
temple in the evening—if only in twos and threes during the
heavy work season—to sing bhajans and offer prayers to Lord
Bharateshwar at the appointed hour. It is a matter of duty and
devotion to keep up this tradition which was begun only about
eighteen years ago, and the women are very proud of it.

Men also have their own bhajan mandal, congregating in the temple each night, a couple of hours after the women. But the two groups are quite distinct and separate. The Mestrys have their own ruling deity with Her separate temple at the back of their wadi, but they have come to accept the primacy of Lord Bharateshwar, the Village King, with great dread and devotion, and they try not to be remiss in offering daily bhajans and prayers in the very hardest of times.

Today men and women are gathered together in the temple in the afternoon to sing bhajans amid a larger group of visitors from Bombay and Malvan, as a part of the week-long special bhajan *sapta*. Although men too join them on this occasion, it is women who lead the singing and the recitations. There are about thirty women of various ages, from the old to the very young, seated on the floor in the open hall of the temple under an arched roof. The men are huddled on the outer edge, some ten to twelve of them, including respected elderly visitors from the city. A Bramhan woman preacher from the town of Malvan has been specially invited to give a religious discourse and to lead the recitations and songs from the books. No caste barriers are observed, and we will all be invited to tea at Savitri's house, since this is a special event in the year.

The women make room for me in their midst without undue bustle, and a girl hands me a tattered copy of a book from which they are all reading. Of course there are many unlettered women in the group, almost all of them older, but they look into the books intently along with the younger women, singing aloud from sharp memory without the slightest hesitation. They all present a fresh, well-dressed appearance, with neatly oiled hair decorated with fragrant jasmine blossoms strung together. This is in a sharp contrast to their usual harried appearance as women of work. Even widows are not debarred from the happy group of bhajan singers, and the women present a rare united front on this occasion.

Surely, they have their full share of petty jealousies and rivalries, but none of that is permitted to intrude upon the bhajan sessions. There is no formal organization behind their activity.

It is only the level of discipline and commitment they bring to
it that has sustained the group over the years. This is all the
more remarkable in a place where no non-traditional grouping
or alliance whatsoever can last past the few days of initial
enthusiasm and hype. Grown up daughters get married and
move on to another village. New daughters-in-law take their
places soon enough. There is no hierarchy of any sort. Young
girls who sing well, with a clear and loud ringing voice, take
the initiative to lead the singers in turns. Some read aloud from
the religious books while others pay attention in respectful silence, and then join the chorus as the singing begins.

Despite all the appearance of cooperation and shared initiative, there is one strong-willed woman, Savitri, who is the mainstay of this group. It is she who has forged the rag-tag group
of women with divided interests into a homogeneous group of
disciplined singers. There are days when no one except she and
her two daughters make up the evening bhajan group, while
others have allowed their spiritual drive and energies to dissipate altogether in back-breaking farm work. She and her brood
return from the farm, take a hasty bath and head towards the
temple. They present a quick yet unhurried obeisance to the
·deity, in the form of bhajans, before returning to their usual
cooking chores. Invariably they are joined in the temple by a
couple of shamefaced older women following belatedly on their
heels. As the farm work gradually recedes from an unrelenting
crescendo of exertion into a more relaxed, evenly paced effort,
they are joined by others repentant about their dereliction from
duty, and the group continues from one year into the next.

Yet most women candidly admit that without Savitri's silent
and unreproachful vigil, few would even be sufficiently motivated to keep up the singing on a regular basis. Once permitted
to lapse, it would surely be the end of that fine activity, particularly since the women have so many demands on their limited time. So they are grateful to Savitri for keeping them on
their toes without being too bossy or officious about it, and they
treat her with a natural respect rare in the life of an ordinary
farm woman or householder.

Tall and well-built, fair-skinned with beaming good looks and an in-born sense of command, Savitri stands out in any crowd of women, always well-dressed, with the neat round dot of kunku on her forehead to indicate her fortunate married status. She presents a somewhat incongruous sight in her open deference to her husband, Satto, a man as short as she is tall, as slight and bent in frame as she is round and bosomy, and as shy and self-effacing as she is confident and forthright. She usually has a smilingly candid air of self-possession, which places him in the role of respected patriarch without the slightest touch of obsequiousness, while at the same time maintaining that delicately assertive air of herself being the controlling nucleus of the family.

She covers her mouth out of a sense of modesty, and tells me of how so-and-so's son accosted her the other day to ask her admiringly what was the secret of ruling her household with such success. 'How is it that old Satto has never touched a drop of liquor all his life? How is it that your grown up sons respect your every wish, never disobeying you to play truant like the other wastrels in the neighbourhood? Why do your daughters appear so genteel and well-behaved amidst all the grinding poverty?'

The answer lies in the fine balance she treads between innate goodness, respect for traditional boundaries, love for her own people, and a sense of creative fulfilment in all that she does. Other villagers also tell me in the passing of how much they admire her for her air of efficient self-sufficiency, the success of her kitchen garden in the monsoons, her untiring efforts at food processing for household consumption in the summer, from making papads to pickling mangoes. These activities are now restricted to relatively leisured aging housewives of the Bramhan caste in the village.

Days of Prosperity in a Bygone Era

Savitri lives in one of the few double-storey structures in the village, that is, in a house with a *madi*. It has a small upper floor beneath the roof, with elaborately carved, wooden lattice-work windows. The house testifies to their status of pre-eminence amidst their neighbours and a better standard of living than most village households in the past. It was a family of ship-builders in the prosperous days when Malvan, the nearest town and taluka headquarters, was a flourishing harbour serving as the nerve centre of communications and transport for the entire district, buzzing with trade and commerce.

Today the town is nothing but a distant satellite solely dependent upon the stellar economic force of Bombay for its measly sustenance. Only the imposing sea-fortress of Sindhudurg from which the district derives its name and sundry other forts along the coast testify to the past glory of the region. Once roads were constructed into the region for the first time some twenty years ago, a network of bus services began to operate through the district, taking the load off sea transport.

This long-needed development of alternative means of communications brought unsuspected blight in its wake. Tree-felling was undertaken in massive proportions throughout the lush subtropical rainforest ecosystem of the Kokan and in the Sahyadri mountains. With the blessings of corrupt officials and politicians, logs were transported in truckloads to the city by out-of-state jungle contractors. It did not take too long to do serious damage to the entire ecosystem, with massive soil erosion which led to silting and blocking of the long-flourishing natural harbour. This was also accompanied by an ever-present threat of serious flooding of the rivers in the district during the monsoons because of heavy silting caused by loads of deposits of precious top-soil washed off the mountains.

There was little political pressure to allot scarce state revenue to dredge the silt so as to open up the channels of navigation. Once the harbour was shut down, the local economy of Malvan town and the surrounding villages simply folded up. As the new roads provided easy access to the regional markets for the mass-manufactured cheap goods from Bombay, local trades and crafts inevitably shut down.

Carpenters, Shipbuilders

Savitri tells of being married into a big joint family of ship-builders, of the bustle of many people in the household, of big enough tracts of commonly held agricultural land, of a large labour force to work those lands, with employed labourers, and even distant memories of prosperity. The carpenters owned rooming houses in Malvan as a base during the shipbuilding season. Here in the village, there was no need to buy foodgrains from the market. Cereals, pulses, oil and even jaggery were all produced by themselves for household consumption.

As an indicator of their prosperity, she tells of the family needing an annual purchase of wood for fuel worth five hundred rupees, a big sum in those days. This is a pleasant memory, since it meant that the womenfolk were saved the gruelling labour of fetching wood for fuel from the mountain slopes.

They always had at least ten heads of cattle, including a cow and two buffaloes maintained just as milch animals. She recalls their yielding up to four litres of milk daily, quite a lot by village standards, and she remembers those prosperous days of having curds, ghee and other milk products for daily consumption. 'We even had servants employed specially to take the animals to graze, while the menfolk were busy at their trade,' she adds with considerable nostalgia. But that was in the good old days when her father-in-law was alive, before the blight shut down the harbour and put an end to the once thriving economy of this coastal region.

Savitri herself belonged to a family of respected shipbuilders from a nearby coastal village. Her father was a skilled carpenter. He had no child for the first fourteen years after marriage, and then, at last, a daughter was borne by his wife. Her second pregnancy was difficult, and at the time of delivery he was asked to choose between wife and child. He refused to accept such an inhuman choice and in the meanwhile both wife and child died. He soon married a second time out of the need to provide a mother to the infant daughter, barely two years old.

Savitri, born to his second wife, had six siblings in all, including two brothers and four sisters, she herself being the fourth among them. There was no great emphasis on schooling in her natal home. She recalls being brought up not only with a great amount of discipline, but also with a sense of equal treatment as a daughter. Her father died a year after the older son's marriage. This brother died of an illness a few years after her marriage, and was followed by their mother within four months. Savitri's brother left a son and a daughter behind to the care of his widow. All the sisters were married by then. Two of her sisters died in childbirth, a common enough occurrence particularly in the earlier days, given the severe malnourishment of the farm women already overburdened with work, early and repeated pregnancies and poor medical facilities. Her youngest brother works in Bombay and supports his family. Savitri mentions that they had good farms and horticultural lands, sadly gone to ruin now with nobody left to tend to the ancestral wealth in her natal village. To her mind, it was inevitable once their old trade of shipbuilding was wrecked so completely.

Her in-laws were a respected, well-educated family in the village. Her father-in-law's brother was a revered schoolteacher then, and even her mother-in-law had studied up to the final or school-leaving level, which was up to Class Seven in those days. This was quite an accomplishment for a house-bound village woman of any caste in those days. Savitri herself has studied only up to the third class, and is just barely able to sign her name. When her marriage was arranged, Satto Mestry overruled any objections from his family on account of her low education by pointing out that they needed a woman to cultivate the lands, education hardly being a point of concern. He was some eight years older than her, and a sickly constitution had prevented his pursuing studies beyond the Final stage in the old school. Poor health had also made him opt to stay behind in the village to tend to the farms in his lackadaisical way, besides doing odd jobs as a carpenter around the village.

Savitri remembers that she had absolutely no knowledge of

paddy cultivation at the time of her marriage. Her father-in-law taught her all the chores with great patience, even as her mother-in-law busied herself with the cooking and other household chores for the large family. Savitri is grateful for her good fortune in getting such good in-laws, and for their tolerance, acceptance, and love for her as though she were a daughter of their own flesh and blood, rather than just by marriage.

She recalls wearing the round-draped city-style five-yard sari at the time of her marriage. Her father-in-law had admonished her firmly, 'in this village the nine-yard sari is the custom', so she changed her mode of dress in deference to his wishes. She continues to respect his words to this day despite her city-dwelling relatives' occasional attempts to persuade her to do otherwise.

Her husband's older brother completed his schooling in the village, and was successful in getting a good, steady job in Bombay. Her father-in-law, whose word was law in the household, wisely decreed that one son should work and live with his family in the city, while regularly providing for the cash needs of the other son's family. It was the duty of the older not to forget his responsibility to his ancestry. The younger son, on the other hand, was expected to sacrifice any ambition to try his luck in the city, by staying behind to care for the ancestral property, living as a farmer and village carpenter. This was a good arrangement for both the households. The brothers and their wives maintained close ties and deferred to each other in important matters, so it has worked to their advantage. It is of particular benefit to Satto because of his poor health and its resultant ill effects on his ability to provide for his family.

Savitri recalls that her sister-in-law, Satto's eldest sister, had lived with them for some time after Savitri's marriage. It was the sister-in-law's sad fate to have been widowed within two years of marriage, returning to her parents' home with an infant son. This son successfully finished his schooling, took up a job in Bombay, and fetched his mother to live with him in the city. He soon got married, and is now well-settled with his mother, wife and children.

After all the land was parcelled off among the different factions of the once joint family, Savitri's household was left with a relatively small share of some four large and four small plots of good farm lands on which they grow rice twice a year. They also have a small plot where they have grown some fourteen choice mango trees of graft Alphonse variety. Besides these, they have fourteen coconut palms on various pieces of land. They own two bulls to run the plough, and a cow still too young to give any milk. Satto Mestry's earnings from carpentry are meagre, since he has very limited skills and almost no business sense.

Savitri has four children. Within three days of the youngest daughter's birth, Savitri, who was in a hospital, had a sterilization operation performed to prevent further pregnancies. She says she took the decision on her own in the hospital, and sent the consent form at home to her husband for his signature, as was required then. He was not too happy about it, but she managed to persuade him by explaining patiently that she could not manage any more pregnancies, particularly since the last one had been so difficult for her. 'Your own health is not so good,' she remonstrated with him. 'We know you will look after us well, but what will become of all the children later?' It was not possible for Satto to ever argue with his wife once she had made up her mind, and moreover he trusted her wisdom and goodness sufficiently to know that she was right. The discussion had been a matter of mere formality, and he had readily signed the papers.

To Guard My Gentle Patriarch

Despite all the hardship, Savitri has propped up her husband's ego as a patriarch with consummate skill. Thus, even though she and her children readily admit that he is no great provider, they are at the same time very respectful and gentle towards him. She is thankful that he is one of the very few men in their community who is an absolute teetotaller, a godly man also, who has never sullied his lips with abuse of any kind.

She is clever enough to understand that while good fortune

has taken care of their needs in the person of her brother-in-law working in Bombay, a carefully nurtured and projected image of the patriarch is good protection for his family in the harsh village environs. While they present a united front, her aura of power and determination behind the weak mien of her husband is sufficient to bring them the respect they deserve. She is a woman of genteel breeding, and will not be able to bear ridicule and taunts in typical village fashion. She attributes it to the blessings of Kalavatiaai that she has avoided that dreaded fate thus far by virtue of her own strength and good will.

Savitri is at peace with herself, and openly admits to having a great attachment to her husband, the good and saintly man that he is. Speaking of her sex life, she mentions that she had absolutely no sex education before marriage. She began menstruating at the age of fourteen and was married at eighteen. She resigned herself to her husband's will from the beginning. She knew that it was not good for her to invite adverse comment after marriage. 'I understood that it was important to bear patiently whatever the husband desired.'

Their sex life did not begin until two to three months after the wedding. The household was full of in-laws and guests from Bombay who stayed over for more than two months after the wedding, and they all slept in common quarters initially. Later it was her sister-in-law who made separate arrangements in a room and locked the wedded couple in. Savitri admits to a sexually fulfilled life with her husband. She says that there is no strict rule about avoiding sex after menopause. Even now her husband asks her once every few months and she willingly submits to him.

'There are some women who are most reluctant to ease up on their husbands, even when approaching old age,' she says with a grin, a palm modestly covering her mouth. As for herself, she admits to her sexual urge having totally declined after the sterilization operation, followed by a bout of chronic illness. Yet she does feel contented about having had her desires fulfilled in youth, so that it does not really matter any more. Religion provides her with greater satisfaction in her middle age, but she continues to be dutiful towards her husband.

'How will it help if he loses interest in me? I have to do as he pleases. A *saunsar* runs well if the husband's wishes are taken care of, or else, it is the end of everything. If both the partners are nice, understanding, caring and well behaved, it makes for much happiness in marriage.' Savitri's mature attitude towards her relationship with Satto Mestry has served her well all these years, making her household the subject of well-meaning envy in the village. By their sweet temper and helpfulness, all the members of her family have become indispensable to community affairs, and few grudge them their preeminent status.

Of Drunken Brawls

They share their dwelling with Satto's cousin and his family. His father, Satto's uncle, was a schoolteacher. This middle aged cousin is an artist by temperament, very good at painting signs besides being skilled at carpentry. All his talent has gone to waste in his addiction to alcohol, much to the family's shame. The artist's slothful, unlettered wife and three undisciplined children are the bane of Savitri's existence. Being forced to share living quarters with them, albeit in different wings of the house, is too close for comfort. His drunken brawls, constant foul-mouthed abuse in the evenings, and his beating his wife and kids in rage, makes it difficult for Savitri to impress good values and discipline upon her own brood of children. That she does it so admirably is a matter of great credit to her.

Most men in the neighbourhood are confirmed alcoholics, having begun soon after graduating to the final year of high school and yet not succeeding in passing the examination. Alcoholism is a modern rite of passage to adulthood and independence from parental constraints, more so if the parent happens to be a widowed mother. There are brawls aplenty in the evenings as the carpenters return on the high street from construction work in the village, passing through Christawadi on their way home. For those gone to work in the opposite direction, home is merely a half-way station to Christawadi.

On some moonlit nights, the neighbourhood hears the sounds of a brawl from afar. Anxious wives and children run screaming to the silhouetted fighting figures, sharply etched against the night sky. No family can afford to have its breadwinner patriarch assaulted, stabbed or otherwise incapacitated in a drunken brawl with his own kin and neighbour.

All the louts wait upon each other to settle one score or another as sharp fumes of cheap adulterated liquor rise to cloud the grey matter. One would think that hapless women and children might appreciate the poetic justice in having the perpetrators of domestic violence themselves battered or abused and shamed, their bursting energies used up on men their own size for a change. That is not so since it is family honour that is at stake when violence against the man of the house is involved.

Risking her own life to save her man, even the worst of abusers, from a sound battering is small matter for a woman. Much as the public despises the sot, all their sympathy will be directed towards the woman and children, and indirectly to the man himself. 'Who will feed these poor critters, what fault is it of theirs that their provider be put out of commission in a brawl?' There will be much head-shaking on this score, with injunctions to the women to go take their men home for the night.

Alcoholism is definitely a gender issue in the village, as elsewhere. Even as social drinking in 'mixed' company becomes the rage in upper class salons in cities, accompanied by lavish media hype, most proletarian and rural housewives are deeply mindful of their good fortune whenever blessed with a teetotaller husband. Such a husband is earned after lifetimes of piety and goodness, and all his other failings pale in comparison. Whether it is Akka, Parvati or Savitri, they thank their lucky stars for having.escaped the ignominy of having a drunken sot for a husband, with his umpteen brawls and battering. They hope their beloved daughters will be similarly blest in getting above all husbands who are *nirvyasani*, free of any kind of addiction.

From Shipbuilders to House Builders

Since the local economy broke down, most carpenters turned to house construction from skilled craftsmanship. It is now rare to find a skilled artisan amongst them. There is little opportunity for training and apprenticeship as the old masters are either dead, decrepit with fading vision or doddery with cirrhosis. Few village carpenters are familiar with more modern styles of furniture. They do not have the expensive tools of trade required for these, such as machine lathes, and not many villagers can afford fancy furniture anyway. Handmade goods produced in the village do not have a ready market, nor can the artisans afford greater capital investment in their trade. Shoddy workmanship is the order of the day, and people who can afford it import workmen from outside for expensive jobs. The poorer villagers can do no better. Bitter quarrels and much breast-beating is evidenced over crooked walls and badly fitted door and window frames in new houses over which lifetime savings and borrowings have been spent.

It is most ironical that the carpenters-cum-construction workers often live in fairly ramshackle dwellings themselves, and even in makeshift arrangements away from ancient homes vacated under the threat of imminent collapse. Often they have little or no land of their own, and consequently no trees or timber for house construction. The materials are getting more and more expensive with each passing day. Few men can manage to undertake repairs of their own dwellings on the basis of what they earn in the village. Very often the homes are in joint ownership with migrant workers in Bombay. The latter have little incentive to help out the villagers left behind, suspecting them of wishing to bilk them of hard-earned cash, and yet never willing to let go entirely of their own stake in ancestral property.

The villagers, then, are left very bitter about the situation, whereby they either bear the costs of repairing a house that they do not entirely own, at great hardship to themselves, or else risk their own lives by living in an obviously unsafe dwelling. Such are the travails of symbiotic living for the villagers depending on the migrant workers in the city servicing the 'money-order economy' of the village.

Rural Development: A New Dawn of Hope

For carpenters, as for most other villagers,' High School Fail', that is, Secondary School Certificate or SSC Fail, is the ultimate standard of scholastic achievement, blocking all meaningful avenues of future livelihood. A few years back, there was a surge of enthusiasm among these boys as the government solicited applications for loans with heavy subsidies under a new scheme for assisting the educated unemployed youth to develop avenues of self-employment, within the Integrated Rural Development Project. The carpenters' sons saw a new ray of hope, and several among them readily completed the necessary paperwork.

Their applications included, for example, proposals to start modest carpentry workshops with a minimum of necessary tools. After due time had elapsed for the review of their applications, cheer spread in their midst with rumours of their having obtained the necessary approval, and of money being on its way. Since nothing further was heard, the boys began to grow anxious. They were sent from pillar to post with enquiries about the papers, as each bureaucratic agency pointed to another for probable directions. So they went from the panchayat to the cooperative society office, to the appointed district bank in another village, on to the block level office in Malvan, with ne'er a bureaucrat being able to shed light on the status and exact location of their sanctioned grant orders.

Each futile trip involved loss of precious man-hours, at a time when many families could hope to eat at night only on the basis of the wages earned by the artisans during the day. Finally it dawned upon them that it was the same enterprising middleman—they always fawned on as a man of action—who had rounded up all the sanctioned grant papers and blocked the release of funds, to settle some petty score. Their hopes of a bright vocation dimmed and finally receded into the twilight of district corruption. According to them, the Block Development

Officer in Malvan was a good man who had promised to bring the guilty to book without revealing the identity of the complainants. He was, however, soon transferred on the completion of his duration of service in the district, and that was the end of this matter.

That was a deep lesson for the entire community. They are usually helpless in the face of such organized harassment. Another time, during the drought two years ago, the village cooperative society had distributed free fertilizers to farmers in the entire village, but the carpenters' names were mysteriously missing from the lists. This could only be amended after several determined trips were made to the panchayat, involving loss of precious wage hours. Needless to add, the same local middleman was in charge of the distribution.

Preserving an Art

The other major undertaking for the carpenters, besides house construction in the dry months roughly ranging from January to May, is once again the seasonal festival duty of sculpting and delicately painting clay idols of deities for worship during the major festivals. The most important, and a relatively lucrative business is of making idols of the elephant-headed God Ganpati, ordered in fancy poses by the villagers a couple of months before the festival.

Carpenters also need to do farming in whatever measure possible, on their own patches of land or as tenants, to provide at least for their needs of rice for home consumption for part of the year. As soon as the heaviest part of the transplanting season is over, they start making the Ganpati idols. They order special clay by cartloads from a nearby village. The women help by fetching water to mix the clay, by pounding the hardened material with grinding stones, and kneading the malleable earth ready for sculpting. Besides this, there is important emotional labour involved, of sustaining their menfolk through the myriad frustrations of soliciting orders amid cut-throat competition from their own kin and neighbours. Besides the Ganpati idols, the carpenters also sell beautifully painted little clay models of co-bras for worship during Nag Panchami; models of Gauri and Hartalika accompanying the Ganpati celebrations; and idols of Krishna on the occasion of Janmashtami, celebrating the birth of Lord Krishna according to the Hindu almanac, all within a few weeks of each other.

The villagers take the idols from the carpenters' houses in a procession, worship them with great fanfare for a set number of days, and then take them out in a gala finale for worshipful immersion in rivers and streams in the neighbourhood. Such times help the carpenters to tide over the difficult wet season until the busy construction period begins again close to the summer months.

Symbiosis and Money Orders

At these times of idol-making, Savitri's eldest son returns from Bombay with his uncle's permission, bringing with him five hundred rupees each year for household expenses. His presence is crucial to complete the customers' orders, since Satto Mestry can manage very little of the work on his own. This eldest son, Ashok, is about twenty-three years old, SSC Fail. He lives with his father's brother and his family, having left home after giving up schooling some six years ago. The uncle owns a small-scale industrial unit in die-making. He solicits small contracts, and has trained his nephew as a die-maker.

He does not pay the boy anything, but sends Rs. 200 per month directly to Satto in the village for maintenance. There is some amount of heart-burning on the part of Savitri and her family because this uncle has been refusing job offers for Ashok on the grounds of their not being sufficiently remunerative. It is a sad situation for the boy, as they all realize well. Unless he becomes independent and establishes himself in the city, in the rough and tumble of city life it will soon become too late for him to put down roots so as to be able to support a wife and family. Yet they are beholden to the uncle for a lifetime's personal sacrifice in providing for his brother's family through all their numerous bouts with ill health.

How long can this carefully nurtured sense of mutual responsibility and family solidarity maintain its strength despite the
swelling push of modern individualism is a moot question.
Savitri hopes that she does not have to face the indignity of
such a break-up in her own lifetime. She bears deep gratitude
to her brother-in-law for keeping his word to his father on his
deathbed to provide well for his brother's family. So many have
allowed such pious resolutions to fall by the wayside in the face
of serious economic hardship. She feels heartsick at the same
time at the thought of blight on her eldest son's future unless
he is soon allowed to strike out on his own.

There is a possibility that because Ashok is so good at his
work, while the uncle's own son is lackadaisical in his attitude
towards die-making, the uncle may prefer to take the former
in partnership and thus resolve this crucial dilemma. Neither
Savitri nor Satto can be forward enough to broach the matter
with the man, should he see it as lack of trust, or worse, as
greed on their part. They can only wait and pray.

Savitri's daughter Kala, who is about twenty-one years now,
has been quite an economic asset to the family in the last several years. Neat, well-dressed and capable, she works as a
teacher at a balwadi in the same hamlet. She also tailors clothes
at home for customers, working at the sewing machine she
owns. An intelligent and hard-working girl, it was her misfortune to suffer from a prolonged bout of typhoid just before the
High School examinations, and she failed in English and mathematics. She was too dispirited after that blow to reappear for
the examinations despite the headmaster's efforts to persuade
her otherwise. She then completed a government diploma
course in tailoring before going to live in Bombay with her uncle's family for nearly a year. On her return from the city she
purchased the sewing machine under a loan programme with
the encouragement of her sewing class teacher and her parents,
determined to make a good living plying the trade of a tailor
in the village. At that point it was her good fortune to land the
job of balwadi teacher. This coincided with her father's illness,

when they found out that he had a brain tumour. Her job helped
to relieve the financial tensions, and she has contributed a fair
and regular share to the family income ever since.

Teacher, Tailor

The job has earned Kala great admiration from the village community. It has considerably enhanced her status as a woman
with a mind of her own, with talents of service to her natal
family. It has also served to enhance her status in the marriage
market, and her family has had to turn down several proposals
already because they want to be choosy about finding the right
alliance for her.

She pays the monthly instalments on her sewing machine
out of her part-time salary of Rs. 150. She also shares the financial responsibility of the household. She proudly tells me
that they have stayed out of petty borrowing, particularly for
household grocery supplies, ever since she began to earn. The
job has overseen her rite of passage from a girl free of too many
cares in the world to a full contributing adult member of her
household. She says that she is made much of at home and in
the community, treated with a lot of respect ever since she found
outside employment. Her parents are very particular about consulting her in all big and small affairs of the family, although
she is only twenty-one years old.

Apart from all this, Kala of course shares the full burden of
housework and farm work with her mother, 'as a good daughter
should', and also because her mother has frequent bouts of ar-
thritis. This work includes everything from lighting the mud
stove and putting on the tea to boil for all the family, first thing
in the morning, clearing the manger of accumulated manure,
to cooking, washing, and working in the fields.

Kala adds that her job has given her financial independence,
since she has a certain amount of sanction to spend as she
desires out of her income from the job and from tailoring.
She spends for her younger sister's clothes and other school
expenses. She has purchased two wristwatches, one for her

brother and another for herself. Kala has also bought with great delight silver anklets and a decorative silver key ring for herself, no doubt as a part of her future dowry. Apart from all this, there is the pride that she feels over her parents fully sharing their financial trusteeship with her. Earlier her mother alone held the key to the money box, and her father asked her for money whenever he needed it. Now Kala can not only inform her mother and take money out of the box according to her needs, but her parents also make it a point to tell her when they take any money out, so that all three know about the exact state of finances in the household. Kala has begun to take a more active role in family budgeting and in monetary transactions, particularly in view of her father's lack of business sense. All this has greatly added to her poise and self-confidence, and she carries herself with an air of assurance rare among girls of her own age.

Savitri's third child is a boy of about eighteen, good in sports and drawing, who graduated to SSC Fail this year. They are trying to convince him to reappear for the examinations, and hope that he may push on for a couple of years of college so as to slightly improve his chances as an 'educated unemployed'. Her youngest child is a beautiful, timid and meek-mannered daughter, about sixteen years of age, who is studying in the ninth standard in high school. She is clever at studies, and Savitri hopes that she will make a good marriage after completing her education.

Savitri is worried about finding a good bride for her oldest son. She hopes that he will settle well in the city and keep his wife with him, rather than undergo the sorrow of a split household with the wife left in the village under her own tutelage. She shows in this the wisdom and selflessness of a truly content woman, for who does not crave for a daughter-in-law at her beck and call in old age?

She first hopes to settle Kala in marriage, for it is considered more respectable in village society to get a daughter of marriageable age married first, even if the son is a few years older. This is so because a son, once married, may get too engrossed in caring for his wife and children, and neglect his duty towards his natal family, to the detriment of his sister. No doubt it is a custom born of mellow wisdom, and has served village daughters well thus far.

A Godwoman's Blessing

It was following the chronic debility suffered after the birth of her youngest child, and after having spent nearly a year as an invalid in futile search for a cure, that Savitri's brother-in-law sent her to Belgaum with his wife, to ask for Kalavatiaai's blessings to ease the pain. The woman Kalavati, with the suffix *aai*, meaning mother, conducted a group of bhajan singers called Kalavatiaai Hari Mandal.

Earlier when Savitri's sister-in-law had suffered from fibroids which had continued despite two operations in Bombay, she had first visited the Belgaum bhajan group with a friend. She was miraculously cured at the time. Her son, who used to suffer from fits was also cured of the ailment with the blessings of Kalavatiaai, according to Savitri. When Savitri's husband had his operation for urinary blockage, he too recovered well with the holy woman's benediction.

'I was very headstrong and sceptical in those days. I used to laugh at all their madness and seemingly foolish faith in all the mantra and chanting. I had refused to accompany them to Belgaum for a cure during a year of suffering. It was only after umpteen doctors did not provide any relief that I gave in to their pressures.' This is how Savitri laughingly tells of her initiation into Kalavatiaai's inner circle. The holy woman blessed her, and soon after that Savitri began to feel well enough to resume a normal life as a householder, mother and farm woman.

Soon after that the brother-in-law, ever grateful for all the cures in his family, decided to invite the Belgaum group for a session of devotional singing and prayers in the village. He spent some five thousand rupees out of his own pocket to defray the costs of the event. It was a sapta, a week-long happening,

and about five hundred people from all over the village participated in the bhajans. From then on it became a regular annual
event in the village, with people congregating from Bombay,
Belgaum, Malvan and other towns in the district. This has been
kept up unfailingly over the years, even after the death of
Kalavatiaai.

At first, the bhajans were conducted in Savitri's house, but
later the venue was shifted to Lord Bharateshwar's temple
across the street. It was the first event of its kind in the entire
village that first year, as Savitri tells it. A Bramhan widow
from Malvan, a devotee of Kalavatiaai, brought the song books
and photographs of the activities of the Belgaum group to generate interest among the villagers. She also took the initiative
to teach devotional songs to the illiterate carpenter women.
Savitri naturally took the lead from her, particularly inspired
by her own recovery to good health, to become the hostess of
the entire event. All the correspondence concerning each annual
organizing effort continues in the name of Satto Mestry as the
malak, as Savitri explains. Savitri gets the publicity boards
painted by her eldest son in Bombay, and then sends her second
son out to put them up all over the place. Some fifty to hundred
people visit the sapta daily. She spends about a hundred rupees
for the loudspeaker during this period. They also celebrate the
saint mother's birthday with bhajans in a day-long session.
Savitri provides hospitality during these events, and other
neighbours enthusiastically share some of the responsibility as
a festive atmosphere infects the entire hamlet.

I ask Savitri why she goes to all this effort on her own initiative and strength, without much support from the community in
the actual organization of the event. She painstakingly enumer-
ates the benefits she is happy to derive from the whole effort.

'My soul finds fulfilment, all dangers, illness are driven away.
I get new clothes, a sari for the sapta, my children get new
clothes, all brought in appreciation by the visitors from Bombay
... I feel good, respected, important. It is a time of happiness,
of pride over the privilege of outsiders visiting the village owing
to my efforts. The seven days of joy fly by too soon. All our

family congregates together at that time, and we do not feel orphaned any longer because of my mother-in-law's death all those years ago. I truly have good in-laws. All the sisters-in-law are sweet-tempered and loving to each other, and that makes it a special get-together. I get immense pleasure from devotion to God, a great amount of spiritual satisfaction, plus the satisfaction of a task well done. The visitors, the community, my kin, they all make much of me, and that makes me very happy.'

Her list of benefits is endless. She remembers to tell me of other personal advantages she has gained from this organizing effort. 'In the name of good health, I got very good motivation for leadership, and my family's support too. It was only because of this activity that I got scope for developing my special talents. They honour my words, respect my opinion. Even the elders ask me about what I have to say in decision making of any kind. My elder brother-in-law listens to my advice.'

Savitri is very grateful for all that she has received for her involvement in this activity. She revels in the festive atmosphere. But she is also mindful about sharing all this grace with her children, and daughters in particular. 'I always remember to consult my daughters, to take any decision by consensus,' she adds surprisingly, because it is a rare parent who is so far-sighted about sharing authority. 'I want them to develop leadership too. They get good clothes to wear, but it also increases their faith. It is important to have a sense of ritual in your life, particularly in times of stress and danger.'

Savitri is a typical unlettered hard-working village woman, untypical in the level of wisdom and even erudition she brings to each and every issue of living. I have not seen her even once without a broad welcoming smile on her face. Yet life is full of disappointments, trials and tribulations. Her story is an inspiring example of the transformative power wielded by an uncommon individual in the face of adversity, to make flowers bloom while subsisting on meagre fare.

CHAPTER VII

The Myth of the Money-Order Economy

W HEN THE BRITISH developed a new freshwater port in Bombay, a sleepy fishing village until then, to serve their trade and imperialist ambitions, they looked to the densely populated hinterland to supply manpower for the construction needs of the city. It was the labour from the Kokan that was primarily employed in construction of the dockyards, roads and railways in the new city. In the second half of the nineteenth century, a backward agricultural system, low land-man ratio, growing indebtedness and lack of alternative sources of income were coupled with high population density in the district, leading to outward migration in search of a livelihood. By 1880 as Bombay began to develop as the major centre of commerce and industry, the British faced a serious manpower shortage. It was then that they systematically turned to the hinterland.

Communications with the hinterland were opened up to facilitate the movement of people in large numbers to Bombay. Young men were increasingly recruited in the British army, the police, the docks, the railways and the textile mills. There were minimal governmental inputs in the development of the hinterland economy. Since the most able-bodied and talented were the first to be recruited as migrants, agriculture became burdensome to those left behind. The first cracks began to develop in the kinship support systems, even as welfare measures for those left behind, and also for the migrants, were largely absent.

As Bombay grew in leaps and bounds, the hinterland grew more and more impoverished as a result of governmental neglect and loss of the male population. After independence from colonial rule, Indian administrators followed the same policy of focusing exclusively on the development of the city. While paying lip service to decentralized development, they totally neglected the development of the rural hinterland. There was almost no government initiative in promoting a new agricultural policy for the region, in developing its agricultural technology and infrastructure including irrigation, or in setting up measures to support local produce in terms of fiscal arrangements, development of cooperatives, expansion of markets and export of local produce. This sad state of affairs has continued until very recently, in the absence of a coherent policy for the development of the Kokan.

It is ironical that this fertile subtropical rainforest region with a record of heavy rainfall also faces severe water shortage each summer. This has been caused by the total neglect of water resources management until very recently. Railways, the lifeline of industrial and commercial development in the country, are still to be extended to this region, so close to Bombay, although work has begun at long last towards rectifying this serious lapse. Silting has caused many harbours to close down, leaving the Bombay-Goa road as the vital artery for communications and transport.

At one time, 45 percent of the Bombay migrants were drawn from the Kokan and nearly 70 percent of the textile industry labour originated in the Kokan, although this percentage steadily declined over the decades following the depression of the thirties, attaining a further sharp drop after the textile strike in 1982. The Kokan used to be referred to as the police-military reserve in the old Bombay Presidency, since it provided a high proportion of recruitment from amongst its Muslim, Maratha and Mahar population (Buxamusa et al. 1979; Zachariah 1968; Desai 1982; Dandekar 1986). Even now, 42 percent or 1,200,000 of the Marathi-speaking population in the city is said to belong to the two newly separated districts of Ratnagiri and Sindhu-durg (Patwardhan 1987). It is just as interesting that at any given time, over 60 percent of those left behind in south Kokan are women.

The city of Bombay, to emphasize an important factor, is both historically and geographically very much a part of the coastal strip of the Kokan. The relationship between the city and its hinterland was one of close organic interdependence for over a century. The city provided jobs and a much appreciated cash flow to the region while the villages in turn provided much needed labour to the urban enterprise. The city enterprise was often based on extracting high productivity from a vast pool of undernourished and over-exploited workers so as to make the enterprise commercially viable. Work and living conditions were often abysmal, and no humane allowances were permitted to the workers unless they resorted to strikes (Datta 1985). The migrant had been pushed out of the village economy to make a living for himself. It was rarely possible for him to bring his wife and family to the city and the latter were left behind to tend to ancestral lands and home. This was of vital importance since the city did not provide the worker with long-term social security. Nurturing the family home during his absence from the native village was crucial to him, and the women who did this task served to subsidize the industrial empire of Bombay.

As indicated by Desai (1982), more often than not wives had to make a conscious and deliberate choice regarding staying back in the village to tend to the ancestral home, even when it was feasible for them to accompany husbands to the city. Often women in the household were part of 'relay teams', so that one woman accompanied the migrant to cook and serve in the city dwelling, while another, often the widowed mother-in-law, stayed back in the village. Following her death, it was the mi-grant wife's turn to attend to the ancestral home in the village.

It was again the thriving support systems generated by mi-grants that served the needs of the workers more than any statutory services available in the city. Thus whether he needed to find a job for a grown lad or a loan for his daughter's wedding, it was the old village network that helped him out with timely hints and assistance.

Today, the fact that the migrant does not send regular or substantial remittances to his 'dependents' in the village is well-documented. It is obvious that the 'dependents' are holding aloft his fragile patriarchal status as breadwinner, at considerable hardship to themselves, including periodic starvation. They are at the same time ensuring old age and retirement benefits for him in the abdication of that role by industry and the government. Yet the myth of the money-order economy dies a hard death (Burawoy 1976). Many of the authors cited earlier, despite sensitivity to the plight of the migrant and the rural women left behind, continue to cling to this concept. Misperceptions have led to a distortion of the reality, thus subverting well-intended plans for the betterment of an already demoralized population.

The Migrant Driven Out

With the ingress of the global economy in the Bombay commercial-industrial empire, along with massive unemployment throughout the nation, the monopoly of this region on labour supply has ended. The myth of the 'lazy Kokani migrants' serves to illustrate how workers from the far-flung corners of India work much harder and longer, without complaint, as compared to Kokani workers who are active in the trade unions. Entry into the fast growing service sector is restricted mostly to college graduates, and a majority of village youngsters who are blocked into a 'high school fail' status have little hope of gaining access to these jobs.

A heterogeneous proletariat serves the mighty industrial empire, and individual workers are fragmented amongst themselves in terms of caste, religion and regional affiliations, so that sustained unity for the sake of improving job security and work conditions is rarely possible. This is further compounded by a serious level of unemployment, grinding poverty, extreme politicization in terms of party politics, and criminalization of politics, whether at the electoral or at the trade union level.

The Bombay textile labour was in the forefront of the national union struggles and in organizing strikes over political issues and also to demand better working conditions even under British rule (Gupte 1981). Once the migrant returned to the native village, given the extreme schisms in rural society in the hinterland, very little of that activism manifested to improve conditions in the village. Much of his energy and enthusiasm would also have dissipated in weariness and ill-health. Moreover, his proletarian status in the city was in stark contrast to his position in rural society, and the worker often had a stake in maintaining feudal conventions in the village.

What If He Lives or Dies?

Zachariah (1968) points to the unexpected finding that hidden within an overall high rate of migration to the city from out-lying areas was a strong undercurrent of reverse migration. He notes that mill workers above 35 years in age tended to return to the native village after ten to fifteen years of service in the city, presumably to take up cultivation of ancestral land. It was attributed to the lack of drive and initiative of the lazy villagers who could not bear up to high pressure urban living. It is more likely that a significant group of workers, nearly 18 percent, simply could not withstand the inhuman working conditions, overwork in the mills, low pay, poor and unhygienic living quarters, city pollution, occupational health hazards such as the high extent of cotton fibre in the mill atmosphere and poor nutrition. Datta effectively deals with the fallacy of the established colonial view derogatory to the Indian worker, which labelled indigenous labour as inefficient and lazy in order to justify the harsh exploitation of the latter in British industry. The same myths later conveniently served the interests of Indian industrialists (Datta 1984; also Gupte 1981).

Other scholars raise the issue of surprisingly high male mortality after the age of 35 among the migrants suffering from respiratory tuberculosis, particularly in Bombay, but also after their return to the village. At this level, male mortality rates are supposed to take over from the unnaturally high female mortality rates in infancy and among women in the young child-bearing age group (Dyson 1984; Ramasubban and Crook 1985). It is important to explore further this aspect. My own observation of a large number of widows in the village, whose husbands died young of tuberculosis after a relatively short phase of industrial work in Bombay, seems to support the preliminary data cited by these authors.

The debilitating work conditions in the city are glossed over probably because even the villager cannot bring himself to face this issue. The lack of self-esteem, loss of manliness, and the general dishonour that is implied in the gross failure in his breadwinner role are a formidable alternative. Few men choose to return of their own volition; they do so only when fired from their jobs, or because of serious health problems.

In this context, the historic textile strike of 1982 has proved to be a landmark in the sense of breaking the back of the Kokan economy. It stood for a unilateral withdrawal from a symbiotic relationship, with the city reneging on its promise to the hinterland (Lokadhikar Chalwal Karyakarte 1982; Omvedt 1983; Tulpule 1986; Dandekar 1986; Singh 1987).

Their Hopes Dashed in the Textile Strike

Men from the Kokan, particularly the southern region in which Masure is located, predominated among the strikers. About 250,000 workers actively participated for over a year in a strike that has not been officially called off to this day. One of the chief demands was for the government, a third party in the case of most mills, to repeal the anti-labour and antiquated Bombay Industrial Relations Act of colonial times. The workers also demanded improved wages, dearness allowance, daily allowance, scientific standards for management of workload, work conditions and wages, reasonable vacation provisions, housing and daily travel allowance, provision of secret voting in union elections, work benefits to women employees, and opening up all departments to the segregated dalit or untouchable caste.

The textile mills had worked with very old machinery for a long time, and an antiquated, labour-intensive production process was no longer profitable to the industrialists, particularly in view of rising labour unrest. They were beginning to lose the market to the latest synthetic products from Japan, for example. Modernization was a complicated issue, since that meant they would have to invest in training vast numbers of workers past their prime. In any case, the retrenchment of a large proportion of the workforce would be called for.

Most industrialists were not even happy with the textile units any longer, itching to diversify into more profitable ventures such as chemicals, fertilizers and electronics. The age-old textile industry had turned into a dinosaur towards the end of the twentieth century. Vast tracts of prime land occupied by the mills in or near the central part of the city were potential gold mines for the owners. Construction activity soared all over the city, in a mega-million industry, for building luxury apartments and penthouse suites even in the midst of the grinding poverty of the slum communities.

At the start of the textile strike in 1982, the official textile union was governed with an iron fist by the ruling Congress party. An 'upstart' unionist had begun to threaten the hegemony of this union, particularly since it was seen to be unresponsive to the needs of the workers, serving merely as a tool in the hands of corrupt politicians already beholden to wealthy industrialists in the city. Threats and terror were used by both sides against workers owing allegiance to each other, and industrial violence reached a peak.

When such a large number of workers went on an indefinite strike in the commerce, trade, and industrial capital of modern India, it did not seem as if anything but victory would crown the striking workers. They were supported by all the leftist splinters of trade unions, who were as threatened as the ruling party-backed trade union by the meteoric rise of this particularly radical unionist. There were innumerable token strikes in support of the textile workers across the vast industrial empire in the city. Indigenous versions of 'soup kitchens' sprang up in the labour dominated areas, to feed striking workers and their families. The government, however, threw its weight behind the industrialists. Bombay is the state capital, but the rest of the Kokan has very little political clout. A majority of the state politicians hail from the nouveau riche class of rural capitalist farmers belonging to the prosperous sugarcane and cotton growing areas of the state. They have very little stake in the well-being of city residents, their own political base secure within the feudal patron-client relations of their village constituencies.

The force of the strike dissipated as the strikers faced with starvation, left the city with the hope that the strike would be resolved in their favour. Those who stayed behind were beaten up or stabbed by hoodlums while picketing at factory gates, even as factory managers hired scab labour under police protection. A fierce debate raged on among city intellectuals for a while, then died a natural death. The government has now launched forth on a liberal initiative granting industrialists permission to sell off factory lands in central areas of the city to the builders and developers and to move their units outside the polluted city environs.

The revamped textile industry is once more a thriving industry, in its modernized version, using the technology of Du Pont and other multinational companies. The scab labourers, mostly recruited among migrants from the more politically influential northern states like Uttar Pradesh, have got permanent jobs in the new industry. For the workers from the Kokan region, the textile industry was a mother-provider for over a century, and the strike was a matter of honour, over just demands. All that is past history.

The migrants from the Kokan had constituted almost 70 percent of the labour force in this sector, and had contributed to the great wealth of the city. Their work had earned the Kokan region the derisive epithet of being a money-order economy. As politicians and scholars remarked contemptuously, the lazy peasants who stayed back, the women, the aged and the chil-

dren had thrived into indolence over the earnings repatriated
by the migrant workers. Also, they were quarrelsome, unable
to cooperate to the least extent for the sake of mutual benefit.
Tuka nay, maka nay, ghal kutryak, was the oft-repeated proverb that pithily encapsulated the dog-in the-manger mentality
of people in this very backward region.

Intellectual leaders and politicians cling to this colonialist
labelling without ever bothering to inquire into the reality behind the seeming intransigence of people from the Kokan. It is
all the more shocking considering the cultural history of this
leading Indian state. A majority of its leaders who had come
up through the nationalist struggle against British rule, as well
as its litterateurs, poets, novelists, playwrights, intellectuals
and activists, had their origins in the Kokan. Few of these intellectuals or politicians ever returned to their native region to
investigate the myths.

The migrants from the Kokan had lost considerable ground
over a couple of generations, even as the tales of the fabulous
city with rags-to-riches stories multiplied by the hundreds.
They had worn away the prime of their lives far from the comforting warmth of their women and families, in the grime and
pollution of the city, blackening their lungs with industrial
fumes, in an air thick with cotton particles.

Families of Migrants

It is a separate issue that village families consisting of the aged,
women and children could hardly have survived day-to-day on
the basis of the paltry and irregular remittances from the migrant workers. Alcohol, tobacco and visits to sex workers in the
brothels in the poorer sections of the huge red light district in
the city on pay day further served to undermine his health as
well as his financial contribution to his family. It was not as if
the worker could afford decent nourishment and medical care to
start with. There was also the burly Pathan, a loan shark, to pay
at the factory gates on pay day each month.

Earlier migrants could afford reasonable accommodation

close to their place of work in the heart of the city, often managing to bring their wives over, if they could be spared from farm work. They even raised families in those dwellings. But conditions had deteriorated. The city had reneged on its promises to the workers, until fine city accommodations turned into hovels of misery. This was even as the city was expanding by leaps and bounds towards a modern utopia. Rent control, a well-meaning measure, has probably contributed to this. Rents have remained static over decades, failing to keep pace with rising costs of construction and maintenance, even as real estate prices in Bombay become the highest in the world. There is little incentive for landlords of old tenanted buildings to undertake proper maintenance. Some of the rickety old buildings have become death traps as they come crashing down during heavy rains. The government has undertaken notification of such buildings, with offers of alternative accommodation to the tenants in distantly located 'transit camps'. Such a move is often resisted by occupants of buildings in the heart of the city, since it involves extensive commuting, and a concomitant loss of earnings. Sometimes basic amenities are most inadequate at the alternative sites that are themselves no better than slums. There is also well-founded suspicion on the part the of the tenants, that such notification will be misused by the officials in league with the landlords and builders, to dupe them into vacating the premises, in order to profit from subsequent land development, a veritable gold mine.

The newer migrant did not have hidden sources of wealth to pay the ransom amounts needed for a nice respectable flat or even a room in the sprawling slum colonies in the suburbs. Lucky government employees were often accommodated in government housing colonies, but the textile industry was a private enterprise fueled by the labour of undemanding rural multitudes. Housing was simply not an issue, nor were pensions or retirement benefits a part of the deal.

It was imperative then for the wives and the families left behind in the villages to tend family lands and homes. Always short of male hands, they had to work hard to ensure not only their own survival, but to provide secure retirement benefits to the worker once the city had no use for him. This was the only known security in a textile worker's life. To have a few scattered pieces of land in his name, a humble dwelling and a progeny to perpetuate his name, all preserved for him by a devoted and generous wife who did not complain of deprivation, hardship, insecurity and the loveless existence a migrant's wife. All this, usually, without her direct legal ownership of their assets.

At that level of existence, people are heroic enough to deny themselves gratification of the senses even while living amidst a riotous burst of sensual imagery in the village and in the city. Their senses are not dead, only sufficiently submerged with the promise of occasional channeling out, particularly during festival times and when the migrant returns home in rare forays from the city. It is not so surprising that festivals, and other occasions for celebration, such as weddings, are a perennial source of indebtedness and abandon.

Village living in particular is not grey. Within a rich textural tapestry of the exuberant natural and cultural matrix, work is the anodyne, narcotic and inspirational medium in the sad lives of the women left behind. It creates their sense of security and worth. It is what binds their lives together in a self-respecting community of people banking the fires of poverty and destitution for themselves, their children, and for the migrants. They help each other out with a deep and committed sense of compassion in times of need. A sense of shared humanity and goodness is the life blood of most village communities, despite severe strains. There are also times when they rage against injustice and turn against each other in the true manner of powerless underdogs.

Money-Order Economy?

When city intellectuals loosely and derisively talk of cash flow from the city to the 'money-order economy' of the Kokan, they are perhaps referring to the total bulk of money orders received by the General Post Office in Bombay each month for remittance to village families, by thousands of migrant workers. It adds no doubt to the sense of male pride and prestige to think of how male breadwinners are supporting entire rural economies with the sweat of their brows.

Unfortunately there is no systematic investigation into the quantum and frequency of money sent by each migrant to his family of 'dependents' and what portion of the household budget in the village is served by the said remittance. The myth of the lazy inhabitants of the Kokan at once serves to emphasize the benevolent indulgences shown to the good-for-nothing migrant worker by industrialist-employers in the city, and to underscore the patriarchal-colonialist ideology of male breadwinners furnishing the money-order economy for the benefit of the peasants left behind in the village. If the region is still extremely underdeveloped, the government can always point out to the useless, lazy and illiterate rural inhabitants who make the task so difficult for the implementers of well-meaning policies and schemes.

Out-of-state migrants including the working class from Uttar Pradesh, Andhra Pradesh, Kerala, Karnataka, Goa and Tamil Nadu as well as those from other regions in Maharashtra have already surpassed the number of Kokani migrants in Bombay. Presumably the volume of money orders sent by the former groups must also considerably exceed that of the Kokani migrants. Yet the Kokan alone is regarded as a money-order economy, which implies that its inhabitants are parasitical, lacking initiative. It is probably the self-serving and short-sighted leadership and the absence of political patronage that is usually available to migrants from other places that is to blame for this undeserved reputation.

The Kokan indeed has no 'economy' to speak of. There has been a lack of comparable government investment in infrastructure, growth, development. The service-delivery systems are poor. Caste, class and communal divisions have played their role in perpetuating backwardness as has the difficult terrain since communications are not easy in an area riddled with hills, rivers, salt marshes and creeks. The heavy monsoons also add to the isolation. At the same time, the absence of development and the isolation have served to prevent the sustained growth of a mass movement for change or for the growth of an alternative leadership. This prevents the growth of a strong lobby at the state capital, Bombay. It is the extreme lack of resources, the sharp polarization of the grassroot population on the basis of party politics and the corrosive effect of widespread corruption that have served virtually to 'emasculate' the population, putting an end to much of the drive and enterprise even among talented aspirants. All of this has fed into the malicious myths and stereotypes of the Kokani and the Malvani people. In turn, these are internalized by the people themselves, undermining their own confidence and self-respect when competing for scarce jobs in the city. The strong identification with their own age-old culture and traditions serves as the only source of pride in their lives, even as it undermines better assimilation with the cosmopolitan milieu in the city.

The famous textile strike was never formally withdrawn, but textile industries continued with new optimism, newer technology, and a different, newly trained workforce. Thousands of former workers lost their jobs, and the hinterland economy was once again delivered a body blow. It was, finally the toil of the peasants, particularly of the women who stayed back which as usual, served to support families and unemployed men.

Conclusion

THE VILLAGE BEGAN its transition towards modernization in the early part of this century, from a relatively isolated, self-sufficient subsistence economy, through growing male out-migration to the city. This shift created demographic imbalance on a gender-basis, so that nearly 70 percent of the village population was female. Meagre earnings of city migrants did not make any dent in the phenomenon of rural poverty and technological backwardness. Subsistence agriculture and mutual co-operation within the traditional support systems continued to be the mainstay of survival in the village. Over the years, scarcity of male labour in agriculture and allied tasks began to have an adverse impact on farming so that increasing tracts of land were allowed to lie fallow even under good climatic conditions. As the money economy began to infiltrate into the village, along with the accompanying individualism, the old support systems in turn started developing irrevocable fissures. This was especially so in the case of the joint family system. Earlier, more than five or six quasi-nuclear family units spanning several generations had lived under one roof, sharing a common hearth. It was not unusual for such a family grouping to consist of more than twenty people, all living together, with the commensurate wealth of livestock, granaries and other family resources. Some family members bore a greater share of the burden of work, while others did little or no work. Children were almost communally brought up, with a strong sense of identification with the kinship network. The family took care of basic necessities for all, within a wider cooperative system in the neighbourhood. Arbitration of individual disputes in each hamlet was delegated to a community of male elders whose dispensations were final, and non-compliance involved ostracization. Such a fate was abhorred even for a limited period. Apart from loss of status, it implied considerable hardship given the close-knit cooperative nexus of subsistence and ritual interaction.

As migration in search of individual salaries took root within this system, there was an inevitable, gradual shift towards monetization and accountability on a comparative basis within each family. Sharing the costs of repairing large dwellings became a contentious issue, and almost each joint family was split into several smaller units. This was accompanied by the division of joint property including dwellings, mangers, farms, orchards, grazing grounds, trees, cattle and equipment. It also gave rise to bitter feuds amongst kinsmen, leading to increasing civil and criminal litigation in the taluka and district courts. The break-up of the older version of the joint family in the village was already a fait accompli by the middle of the twentieth century. Kinship networks and other traditional systems of support and arbitration of disputes, however, continue to exist in a much diluted form to this day.

A high premium on available male labour, and the very low productivity of bits and pieces of cultivable land parcelled off amongst relatives, became the bane of subsistence agriculture in the village. Government intervention in the development of infrastructure and services was almost non-existent earlier, and the role of governance was restricted to the revenue and judicial systems well into the sixties.

The level of mistrust between the city migrant and close relatives in the village was fairly high on account of the unequal ownership of land and property amongst them. This was one of the major reasons for lack of private initiative in undertaking development, particularly in agriculture. For several generations, the eldest son was sent out to work in the city to earn and provide for the cash needs of the household, while the younger son had to stay behind to till the land and manage the property. Again traditional custom demanded that the legal deed of the land was in the eldest son's name. This gave rise to the paradoxical situation where no matter how small the land or house was, it was held by an absentee owner while the actual tiller and user who had spent a lifetime farming and looking after ancestral dwellings, had no de jure ownership rights. The money orders that contributed partly to the upkeep of ancestral property assumed the overtones of a generous dole to the peasants on the one hand, while on the other, the considerable love, labour and skill exercised in 'husbanding' the same properties remained invisible.

A hardworking farmer with no cash reserves, was not eligible for development loans if the land was in the name of a migrant relative. He could not afford irrigation pumps or farm machinery to improve agricultural yield. There was little incentive for him to develop small horticultural plantations on fallow land. He could not even cut down a tree without the migrant's permission. He could not replace a head of cattle unless the migrant sent him money, in dreaded emergencies during the peak agricultural season. The migrant often saw this as endless charity, while also demanding his rightful share in the agricultural produce harvested by the farmer.

Earlier, through successive transfers of power in the Kokan region, and well into the British period, a single clan belonging to the dominant Maratha caste had consolidated its hold over the village as the ruling family. Its power accrued mainly through its authority over the temples through an elaborate hierarchical system of ritual worship, linking all the caste groups, and also through its control over vast tracts of land all over the village. There were a couple of other big landlords in the village who had received grants of hundreds of acres of forests and agricultural land from the British. Demographic shifts in the population, given the fragmentation of families and land and the depletion of the male labour force, meant that the power of these families too began to be severely eroded. Managing huge tracts of land became increasingly untenable, so that these were often divided amongst small farmers as tenants.

The system of feudal ownership came under severe stress after progressive land reforms were introduced in the state a few decades earlier, so that erstwhile tenants could stake a claim to the ownership of the land they tilled. Similarly, the introduction of local self-government through Panchayati Raj in 1960 saw the technical shift of political power to the newly created *gram panchayat* with elected members. The sarpanch, who was the elected chief of the panchayat, came to wield considerable influence particularly in matters related to development. Successive elections and the emerging integration within the district and even state-level mainstream preoccupations over broader social and political issues served to undermine the hegemony of the ruling family in the village. The recent government policy of taking over temple lands and favouring the formation of democratic temple trusts regulated by the Charity Commissioner at the state-level, may also provide additional impetus to the dissolution of traditional control in the village. The judiciary and the police had already eroded its powers of arbitration in the event of major disputes. The authority of the dominant caste also faced similar erosion in the village.

The interregnum of transfer to a monetary economy saw an alarming increase in rural indebtedness, giving rise to a new class of moneylenders, usually belonging to the literate Bramhan and Saraswat families. Such families had come to appropriate lands belonging to bankrupt borrowers, and they amassed large land assets. Ingress of fiscal services through banking and loan facilities provided by the statutory agricultural cooperative in the village as a part of Panchayati Raj began to erode the role of the moneylender. These families also faced fragmentation and impoverishment. They were quick to seize upon opportunities for better jobs in the city through education, their traditional preserve. A majority of them have shifted permanently to the city after selling off their lands and dwellings.

A gradual weakening of the traditional system of governance and arbitration in the village and also of the caste hierarchy and kinship networks over the decades has perhaps contributed to an extreme level of contentiousness and lack of sustained cooperation for the common good of villagers. A new elite consisting of petty officials and government employees beholden to the traditional elite, while at the same time beyond the purview of caste and kinship networks, has remained impervious to the needs of the large mass of impoverished villagers. Small thefts, quarrels and fighting amongst themselves, harassment by corrupt officials, and at times even misappropriation of lands through the doctoring of land records in the village have become the bane of rural living. It is often the migrants' mothers and wives, who bear the brunt of such injustice over and above their sufferings caused by deprivation on account of scarce male labour resources.

As documented earlier in the study, once thriving trades and crafts that catered to the needs of subsistence living in the village yielded ground to mass-produced goods from Bombay and other urban centres. The village was earlier renowned for its sugarcane and jaggery production. This enterprise also died a natural death because of the fragmentation of the households and scarcity of manpower. The sustained development of the sugarcane industry with large government inputs and strong political patronage in the region east of the Sahyadris was another reason. As the rural economy became increasingly dependent on an in-flow of foodgrains, goods and services within the cash economy, the once prosperous Kokan region began to face greater marginalization and impoverishment, while other regions of the state prospered on account of better nurturance by the government and the political bosses. It is interesting that this primarily rice-growing region has to import rice through government machinery to provide for its needs.

It was only in the area of school education that Kokan maintained its lead over other regions. Sindhudurg district was the first in the state to declare 100 percent literacy under a new education policy. Even earlier, private educational institutions which were managed from Bombay established and maintained primary and secondary schools all over the district. The final examination at the high school level (SSC) is conducted by a centralized and urban-oriented examination board at the state-level, common for high school students all over the state. It is at this juncture that the majority of students in the villages of the Kokan get sifted out of the educational system, as 'SSC Fail'. Good teachers in English, mathematics and science are at a premium in the villages that offer few incentives. A majority of the students fail in English and mathematics. Thus the high school pass percentage ranges from anywhere between 0 to 30 percent, only rarely exceeding that in village schools. Facilities for vocational and college education are sparse and expensive in the district, often drawing better-off students from other regions in the state. Admissions to private institutions of higher learning depend on a high percentage of marks and payment of large sums as donations, which few peasant families can afford. This has served to undermine the confidence of the Kokani populace that was once considered to be in the forefront in education. In any case, poor opportunities of employment in the region assure greater migration of the educated unemployed to the city. An interesting fact emerging from the 1991 census is that the total population size in the village has actually declined, despite natural growth on account of the birth rate. This is in contrast to the overall increase in the state population. Village schools are threatened with imminent closure as the student population is also on the decline.

Earlier, a single high school used to serve the children from several far-flung villages. The children often trekked more than 10 kilometres every day, under all weather conditions, in the absence of proper roads. Naturally the schools were not hard put to find a reasonable number of students enrolled each year. From the last decade onwards, there has been a mushrooming of private-run high schools in most villages. While this does provide much better access to schools, it also leads to a division of the student population across several schools. District government grants to individual schools depend on a minimum number of students being enrolled, and this target is particularly difficult to achieve in the tenth class, that is, the SSC class. The threat of cessation of grants and the consequent closure of schools is very real for almost every rural-based school in the region. Most schools have followed the stratagem of passing almost every student in all the lower classes up to the SSC level. Even then, the drop-out rate for boys and girls in each successive class is fairly high, so that achieving the target of minimum enrollment is rendered difficult.

Many students who are automatically promoted to the tenth class are often untutored in the basic medium of instruction, that is, Marathi, besides subjects such as English and mathematics. An important aspect of rural schools is that the number of holidays easily outstrip those for urban schools in multiples. This is in addition to uncontrolled absenteeism. There are no special coaching classes, tuitions or guide books available for rural pupils, and it should be remembered that sending children to school is itself a matter of deprivation for most families. The teachers, especially those at the primary school level, are overburdened with an array of non-educational tasks, as government 'servants'. Such tasks include preparation of voters' lists on a door-to-door basis, and achievement of sterilization targets in the drive for birth control, which are often linked to promotional opportunities. This certainly affects the motivation for achieving excellence in teaching and also for paying special attention to students on an individual basis. Moreover, the students are mostly first generation learners, often attending school for long hours on an empty stomach. They start with a weak educational foundation, which is further stressed progressively from one class to the next. Thus success at the SSC level is usually a distant dream for a majority of the students, who in any case cannot afford further education at the expense of their farming responsibilities.

The drop-out rate of girls between Class 5 to Class 10 in schools is very high. Little confidence in the educational system combined with pressures of subsistence living ensure that girls are drafted into the workforce at an early age. An overall cultural bias that perceives girls as burdens and boys as potential providers deters investment in the girls' future beyond mandatory dowries at the time of marriage. At the same time, economic pressures have perforce extended the age of girls' marriage to anywhere between 18 and 24 years. These girls share a major burden of agricultural labour and allied tasks in the village.

Apart from the prevalence of large-scale male out-migration from the region, there is the unacknowledged phenomenon of extensive female migration from the natal village to that of the in-laws after marriage. Such a demographic shift serves to undermine the sense of security of individual women within a rigid system of interchange. It also undermines their sustained participation in cooperative activities and employment before marriage.

Submerged within an overall picture of contentiousness and lack of cooperation amongst people in the Kokan, is the fact that it is the impoverished peasants who have contributed more than a fair share to the development of infrastructure in the village. In the absence of government initiative, it was the villagers who donated their lands for developing roads, schools, hospitals, temples, and even for the statutory services attractive to them. They donated precious trees and free labour for construction purposes so that such services could serve their needs. It is a different matter that poor management and sometimes misappropriation of funds undermined the effectiveness of these services initiated with considerable goodwill from the villagers. This has in its turn contributed to a certain amount of cynicism and lack of sustained cooperative effort. Yet even now a fairly high proportion of the household budget is spent as contribution towards cooperative community events on a year-round basis by the villagers.

A major network of mostly dirt roads traversing remote areas in the district was constructed as a government initiative towards development of the region only from the early-seventies onwards. Most of this construction activity was under the well-intended employment guarantee scheme of the state government. It is a different matter that labour for construction work has to be engaged from outside the Kokan, and even from outside Maharashtra. Scarcity of labour, both male and female, beyond traditional agricultural work in the village, is one reason. The other reasons are simply that undernourished peasants are neither physically fit for the long hours of hard construction work nor willing to face the implied loss of status in the natal village. In addition there is the adverse experience of corruption in the payment of wages.

Among the earliest entrepreneurs to benefit from the development of an extensive road network were often out-of-state forest contractors engaged in supplying valuable timber for construction, carpentry and coal in the city. Massive deforestation was undertaken all over the district in the past two decades so that what remain to this day are largely degraded and sparse forests. Such activity in cohort with corrupt government officials also brought increased criminalization in its wake as large sums of unaccounted wealth were involved in this illegal enterprise. Cash-starved villagers were often plied with liquor and threatened, or induced to steal timber for the forest contractors.

Ill-advised government initiative, in the late sixties and seventies, towards clearing of forests for large-scale planting of cashew and mango as cash crops, even in the absence of adequate trade and processing facilities, further added to the deforestation. Villagers were cheated out of their produce of mangoes and cashew nuts by a chain of roving middlemen feeding into the external markets in cities. While prize Alphonse mangoes were chiefly a product of this district, the thriving mango trade in Bombay, including export, was monopolized by traders from other regions.

Extensive deforestation in the district caused untold misery in this region, with silting of waterways, giving rise to frequent floods in the monsoon season. Soil erosion assumed serious proportions, while the lowering of the water table in the absence of forest cover led to the early drying out of once reliable forest streams. Drought in summer is now a permanent feature in the Kokan. Total reliance on the monsoon rains for agriculture and the absence of a coherent policy for irrigation and watershed management added to the backwardness of the region. Increasing reliance on costly fertilizers in subsistence farming and the absence of marketing development added to the unviability of agriculture.

Following hard on the heels of large-scale ecological devastation, depredations wrought by large troops of monkeys, once forest dwelling, upon agricultural and horticultural crops and on kitchen gardens alike, also assumed alarming proportions. In the absence of government intervention in terms of well-thought out measures to combat this menace, poor farmers simply gave up cultivation in the out-lying farms to avoid extensive damage from monkeys and also wild boar. The growing of vegetables was also on the decline for the same reason. Marauding monkeys destroyed roof tiles often causing serious damage to the mud and timber dwellings during the heavy rains, and heavy termite-infestations did the rest. Lack of money and manpower for repairs simply added to further degradation of the living environs.

The pollution of the sea as a result of effluents from large chemical and mining industries in Goa and North Kokan, has begun to affect fisheries on a periodic basis, particularly on the Malvan coast. Moreover, the carte blanche provided to the better equipped and mechanized out-of-state and foreign trawlers for fishing off the Malvan coast is a serious irritant to local fisher folk. Plans for developing a one-of-a kind national marine park in Malvan with international funding has caused a sharp polarization amongst the local population. One group, led by local traders and the state's political bosses, is excited by the prospect of unending economic progress, on account of the growth of international 5-star tourism in Malvan. The other group, led by a solid phalanx of fisher folk, has strongly resisted the marine park, which is expected to displace their dwellings and livelihood from the coastline. The government's assurances have poor credibility, which has not helped its cause. There is already a total ban on construction and major repairing activity in Malvan town, a first step of the juggernaut towards the marine park. In addition, even as the populace in the neighbouring state of Goa has begun to realize the ravaging effects of uncontrolled tourism on its culture and ecology, accompanied by a growth of organized resistance to further development of tourism in Goa, there are high level plans afoot in Maharashtra to siphon off excess tourism from Goa to the 'virgin' beaches of Malvan.

The costs of land in Malvan have escalated considerably and vacant lands have already become scarce, with an acre of land costing over Rs 800,000 in the early nineties. Several national and state politicians are known to have made quick investments in hundreds of acres in this coastal region. That the locals do not have the resources, management skills and any entrepreneurial base to cater to the needs of 5-star tourism is ignored in these plans. While such developments will certainly cause a growth in the state revenue, they will also add to the miseries of the local people with a consequent growth in the activities of the land sharks, builders, criminals, smugglers, sex workers and drug peddlers. The locals will find that while a 'base' in Bombay is no longer feasible, such 'development' will increasingly displace them out of their native land, most probably to the new slums and ghettoes in the Kokan. For instance, a prominent leader of the fisher folk has reported that the district government has already stopped assistance in the form of grants for the development of fishing to poor fishermen.

Besides these incendiary issues, there is growing ingress of the sea into some of the coastal villages around Malvan, along with widespread coastal erosion, probably on account of unbridled land reclamation in the urban centres along the coast. This has created a serious threat to dwellings and farms in these villages. Similarly, increased salinity in previously fertile agricultural lands around the creeks and a depletion of the rich mangrove swamps have begun to cause serious damage to the local ecology. There is very little cognizance of these issues on the part of the government.

Such ecological ravages have brought about a direct decline in the nutritional standards of once self-sufficient peasants. Shrinking of agricultural as well as forest produce has led to a near total reliance on rice as the staple diet. The export of fish to the Middle East, and a concomitant rise in the cost of seafood—which used to be almost freely available—also contributed to this. Childhood malnourishment is on the rise, so that the sons of enlisted soldiers and policemen of the earlier days fail to meet the physical standards of recruitment. Such malnourishment of course affected productivity at work, whether in agriculture or in urban employment. Such ecological degradation is primarily a women's issue since consequently women have more onerous workloads, and they also find that their efforts to maintain their families' subsistence levels are undermined. This has been further borne out by major ecological studies world-wide. A factor contributing to malnourishment of children at a critical period in their growth is the pernicious practice by farm women of denying nourishing solid food to children up to two years of age, and above. During this period they survive basically on mother's milk and occasionally on rice gruel. The mothers are themselves malnourished. They continue with their back-breaking workload almost until childbirth, and often immediately after delivery, since there are no spare hands in the household. Little attention is paid to the mothers' 'special nourishment', leading to the under-nourishment of infants. The children become irritable and throw tantrums when they are introduced to solid foods at a late age. Infants below two years develop persistent diarrhoea in the absence of adequate nourishment. Drinking water is often denied to them out of ignorance despite symptoms of dehydration.

Similarly, while drinking plentiful amounts of water is recommended in several illnesses, it may be denied to the sick out of superstition. The public health care system is too bogged down in the birth control programme to address itself to such issues. Greater sensitivity towards specific local health issues is sorely needed in combatting widespread ignorance and superstition in health matters.

There is a high incidence of infant mortality, female mortality in childbirth, and also among young male migrants on account of tuberculosis. Apart from tuberculosis, skin diseases, malaria, filariasis and leprosy are endemic to this region. Respiratory illnesses, high blood pressure, heart disease, cataracts and, given the stress of survival living in the village, mental illness are also fairly common, besides the physical ravages of alcoholism among men. Also varied infections causing fever, colds and dysentery occur seasonally. Malnourishment because of chronic worm infestation is very widespread. Poor hygienic conditions and periodically raging epidemics serve to undermine health in the village.

The under-staffed and ill-equipped primary health centre in the village focuses on vaccinating infants and on birth control measures. Random diagnoses by private doctors have undermined their credibility in the eyes of the villagers. Pathological and radiological services are now available in the district, as are medical specialists. In any event, patients suffering from chronic maladies requiring thorough diagnosis and treatment, including surgery, are commonly routed to Bombay or Panaji in Goa. Ill health is often a serious drain on the peasants' financial resources, in addition to the loss of labour potential, given the total absence of health insurance and social security measures.

A certain measure of success in the family planning drive is indicated by the acceptance of the small family norm by young couples. Economic necessity and rising aspirations have played their part in this. Families are generally restricted to three or four children, in contrast to the endless procreation of earlier times. It is the high value placed on producing sons, however, that leads to continuing pregnancies in families where there are only daughters. This creates a vicious cycle where a son is deemed desirable, if only to take over the burden of all the daughters, should the male parent be incapacitated in any way. The cultural undervaluing of women thus serves as a hindrance to limiting the family size. It is a different matter that often enough sons turn wayward through unemployment, alcoholism and criminal activity, or even if otherwise fit, refuse to take over the responsibilities of the parental family once they have set up a separate household after marriage. The ever-present spectre of on-going micro-division of family assets amongst sons is not to be considered. While it is privately agreed that daughters are greater assets to overworked mothers from an early age, sharing in the overall workload, the overarching cultural stereotypes serve to negate their worth to their natal families. Money spent on sons' education and upbringing is viewed as investment that will bring returns once they achieve adulthood and its concomitant responsibilities. The grudging amount spent on daughters is seen as wasted money, since they will leave parental homes to serve strangers after marriage. The threat of increasing demands for dowry at the time of daughters' marriages, apart from legitimate wedding expenses, always serves to show up daughters as nothing but a cause of woe to their families.

Besides this aspect, there are always the diehard men who refuse to contemplate restricting the family size even under dire economic distress. At other times fears of sterilization affecting the work potential of men and women performing hard physical labour are not weighed with the adverse effects of repeated pregnancies on the women's health. There is no indepth counselling by health professionals on a one-to-one basis in the short-sighted chase for achieving macro-targets. Men are in any case free to get a second wife if the first wife dies as a result of recurring pregnancies, but widows are prohibited from remarrying, despite progressive legislation to the contrary.

The incidence of childless couples is fairly high in the village. This is because of male out-migration, with wives being left behind in the village to serve aging in-laws and to look after farms and ancestral dwellings, bringing about a separation of couples in their sexual prime. It also explains the high incidence of childless widows in village society.

Men from many families all over the village served in World War II as a part of the Indian army, under British colonial rule. A large number of these men were long dead and their widows in their sixties and seventies clung to a pitiful existence. A belated move on the part of the government to provide retroactive pensions to these veterans, and later to their widows, has suddenly provided a surge of cash in-flow into many households. The widows are now in the happy position of being prize assets to the family, at last affording the health care and special nourishment that they deserve after a lifetime of hard toil. Their families have acquired a stake in keeping them alive, since the pensions will lapse upon their deaths.

It is a surprising observation that there are quite a few single women past the usual age of marriage in the village. These are women working as teachers and nurses, who might have taken over the burden of providing for their families until it got too late to find a suitable match. There are also other women in some upper caste families for whom a groom of higher status was simply not available, particularly in the absence of elderly male relatives who would have arranged a match at the right time.

Decision making and arbitration in matters of ritual is an exclusively male domain. Women are sidelined as facilitators and observers of ritual worship and celebration in the public domain. Communal temple rituals are mainly men's preserve, although special allowance is made for worship by women. Thus women's participation in religious ritual is a more private affair, within the precincts of their respective hamlets and within the kinship network. Occasionally there are men's rituals where women are totally debarred, and they are only permitted to partake of the offerings specially cooked by men after the latter have returned home. While cooking and serving wedding feasts is shared by men and women, albeit in turns, temple feasts are entirely men's responsibility, with men serving food to women as a part of the community event.

While men take the entire day off from work during festivities, women have to make space in their already busy lives to be able to engage in women-only celebrations, often at nights after the rest of the household is taken care of. While men may doze off after a heavy repast following the daytime rituals, or engage in gajali, women change into working clothes and plunge into never-ending work, more so on festival days.

Constantly mouthed aphorisms underscoring cultural stereotypes concerning the lowly status of women and the appropriate modes of female conduct are a part and parcel of daily existence for village women. These stereotypes conform to the 'greater tradition' in India, and are a part of the process of 'Sanskriti-

zation' brought about through the reading of Hindu religious
texts, pravachan, bhajan, kirtan, dhaikala, and increasingly
through popular plays and cinema. Rigidly performed religious
rituals also serve to emphasize the secondary status of women.
Such values are internalized at an early age. It is interesting
that it is women themselves who serve as agents of indoctrination to patriarchal values. Overt objectification of women as
commodities of labour and reproduction may be verbalized. The
growing perception of women as 'sexual objects' is a modern
phenomenon, filtering in from the city.

For women, bodily shame is stressed at a time when there
is little privacy even in the performance of daily ablutions. An
exaggerated display of modesty and decorum is a part of their
burden. Self-control over bodily functions is learnt by girls at
an early age, as also the deferment of gratification of basic
needs. They are expected to step into exacting work roles on
farms and in the household long before the age of menstruation.
This latter stage marks a period of sharp transition to womanhood and reproductive capacity. There is a consequent change
in modes of dress and behaviour, and an even greater familial
control over the moulding of attitudes and identity. A rigidly
adhered to menstrual taboo against ritual pollution and the
defilement of living environs continues to underscore the biological inferiority of women. This taboo, with all the supersti-
tious lore surrounding it, serves to undermine women's sense
of sanctity and wholesomeness. It also contributes to the overt
denigration of their status in social interactions, so that fears
and phobias related to social transgression become a part of the
female identity at an early age. This is in addition to the considerable inconvenience caused within the household over ob-
servance of safeguards against pollution. A natural biological
function marking the onset of valued reproductive ability paradoxically serves as an instrument of shame and denigration in
the lives of women.

It is quite appropriate that village women experience a tremendous sense of liberation from constricting biological bondage upon attaining menopause. This often brings about the

cessation of sexual activity, a development looked forward to by most women, given the lack of privacy and any real intimacy between men and women past their prime. There are fewer demands on their time as children grow up, and menopause serves to free them in an important psychological sense from the intense reproduction and nurturing responsibilities. Most village women begin to assume greater assertiveness in domestic and community concerns at this age, with an improvement in overall authority and status.

Traditional cultural values have served to de-emphasize the affectional bond between married couples. It is the continuation of the lineage and performance of duties and responsibilities within the matrix of kinship networks that are considered to be of primary importance in marital relationships. A wife is first expected to serve the in-laws' demands and those of the children as a matter of decorum, relegating the husband to the third place in her attentions. Similarly a husband is expected to underplay the demands of his wife upon his time, in the traditional set up. Her excessive workload and the absence of privacy in the household are other factors that contribute to a dilution of intimacy between the two. Male out-migration itself undermines this bond during a major portion of their youth. Apart from this, sharp gender-based schisms within the struggle for survival often create a psychological rift between husband and wife. Women use alliances within the household in subtle manipulative ways to undermine their husbands' patriarchal authority and position of eminence at home.

Women's mobility is not restricted by and large, except among a few 'privileged' families still clinging to an out-dated feudal pattern. A psychological rather than actual separation exists between the men's domain and that of women, by virtue of diversified work roles and ritual functions. The pressures of survival entail greater mixing between the sexes, with a relatively egalitarian form of interchange between the two. Rituals serve to emphasize traditional roles and rigid exhortations of behaviour. Villagers threatened by the dissolution of the familiar schema closely interwoven within their identities and world-view, have a definite stake in maintaining the facade of adherence to the age-old norms and prescriptions of behaviour. It is important to don this mask on formal occasions particularly in the public sphere, discarding it in favour of greater freedom of interchange in the private sphere, in the household and at work. There appears then, a certain lack of congruence between formal expectations, and the realities of existence. Women, in fact, have benefited from the loosening of rigid feudal and kinship structures, even as persisting misogyny continues to undermine their freedom and sense of worth.

Another surprising observation concerns the prevalence of pre-marital and extramarital alliances, sometimes within the same kin group, and at other times, intercaste. Relatively mellow attitudes towards such undercover affairs exist despite rigid cultural injunctions emphasizing female 'virtue' and 'honour'. A public scandal however, is greatly abhorred, and the earlier tolerant attitudes do not translate into condoning such transgressions once they become a matter of public cognizance. Cultural prescriptions of behaviour must be followed in public as a 'matter of form', even as their substance may be allowed to be contravened in privacy. This is probably a matter of creative adaptation to wider cultural norms. Women's labour potential is of crucial importance in the subsistence economy, so that it is not feasible to shut them away for their own good. Given the absence of male protectors due to out-migration, and also the primacy of work in the lives of women, such affairs merely serve as temporary diversions. They are tolerated as long as they are discreetly conducted, and do not hamper work roles. There are no comparable injunctions and safeguards against men indulging in affairs. The prevalent double standards in fact ensure that rules will be broken, although it is the women who are chastised and sent away by way of hasty and unsuitable marriages, or simply cast off by the incensed in-laws, if they are already married.

Forces of inexorable change and modernization have begun to prevail with the consequent weakening of rigid kinship networks in the village. Recently there has been an increasing

acceptance of love marriages that have resulted from elopements. Such couples return to the village once the scandal and
sense of shock has quietened, and they are usually meekly accepted within the family, specially after the birth of a child.
Women are, however, handicapped to a certain extent following
such a marriage, in terms of negotiating their status within the
new household, having forced their entry into it. Lack of parental support for the women is an additional factor contributing
to this. Registered marriages are still looked down on as 'non-
marriages'. Finally it is their ability to share in the burden of
work and to produce children that brings about a reconciliation
in the household. Over the last five years, there have been several marriages mostly following elopements at the intercaste
and intra-kin levels, all within the single larger neighbourhood
of which the hamlet under study is a part. These include marriages between a Bramhan youth from a distant town in the
Kokan, who lived in the village because of his government job,
with a local Kunbi girl, which was well accepted by both the
concerned families; between a college-educated local Bramhan
girl and a less educated small Kunbi peasant and labourer,
where the girl suffered severance from her natal family but was
accepted totally by her husband's family. In the latter example,
both households were located within a close range and hence
were extremely well known to each other, within the cooperative nexus of cultivator-labourer relationship.

Similarly, there were other marriages between the higher
born Marathas and the lesser Kunbi peasants, and also
amongst the former caste group of shared kinship, that is, those
related by virtue of sharing the same neighbourhood and caste
linkages. While the families concerned were perhaps aware of
the attraction and closeness between these couples prior to marriage—although not expecting the drastic consequences—it
seems that many in the neighbourhood and community were
hardly surprised by these developments. I am impressed by the
level of compassion and acceptance of these couples in the community, once the privately expressed shock and amusement has
died down.

Patriarchal biases against women ensure an unfair distribution of resources on a gender-basis within the household. Ownership of property is the sole prerogative of men, and most village women are unaware that they legally own even the gold ornaments bequeathed to them at the time of marriage, whether by parents or in-laws. A lifetime of hard labour in the fields and in the household is little better than bonded labour for the women. It is they who ensure the preservation of ancestral properties, while many men end up selling property to pay for their vices and debts. Widows are viewed as usurpers with no right in the husband's property, and are often severely harassed by male relatives with an eye on their holdings.

Even under normal circumstances the interests and priorities in allocation of scarce resources may diverge sharply on a gender basis. Much manipulation takes place to do women out of hard-earned savings stashed away for a rainy day. Men are on the whole better-fed, and well-clothed compared to women and children in the house. Men afford greater leisure. Trading of excess grain and produce is often monopolized by the men, so as to gain access to cash that may be as readily spent on drink, gambling and travel, as on household needs. Women usually end up selling their personal jewellery to provide for the needs of the household in times of crisis. Women pinch and save and indulge in bartering to take care of expenses for running the household and for feeding the family. Such divergent attitudes and the consequent manipulation to gain control over scarce resources often creates sharp schisms within each family.

The village, in its sharp albeit shifting and at the same time flexible division between the public sphere and the private sphere —and not necessarily in the gendered sense—permits a distancing from a horrendous outer world of corruption and exploitation, to withdraw into a more secure inner world based on human interchange. It is a strange kind of permissiveness that provides acceptance to the failures and dropouts of a harsh society at a warm and compassionate level, with unshakable faith in the slow yet inexorable justice of ancient village deities. It is a highly egalitarian world in which people guard a classless existence in a hawk-eyed manner, to peg down the pretensions and self-styled affectations of the deluded to a more comfortable and even level with delicious wit and humour. Quite paradoxically, and not to romanticize a harsh reality, it is also a highly contentious world full of malice and lack of trust, particularly among neighbours of the same caste and kinship group, and within a single household. There exists at this level a high degree of mutual exploitation that adds to the stresses and strains of daily living.

There are many de facto female-headed households in the village, given the absence of adult males, although the overall incidence is on the decline following the textile strike and the scarcity of employment and housing in the city. In households where there are no men and also no elderly women, young mothers are seen to enjoy greater mobility and a general sense of liberty in decision making. Yet the absence of a male representative to negotiate better status for the household in community affairs is a definite handicap. Similarly the lack of a rightful male protector in the event of frequent disputes is problematic, since women cannot cope with the exaggerated machismo displayed on occasions of serious confrontation. It is better for them to use male intermediaries in dealings with the government, since the officials possess the same negative patriarchal values against women asserting their rights as do the rest of the villagers. The worst handicap is faced in agricultural tasks when the absence of manpower within the household must be compensated with entreaties to already overburdened kinsmen. Often an unequal exchange of grains, labour power, at times even money, can be the result. Female headed-households then, are generally poorer, suffer from low status, and there is an overall subjugation of the women and children belonging to these families. 'Feminization of rural poverty' is a valid concept in the light of these observations. These families are also the targets of maliciously motivated thefts and other such acts that underscore their vulnerability in the absence of male protectors.

Feudal-patriarchal values ensure that even young boys above

five years of age are treated on an equal footing in matters of
attending formal meetings for decison making on the wadi and
in ritual celebrations, as representatives of the family in the
absence of adult males, rather than women themselves, whatever be their age. The women are, however, expected to accede
to these decisions, even meekly paying up the pre-determined
and frequent subscriptions for cooperative ritual undertakings
on the wadi.

It is important to understand that the secondary status of
women in traditional society essentially derives from an overtly
stated view of women as possessions rather than as partners
in the family and kinship networks. Thus parents refer to
daughters as 'alien wealth' in a literal sense, and not as mere
metaphor. While men are being inculcated with greater individualism as a result of social change, women are not supposed
to have independent concerns and aspirations beyond providing
for the needs of their families. Underscoring the suppression of
female identity as autonomous individuals is the common usage
of women's relational status as the primary mode of identification rather than their rightful first name. Very often the
women's names are not known in the neighbourhood. Even
amongst women they are better known as so-and-so's
mother/wife and so on, and that suffices. They are mere resources within the household, and are expected to earn their
keep through old age and sickness, unlike men. Naturally there
is no question of their having individual rights within the formal structures of village existence. The same perception also
serves to negate the contribution of women in farming.

The nomenclature of 'farmer' is itself extended to young
boys, even though men's engagement on farms is of a shorter
duration than that of women at all times. The cattle-drawn
ploughshares, wielded only by men, have come to serve as a
powerful masculine archetype, perhaps comparable only to the
feminine archetype of mother and nurturer within the domestic confines. The absence of any symbolic representation
of women as workers, as farm women or as partners in economic activity within the cultural schema probably contributes

to the invisibility of this crucial role in common perception.

Culturally honoured tasks of sowing and ploughing the field are an exclusive male preserve. These are the tasks that 'farmers' do in the economists' and planners' visions as well as in common perception. Women do the all-important tasks of transplanting paddy, weeding, harvesting, cleaning and processing of grain, which includes winnowing. Men use chemical fertilizers while women use cowdung and ashes as manure. Men use electric water pumps while women dig narrow channels for irrigating individual plots. With the exception of sowing and ploughing, male labour is dispensable but female labour is not. Women use simpler implements than men, needing less strength but greater stamina. Women labourers are paid half the wages of men, or even less, and less than one-fourth the wages of labourers driving the ploughshares.

It is not the free availability of women workers from a large pool of unemployed females that leads to the vast disparity of wages amongst the sexes, as conjectured by several researchers studying rice cultivation in South India, since women labourers are as hard to find as men in the peak agricultural season, and at other times also. Men's engagement in farming is limited to the important tasks of sowing, ploughing, construction of earthenware dams for irrigating fields—a task shared by women, of course—and the occasional repairing of small *bunds* or raised barriers, dividing separate plots. Besides rice growing in the kharif and rabi seasons, year-round agricultural work includes raising groundnuts for oil consumption, pulses, vegetables and spices. Most of this relies chiefly on female labour in almost all the tasks including sowing. Foraging for cattle fodder, wood for cooking and gathering forest produce are other tasks that rely on women's labour. There is, after all, a limit on the number of ploughs that small farms can accommodate even in the busy cultivation period. Probably it is the in-built biases against women, as much as the fact that there are fewer young, able-bodied men capable of using the plough or even willing to hire out as farm labourers, that creates the difference in wages. If women dared to organize together and used pressure tactics to

demand comparative wages, all agricultural work would come
to a stop. This is not feasible, however, given the highly cooperative and interdependent existence at that level. Women
probably have a greater stake in subsistence agriculture than
men, and are willing to undervalue their own contribution, as
long as it provides for their modest needs.

Eighteen-hour days are very common for women especially
during the peak agricultural season as they shore up farm work
and take care of domestic responsibilities. Longer hours are put
in on festive occasions. The important task of preparing and serving huge meals to a large number of farm labourers and the family, in addition to farm work, is not afforded the recognition it
deserves. The typical male workday, even in busy times, is of
nine hours. This merely illustrates how cultural biases serve to
suppress the value of women's contribution, while at the same
time overplaying the primacy of men's work as farmers.

Work on the farm and within the household is a primary
function of the village women's identity and self-respect. Her
role as a worker is on par with her reproductive role. Relatively
little time is spent on child-rearing beyond providing for bare
physical nurturance in the typical village household. Most village women continue to work through illness and old age, with
little allowance for human frailty. Men usually retire from tasks
involving hard physical labour by the time they reach the age
of sixty.

The bigger, and seemingly better-off the village household,
the greater is the women's workload, with the extra farming,
grinding of spices, cooking and cleaning that it entails. Extra
work is involved in feeding farm labourers and domestic servants, if any, apart from looking after poultry and cattle. Cooks
for hire are simply not available in the village, nor are domestic
servants, given the severe scarcity of labourers. Work serves as
the great leveller in the lives of women. Thus higher caste and
class status is more easily reflected in the lifestyles and clothes
of men rather than women.

Women are the mainstay of subsistence agriculture, which
is rice cultivation in the Kokan. They have a greater stake in

the preservation of ancestral dwellings and property, since their own survival as well as that of their children and other dependants rests on this. Their sense of emotional security depends on the continuation of kinship networks and village traditions within a highly cooperative system of interchange in the face of further impoverishment and growing crime in the countryside. It is ironical then that all their contribution to maintaining this system is considerably underplayed, even as they are denied access to the formal structures of power, decision making and status, within the over-arching traditions of feudal-patriarchy in the village.

An interesting observation is that patriarchy also serves to dehumanize individual men who are unable to conform to rigid role expectations as providers and protectors in the face of poverty, out-migration and growing corruption and crime in the countryside. The breakdown of traditional support systems merely serves to highlight individual failures on the men's part, with a consequent loss of status within the household as well as in the larger society.

The case studies present aspects of the real world of women farmers belonging to the poor population group in Masure. It is a high-stress environment with very little that is sure and secure from one day to the next in the hand-to-mouth struggle for survival. The villagers live very interdependent lives of mutual exploitation and cooperation, to enhance the stakes for survival. Yet earlier secure ways, and phenomenological equations about their universe do not seem to work amid changing times, and this brings on an intense level of tension and insecurity about the future.

Very few stereotypical notions about poor women are borne out by the grassroot reality. Rather than being passive acculturated creatures silently suffering the yoke of an oppressive system, village women are creative and mature individualists. Each woman is seen to make unique interpretations of the given cultural norms as they impinge upon her own existence, giving individual shape to abstract, amorphous ideologies and in adapting to external changes in her circumstances in her own way, quite distinct from others in the same milieu.

Even at a harsh level of poverty and deprivation, most village women derive considerable satisfaction from the sense of creativity in their lives and from being in direct touch with the productive and regenerative aspects of nature and existence. The level of physical mobility, relative autonomy, creative satisfaction and psychological independence enjoyed by many women, despite the grinding burdens of poverty and misogyny—both traditional and modern—are rare and valued facets of village life. They have few illusions about gender relationships in an atmosphere of obvious and direct misogyny, which differs from the insidiously subtle misogyny that is particularly practised in the West. It appears that there is much to be salvaged from the farm women's experience, which is directly strengthening, empowering and self-affirming.

In organizational work, village women across all castes tend to be less emotional, more pragmatic and more militant than men on issues of concern to them, an observation borne out by most cross-cultural studies of women. The poor level of literacy, lack of experience in group activities, or the extent of indoctrination to traditional gender roles seem immaterial when women rally around specific issues. Direct organization of women accompanied with practical programmes for strengthening their economic roles so as to empower them might prove effective in improving their overall status in the long run. To enable village women to make their voices heard, to assert their own view of what is good or bad for themselves, rather than being subject to well-meaning yet destructive paternalistic interventions is what is called for at this time. I think it is important for middle class or westernized city organizers first to question their own assumptions and biases about village women which may have arisen from an untenable superior standpoint. Another major observation particularly in terms of gender research, is that individual men are also oppressed by women in many subtle or overt ways of manipulative dehumanization.

Ultimately, it is not so much the lack of resources that obstructs progress but rather wrong priorities. The lack of development and overall progress in the villages are to be blamed on the denigration of village culture, particularly in its more positive egalitarian and cooperative aspects, within a neocolonialist external cultural domination, petty political machinations, harassment and the general ambience of corruption and exploitation that governmental 'change agents' bring.

There is a narrow dividing line between most households in poor villages, less so among women. As in the village under study, the divide on an economic class-basis is narrow and confused, given the complexities of land ownership and usage. Inherited distinctions of caste and religion are unambiguous and well-internalized on the other hand. Without undue romanticization of the schisms in village society based on divisions such as caste, class and religion, it is of critical importance to focus on common areas of linkage for unified action as a part of organizational strategy. Perhaps, it is more fruitful in the long run to develop and strengthen shared bonds and cooperation. This is not to deny the overwhelming need for advocacy on behalf of traditionally powerless groups. Yet women constitute the largest single group discriminated against and victimized across all fragmented groupings, and forging alliances on common issues can certainly create pressure for wider social change and equity.

Rapid change over the last decade has occurred within the overall abysmal picture in the village. The bullock cart has yielded ground to auto-rickshaws, three-wheelers and truck transport, even a few tractors, power tillers, dumpers and motorcycles mostly belonging to the rural elite, the educated professionals 'gentlemen farmers', the bigger commercial traders, budding public works contractors, and especially, the new politicians. Privately owned jeeps and cars are still rare. Electric irrigation pumps, thriving flour mills and saw mills, also television and video sets are not uncommon. Farmhouses and orchards—usually owned by urban investors— have begun to dot the countryside. The educated unemployed youth are encouraged to set up small business enterprises with government loans, as a part of the integrated rural development policy.

Thus, tea and snacks 'hotels', as tiny eateries are termed in these parts, small-time grocery stores and electrical, mechanical repair shops have begun to mushroom all over the village.

There is a growing 'encroachment' of women on public spaces. Thus a welcome dilution of gendered spatial arrangements is now evident. A large number of women, including teachers, nurses, anganwadi workers and school and college students are visible on the streets and on buses, in contrast to their earlier restriction to homes, farms and occasional forays to the market. There is tremendous respect among peasants for the few working women who manage homes, farms and in addition contribute cash incomes to the families. This transition in women's lifestyles has been fairly rapid over the last five years, as a result of positively directed state programmes (part of the Integrated Child Development Services [ICDS], Integrated Rural Development Programme [IRDP], Training for Rural Youth in Self-Employment [TRYSEM], Maharashtra Centre for Entrepreneurship Development [MCED], and so on) favouring women. Thus impetus towards the formation of mahila mandals in a loose alliance with anganwadis in all hamlets, as also the formation of women's cooperatives, special loan facilities for women, training for income-generation activities and for developing channels for marketing their produce are welcome measures. The women and child welfare departments at the district level are expected to provide dynamic leadership in promoting the entry of women in non-traditional avenues of earning a livelihood. Special camps organized at the village, taluka and district levels have served to ensure greater mobilization of woman beneficiaries.

Yet there is a high amount of leakage in the implementation of all these programmes on account of corruption, besides being undermined by disdain on part of the lower officials. Lack of proper step-by-step guidance to poor women on matters of management, accounting and financial aspects leads to an inability to overcome the fear of incurring losses. The poor faith in government programmes and fears of government takeover of scarce assets in case of failure is another handicap. A majority of the beneficiaries include the better-off protégés of local politicians. Overall political interference by local bosses, and caste and class biases within a semi-feudal structure negate the benefits to women from the poor strata. Other such factors include inadequate provision of elementary resources to officials implementing these programmes, including staff, vehicles and essential office equipment for the monitoring, supervision and follow-up, in the context of the low priority given to women's schemes and the overall apathy of the people. It must be mentioned here that the appointment of a high-profile, sincere and upright young woman administrator to head the district administration in a brief tenure of three years helped to a considerable extent in popularizing and imparting dynamism to the task of women-oriented development.

The economic liberalization policy of the government and its new economic policy package prepared under pressure from the international agencies and foreign investors appears to negate the need for according priority to the welfare of the poor. Feminists have strongly criticized this skewed policy since it is expected to undermine the work and security of women workers in both organized and unorganized sectors, with disastrous consequences for their own well-being and that of their households.

The recent measure introduced in Maharashtra in 1991 of reserving 33 percent of electoral seats for women and their inclusion in a few committees at various levels in the district has served to overcome the bias against women's participation in public affairs. On the other hand, such a leap in affirmative action policies favouring women may be viewed as a populist sop in response to the pressures generated by the widening impact of the women's movement on the urban-centred middle classes. It is important to see that such policy imperatives do not merely boil down to a cynical manipulation of women who constitute 50 percent of the voters, following the dawning realization of the importance of gendered differences in voting behaviour on the part of women and men. In the past, Mahatma Gandhi, followed much later by Indira Gandhi and currently by Jayalalitha in Tamil Nadu and N. T. Rama Rao in Andhra

Pradesh in the state elections, have successfully demonstrated the political impact of making 'gender-sensitive' appeals to women. At the same time they ensured that the fundamental causes and issues of gender inequity in social relations and in the family are left untouched so as not to alienate men. In the absence of any significant change in male prejudices and in gender relations, such measures will fall short of developing the desired level of improvement in women's status. Again, in the absence of improvement in the condition of women from the deprived castes and minority communities, such policies can only favour women belonging to the privileged sections. Finally, given the absence of integrity, accountability and transparency in public affairs, and a genuine concern for the poor in the present political system, electoral politics offers a no-win situation to most women, excepting a handful of blessed women who are in essence determined political survivors.

As elsewhere, women in politics are also handicapped by a dual set of commitments, which include the nurturance and well-being of their families, and the need to withstand the killing pressures of mainstream electoral policies. Unlike men, women are trapped in rigid gender expectations of behaviour, and this is considerably magnified in the public sphere. They must tread a fine balance between appearing docile, subservient, dutiful and self-abnegating, while at the same time also project a honed image of intelligence, guts and dynamism to overcome the opposition. They must respect and accede to male authority in public and party fora, in the accepted gendered mould, if they are not to alienate either the voters or the party workers. They must not appear too forward and ambitious, and especially guard the limits of feudal norms and conventions within most mainstream parties. A major handicap faced by women is the political ethos governed not only by male chauvinism, but also excessive corruption as an intrinsic element of the democratic electoral process and the consequent criminalization of politics, a no-holds barred level of political manipulation and horse-trading. Cut-throat competition and the settling of scores is essential to the process. Independent women are also easy victims to the unscrupulous stratagems of venal politicos and to character assassination in particular. The closer they are to the electorate, the worse are the effects of such tactics, particularly in the district and rural milieu.

Women participating in the local self-government elections as almost an entire class of new entrants are ridiculed as novices and bunglers with the willing help of the press. Their lack of political savvy, experience and manipulative skills are played up to strengthen male prejudices and serve the ends of political scapegoating. Ultimately, women are used as a convenient front to further the ambitions of dominant male relatives and the party bosses. They often serve as rubber stamps and as captive votes in statutory debates, and independent initiative is not encouraged at this level. The paucity of capable and willing candidates in rural constituencies leads to the import of urban women, and the absence of a local base or support lobby renders them totally dependent on male party workers and their machinations in the electoral arena.

Separate reserved constituencies pit one woman against another, contributing to insidious and personalized warfare between the women aspirants, a spectacle of prime entertainment in the electoral process. Deserving women of independent achievements and genuine commitment to the people generally tend to fall by the wayside, as is often observed, especially because individual merit and principles have no value in this context. Moreover, women are basically usurpers in what is a sanctioned modern version of warfare for state or local rulership, supported by all the elements of basic machismo that is evident in such an enterprise.

Women in politics are often excluded from a role in decision making in the formulation of policies, strategies and programmes both in politics and in government. They are naturally excluded from male croneyism and also from the nightly parleys in secluded spots where important male politicians reach major consensus on policies and issues. The special posts reserved for elected women belong mostly to low priority, low budget committees and ministries, the women and child welfare ones in particular. In any event a genuine prioritization of women's issues and concerns is not desirable as it is perceived to work against male privileges in the household, in society and in politics.

Considering the realities of the grassroot democratic processes within electoral politics, it becomes obvious that women's inherent qualities—born out of their gender-specific experience in society—emphasizing cooperation, harmony and nurturance are eroded maximally, rendering them no better than men in the prevailing dog-eat-dog world of contemporary politics in India. It is small wonder that women's participation in politics peaked in the popular anti-colonialist struggle prior to independence in the first half of this century, including revolutionaries espousing violence to overthrow colonial rule and the Gandhian followers of non-violence. It has now reached an all-time low in terms of women occupying the public party platform in leadership roles and in terms of the number elected to the state and national assemblies and in the corresponding government ministries. The same situation prevails in the supposedly 'progressive' state of Maharashtra, as for the rest of the country.

Similarly, the new Policy for Women proposed in Maharashtra, while offering an excellent set of measures aimed at improving the quality of life of women and their greater empowerment has invited controversy. Feminists assert that it will be ineffective and limited in its scope of implementation. More important, the economic liberalization policy of the government and its new economic policy package is particularly expected to undermine the work strengths and security of poor women, with disastrous consequences for their own well-being and for that of their households.

This is not to say that these measures are of no value, but it must be emphasized that their implementation can be very problematic. At times such policy-formulations can be overly simplistic, when influenced by women's groups with a narrow perspective, without clearly considering major aspects of the ground reality, particularly in the villages. Such over-simplification of the policy perspectives can, in fact, hamper the process of bringing about some of the more radical changes necessary

within the multiple systems interacting together as they impinge on gender relations in the cultural, socioeconomic and
political arena. It is important to understand that patchwork
solutions cannot significantly improve the lot of immiserized
populations, women in particular. Change imposed from the top
in the matter of progressive policies and legislation cannot suc-
ceed unless it is preceded by education and consciousness raising. Also, greater autonomy in decision making leading to
women's control over their lives cannot be imposed from the
top. If it does not evolve as a result of changes at the grassroots,
then only women from a few privileged groups may benefit from
the new policy, leaving the greater mass of underprivileged
women far behind.

It is not enough merely to recommend policy measures;
women must also take the lead in its implementation and consider the range of options and variations at the local level. Thus
we must work towards decentralization, people-oriented planning and policy making. The target groups of these policies must
be involved at all levels, and respect for the local languages and
idiom is essential since this would popularize the development
schemes at the people's level. Not only does this require the use
of indigenous forms of media and communication, it also involves a wider representation beyond the privileged groups, including grassroot organizations, the non-governmental
organizations and special advocacy groups, who may all participate in planning, policy making and implementation.

Because feminists are either urban-based or thinly spread-
out in the mofussil towns and a few villages, wider issue-based
strategic alliances of groups of women and men are called for.
Aspects of close supervision, monitoring and evaluation leading
to improved feedback and timely modification of existing
schemes at each stage of implementation on an ongoing basis
and the encouragement of the involvement of the target groups
are often ignored totally. The politicization of such schemes and
policies and political interference in their implementation at
the local level must be checked as far as possible to avoid their
being hijacked by vested interests. The issue of accountability

to the target groups themselves is a very critical matter influencing the credibility and acceptance of policies and programmes.

One of the pitfalls that feminists face here is the superficial glorification of work with rural women, particularly with women from the lower caste groups, tribals and the urban working class. Working with women facing various forms of oppression and exploitation, or to develop alliances with women of the upper castes and classes, including professional and employed women or homemakers uncommitted to leftist ideologies and organizational efforts are seen as simply not good enough. This seems to be a very short-sighted view. If the women's movement as well as gender studies are to grow in terms of sheer size and to generate sufficient pressures to alter entrenched structures and systems in society—which are often supported by women too besides the men—women from all sections of society must be brought together even when the primary goal is to help deprived people.

Similarly, changes in gender relations cannot come about by neglecting the involvement of men in toto, as we evolve from experiences of injustice in organizational politics to a confident position in leading mass movements and in theorizing and research on gender relations in society. Most women value their relationships with men in and outside the family, and men's active involvement and cooperation is essential to the successful achievement of gender equity. Men are also harmed by the cast-iron moulds of gender-appropriate behaviour under patriarchy, which has as many male victims as women. A greater sensitization of men to the corrosive effects of inhuman patriarchal values on freedom of choice, on the quality and substance of their own lives as well as on the women and relationships within the family and in society is essential in bringing about meaningful change. A 'reification' of human values that were earlier identified as weaknesses and associated with women, including the bonding, bridging and harmonizing influences of sensitivity, sharing, caring, nurturance, respect for different cultural practices, attitudes and modes of behaviour, cooperation and a peaceful way of negotiating dissensions must be emphasized for both men and women. This certainly offers a humane alternative to the restrictively constructed macho ideals that value competition, aggression, appropriation of resources and male supremacy that have wrought so much misery and strife in all societies. Thus willing cooperation between women's and men's groups from a broader range in society can surely help in consolidating meaningful alliances in the struggle for gender equity. This is what we have to aim for as part of a gender-sensitive theory and strategic intervention.

Finally, as we advance in gaining theoretical insights regarding women's work and general existence, we can reassess their strengths and weaknesses from a qualitative grassroot perspective combined with the insights gained from macro-level data including census figures. It is then possible to identify crucial areas of empowerment whereby the tide of female pauperization and general victimization can be halted.

This is a plea for a unified theory and action orientation to the studies of rural women and to warn of the dangers inherent in the self-perpetuating fallacies and wrong assumptions that are commonly found in the traditional approach to studying rural societies. Gender studies on women are not only concerned with facts as facts, but also with the larger issue of helping women achieve a more equitable status. Interdisciplinary women's studies can then become a dynamic double-edged sword in the battle for a just and humane society. It is hoped that academic work particularly in the social sciences will increasingly evolve as a process of human sharing, and that artificial walls in intellectual enterprise will be dissolved in favour of a more holistic, humanizing approach to understanding complex schema.

Appendix

Several ovya and ukhane are used in Chapter 2, 'Folklore and the Malvani Ethos'. The text has taken some liberties with the translation in English to achieve greater fluency. The original Malvani form in the Devanagri script, along with an English transliteration follows.

OVYA

परायाची बाळा	Alien Daughters
'चौघी आमी जाऊया एका देवा.'	'chowghi ami jowya eka deva.'
'चौघी आमी जाऊया एका देवा.'	'chowghi ami jowya eka deva.'
तिथे भेटला सासूमावा,	tithe bhetala sasoomava,
त्यांच्या पायाचा तीर्थ घेवा.	tyanchya payacha tirtha gheva.
आमी तिसऱ्या कामा जावा.	ami tisarya kama java.
सासू नी सासरा,	sasoo ni sasara,
दोन तुळशीची गे झाडा,	don tulshichi ge zada,
आमी परायाची गे वाळा.	ami parayachi ge bala.
माझ्या आयेनी वापानी,	majya ayeni bapani,
'ऱ्हानाची गे मोठी केली,'	'nhanachi ge mothi keli,'
'ऱ्हानाची गे मोठी केली,'	'nhanachi ge mothi keli,'
कडेखांद्यावरी खेळविली,	kadekhandyavari khelavli,
सासूसासऱ्यांच्या पल्लवी घातली.	sasoosarayanchya pallavi ghatali.

जाईसारकी गे फुलविली,
केळीसारकी गे वाढविली,
आणी पराची गे धन केली.

jaisaraki ge phoolavili,
kelisaraki ge vadhavili,
ani parachi ge dhana keli.

कावळा कीत करी

The Crow's Lament

कावळा कीत करी,
कावळा कीत करी,
सासरी जाच भारी.

kowla kita kari,
kowla kita kari,
`sasari jacha bhari.

पुन्याईच्या मायवापारे,
लेक कशी दूर दिली,
लेक कशी दूर दिली ...

punyaichya mayabapare,
leka kashi doora dili,
leka kashi doora dili ...

न्हाय लेकी दूर दिली,
पन वांगडयालां भूल पडली,
का वांगडयांला भूल दिली ...

nhay leki doora dili,
pan bangadyanla bhoola padli,
ka bangadyanla bhoola dili ...

न्हाय लेकी दूर दिली,
पन हाराला भूल पडली,
का हराला भूल दिली ...

nhay leki doora dili,
pan harala bhoola padli,
ka harala bhoola dili ...

न्हाय लेकी दूर दिली,
पन मंगलसूताला भूल पडली,
का मंगलसूताला भूल दिली ...

nhay leki doora dili,
pan mangalasootala bhoola padli,
ka mangalsootala bhoola dili ...

वंसा

नवीन वंसा भरला गे ताई, देऊ कुनाला
गे ताई, देऊ कुनाला?
मामंजी गेले बाजारा, देऊ कुनाला
गे ताई, देऊ कुनाला?

नवीन वंसा भरला गे ताई, देऊ कुनाला
गे ताई, देऊ कुनाला?
सासूवाई वसली पलंगावरी, देऊ कुनाला
गे ताई, देऊ कुनाला?

नवीन वंसा भरला गे ताई, देऊ कुनाला
गे ताई, देऊ कुनाला ?
जाऊबाई गेली शेताला, देऊ कुनाला
गे ताई, देऊ कुनाला ?

नवीन वंसा भरला गे ताई, देऊ कुनाला
गे ताई, देऊ कुनाला ?
ननंद माजी गेली खेळायाला, देऊ कुनाला
गे ताई, देऊ कुनाला ?

नवीन वंसा भरला गे ताई, देऊ कुनाला
गे ताई, देऊ कुनाला ?
दीर माजे गेले शाळेला, देऊ कुनाला
गे ताई, देऊ कुनाला ?

नवीन वंसा भरला गे ताई, देऊ कुनाला
गे ताई, देऊ कुनाला ?
भरतार माजे गेले नोकरीला, देऊ कुनाला
गे ताई, देऊ कुनाला ?

Vansa

navin vansa bharla ge tai, deu kunala
ge tai, deu kunala?
mamanji gele bahjara, deu kunala
ge tai, deu kunala?

navin vansa bharla ge tai, deun kunala
ge tai, deu kunala?
sasoobai basli palangavari, deu kunala
ge tai, deu kunala?

navin vansa bharla ge tai, deu kunala
ge tai, deu kunala?
jowbai geli shetala, deu kunala
ge tai, deu kunala?

navin vansa bharla ge tai, deu kunala
ge tai, deu kunala?
nananda maji geli khelayala, deu kunala
ge tai, deu kunala?

navin vansa barla ge tai, deu kunala
ge tai, deu kunala?
deer maje gele shalela, deu kunala
ge tai, dei kunala?

navin vansa bharla ge tai, deu kunala
ge tai, deu kunala?
bhartara maje gel nokarila, deu kunala
ge tai, deu kunala?

तिळाचे फूल

'तिळाचे फूल वाई मानिकमोती,
गौराये वैनी तुला न्हेयाला येती.'

'येतील पन, येतील पन, कोन-कोन येतील?'
'येतील पन, येतील मामंजी येतील.'

'मामंजी येऊनी काय-काय आनतील?'
'आनतील पन, आनतील पन, हातातल्या वांगडया.'

'हातातल्या वांगडया मी घेनार न्हाई.
मामंजीसंगे मी जानार न्हाई.'

'तिळाचे फूल वाई मानिकमोती,
गौराये वैनी तुला न्हेयाला येती.'

'येतील पन, येतील पन, कोन-कोन येतील?'
'येतील पन, येतील पन, सासूवाई येतील.'

'सासूवाई येतांना काय-काय आनतील?'
'आनतील पन, आनतील पन, गळयातला हार.'

'गळयातला हार मी घेनार न्हाई.'
'सासूवाईसंगे मी जानार न्हाई.'

'तिळाचे फुल वाई मानिकमोती,
गौरायेवैनी तुला न्हेयाला येती.'

'येतील पन, येतील पन, कोन-कोन येतील?'
'येतील पन, येतील पन, भावोजी येतील.'

'भावोजी येताना काय-काय आनतील?'
'आनतील पन, आनतील पन, नाकातली नथी.'

'नाकातली नथी मी घेनार न्हाइ.
भावोजीसंगे मी जानार न्हाई.'

'तिळाचे फूल वाई मानिकमोती,
गौरायेवैनी तुला न्हेयाला येती.'

'येतील पन, येतील पन, कोन-कोन येतील?'
'येतील पन, येतील पन, पतीराया येतील.'

'पतीराया येऊन काय-काय आनतील?'
'आनतील पन, आनतील पन, खोव-याची वाटी.'

'खोव-याची वाटी मी कुरुकुरु खाईन.
पतीरायासंगे मी तुरुतुरु जाईन.'

Sesame Flower

'tilache phoola bai manikamoti,
gowraye vaini tula nheyala yeti.'

'yetil pan, yetil pan, kon-kona yetil?'
'yetil pan, yetil mamanji yetil.'

'mamanji yeuni kay-kaya antil?'
'antil pan, antil pan, hatatlya bangdya.'

'hatatlya bangdya mi ghenara nhai.
mamanjisange mi janara nhai.'

'tilache phoola bai manikamoti,
gauraye vaini tula nheyala yeti.'

'yetil pan, yetil pan, kon-kona yetil?'
'yetil pan, yetil pan, sasoobai yetil.'

'sasoobai yetana kay-kaya antil?'
'antil pan, antil pan, galyatla hara.'

'galyatla hara mi ghenara nhai.
sasoobaisange mi janara nhai.'

'tilache phoola bai manikamoti,
gauraye vaini tula nheyala yeti.'

'yetil pan, yetil pan, kon-kona yetil?'
'yetil pan, yetil pan, bhavoji yetil.'

'bhavoji yetana kay-kaya antil?'
'antil pan, antil pan, nakatli nathi.'

'nakatli nathi mi ghenara nhai.
bhavojisange mi janara nhai.'

'tilache phoola bai manikamoti,
gauraye vaini tula nheyala yeti.'

'yetil pan, yetil pan, kon-kona yetil?'
'yetil pan, yetil pan, patiraya yetil.'

'patiraya yeuni kay kaya antil?'
'antil pan, antil pan, khobryachi vati.'

'khobryachi vati mi kurukuru khain.
patirayasange mi turuturu jain.'

चोरटी सूनबाई

चोरटी सूनबाई कुठेशी गेली?
सासूवाई तुमच्या मागूनी आली.

दह्याचा वुडकूला कोनी सुने खाल्ला,
सासूवाई तुमच्या पायाच्यान, गनोबा देवाच्यान,
मीच सून भली, हो मीच सून भली.

चोरटी सूनबाई कुठेशी गेली?
सासूवाई तुमच्या मागूनी आली.

केळीचा घड कोनी सूने खाल्ला ?
सासूवाई तुमच्या पायाच्यान, गनोवा देवाच्यान,
मीच सून भली, हो मीच सून भली.

चोरटी सूनबाई कुठेशी गेली ?
सासूवाई तुमच्या मागूनी आली.

चुलीवरचा खोबरा कोनी सूने खाल्ला ?
सासूवाई तुमच्या पायाच्यान, गनोवा देवाच्यान,
मीच सून भली, हो मीच सून भली ...

Daughter-in-Law Thief

chorati soonabai kutheshi geli?
sasoobai tumchya maguni ali.

dahyacha budkula koni soone khatta,
sasoobai tumchya payachan, Ganoba devachyan,
meecha soon bhali, ho meecha soon bhali.

chorati soonabai kutheshi geli?
sasoobai tumchya maguni ali.

kelicha ghada koni soone khalla?
sasoobai tumchya payachyan, Ganoba devachyan,
meecha soon bhali, ho meecha soon bhali.

chorati soonabai kutheshi geli?
sasoobai tumchya maguni ali.

choolivarcha khobra koni soone khalla?
sasoobai tumchya payachyan, Ganoba devachyan,
meecha soon bhali, ho meecha soon bhali ...

UKHANE

Note that I have used the name 'Gangaram Rane' in the text as an illustration of a husband's name. The blanks in parentheses in the following ukhane are used by each wife who is participating to fill in her husband's name.

हिमाली पर्वतावर वर्फाच्या राशी,
'——चा' नाव घेतव तुमच्या आग्रहासाठी.

himali parvatavar barfanchya rashi,
'_____cha' nav ghetav tumchya agrahasathi.

खळयाच्या पेळेक उक्शेच्या जाली,
'——च्या' तोंडाक सदीच्या गाली.

khalyachya pelak ukshechya jali,
'____chya' tondak sadichya gali.

दारी होता मेढका,
त्याला वांधली रेडका,
असा 'न्हवरा' रोडका,
तर जल्मी घेत न्हाय फडका.

dari hota medhaka,
tyala bandhli redaka,
asa 'nhavra' rodaka,
tar jalmi ghet nhaya phadka.

तांब्याचे तांवे अबीरबुक्क्याने घासले,
'———ना' पानी घेऊन इले, तर लोक मला हसले.

tambyache tambe abeerbukkyane ghasle,
'_____na' pani gheun ile, tar lok mala hasle.

भाजीत भाजी मेथीची,
'———' माझ्या प्रितीची.

bhajita bhaji methichi,
'_____' majhya preetichi.

नावाची कसली विशाद,
नी '———' माझ्या खिशात.

navachi kasli bishad,
ni '_____' majhya kishat.

काठीत काठी येताची,
वायको केली वेताची.

kathita kathi yetachi,
bayko keli betachi.

खन खन कुदली मन मन माती,
उगाळल्या भिती चितारले खांब,
सासूवाई पोटी आक्कावाईचे पाठी,
जलमले राम; राम न्हाय म्हटले;
नाव न्हाय घितले;
शेरभर सुपारी वत्तीस पाना,
वत्तीस पानाक लावला चूना,
पायात पैंजन चालू कशी ?
एवढे सभेत बोलू कशी ?
सभा सोन्याची नजर पुरूसाची,
जटा जेगिनीची फडा नागिनीची,
उघडया खिडकी जाउदे पालकी '----ची.'

khan khan kudali man man mati,
ugalalya bhiti chitarale khamb,
sasoobaiche poti akkabaiche pathi,
jalamle Ram; Ram nhay mhatle;
nav nhay ghitle;
sherbhar supari battis pana,
battis panaka lavala chuna,
payata painjana chalu kashi?
evadhe sabheta bolu kashi?
sabha sonyachi najar purusachi,
jata joginichi phada naginichi,
ughadya khidki jowde palki '_____chi'.

Glossary

bajar   market

bhain/bhavin   women of the Devli caste who are temple servants

bhajan   devotional song, usually sung in a group

bhakri   type of chapati made from coarse unleavened dough of millet

bhakti   devotion

Bhandari   a caste in the Other Backward Classes group, mainly peasants

Bharateshwar   one of the many names of Shiva

buwa   lead singer in a bhajan singers' group; holy man

Chambhar   dalit caste of leather workers

chandoba   moon

dalit   downtrodden; self-selected nomenclature, referring to the erstwhile untouchable castes; earlier referred to as Harijan

Devli   caste in Other Backward Classes group, temple servants

dhaikala/dahikala   folk plays, costume dramas based on Hindu epics, with men enacting female roles

dharma   religion; spiritual path; ordained way of life

doli   palanquin

Ekadashi   eleventh day after the new moon in the Hindu lunar almanac, when fasting is prescribed, and tilling of soil is prohibited

Ga-ma-bha-na-   letters of the Marathi alphabet (not in alphabetical order); implies the start of schooling

Gauri   one of the many names of the Goddess Parvati

hafta   bribe, often collected by the policeman from petty traders on his weekly rounds

Hartalika   consort of Ganpati

Janmashtami   eighth day after full moon in the month of Shravan, commemorating Lord Krishna's birth *jilha*   district

jodidarin (s); jodidarni (pl.)   female companion/s

khanawal   arrangement of meals for a fixed payment

kirtan   religions discourse interspersed with devotional songs, to the accompaniment of cymbals and drum

kokum   sun-dried processed peels of the seasonal ratamba fruit

Kshatriya   warrior caste, e.g. Marathas

Kunbi   peasant caste, hierarchically lower than the Kshatriya Marathas

madi   upper story, often constructed of wooden material

Mahar   a dalit caste

maka-tuka   derogatory term used to allude to Malvani language; for me (*maka*); for you (*tuka*)

malak   male owner, proprietor; husband

malkin   female owner, proprietor; wife

mandali   congregation of people

Nag Panchami   day for cobra worship, fifth day after the new moon marking the beginning of the month of Shravan

oti   ritual honouring married women; filling the loose ends of their saris with rice, coconut, and a blouse piece; literally, womb

panchayat   village council for local government; earlier, five male elders who acted as arbitrators

Panchayati Raj   three-tier system of local government at village, taluka and district levels by elected councils

porgya   little girl; brat

pravachan   religious discourse

Saraswat   Bramhans, traditionally keepers of accounts and land records

sarpanch   elected chief of panchayat; village chief

saubhagyavati   women of the fortunate married status

saunsar   family; household (as a responsibility)

tai   elder sister; honorific to indicate repect for any woman of higher status

taluka   administrative block consisting of several villages; many of which together form a district

tehsildar   administrative chief of a taluka, also vested with the powers of executive magistrate

tulas (s); tulshi (pl)   better known throughout India as *tulsi*; indigenous variety of basil, worshipped by Hindu households

wadi   hamlet; isolated neighbourhood grouping of several houses

References

Agarwal, Bina. 'Rural Women and High Yielding Variety Rice Technology.' *Economic and Political Weekly* 19, 13 (March 1984): A 39-52.
———. *Cold Hearths and Barren Slopes: The Woodfuel Crisis in the Third World.* Delhi: Allied, 1986.
———, ed. *Structures of Patriarchy: The State, the Community and the Household in Modernising Asia.* London: Zed, 1988.
Allen, Michael. 'Girls' Pre-Puberty Rites Amongst the Newars of Kathmandu Valley.' In *Women in India and Nepal*, edited by Michael Allen and S. N. Mukherjee. New Delhi: Sterling, 1990.
Allen, Michael, and S. N. Mukherjee, eds. *Women in India and Nepal* New Delhi: Sterling, 1990.
Bardhan, Kalpana. 'Work Patterns and Social Differentiation: Rural Women of West Bengal.' In *Contractual Arrangements: Employment and Wages in Rural Labor Markets in Asia*, edited by Hans Binswanger and Mark Rosenzweig. New Haven: Yale University Press, 1984.
———. 'Women's Work, Welfare and Status: Forces of Tradition and Change in India.' *Economic and Political Weekly* 20, 50 (14 December 1985): 2207-2269.
Baxamusa, Ramala, Kalpana Kumbhani, Jyoti Paranjpe, Joseph Pinto, Manorama Savur, and Minal Shah. 'Underdevelopment of Ratnagiri: A Case of Rural Metropolitan Relations.' Part I. A Tentative Report. Bombay: Dept of Sociology, University of Bombay, 1979.
Beteille, Andre. *Caste, Class and Power: Changing Patterns of Stratification in a Tanjore Village.* Berkeley: University of California Press, 1965.

Beteille, Andre. *Studies in Agrarian Social Structure*. Delhi: Oxford University Press, 1974.

Beneria, Lourdes, ed. *Women and Development: The Sexual Division of Labor in Rural Societies*. New York: Praeger, 1982.

Bhagwat, A. R. 'Maharashtrian Folk Songs on the Grind Mill (Songs Embodying Sentiments).' *Journal of the University of Bombay* 10, 1 (July 1941): 138-186; 4 (January 1942): 137-174.

Binswanger, Hans P., Robert E. Evenson, Cecilia A. Florencino, and Benjamin N. F. White, eds. *Rural Household Studies in Asia*. Singapore: Singapore University Press, 1980.

Borooah, Romy, Kathleen Cloud, Subadra Sheshadri, T. S. Saraswathi, Jean T. Peterson, and Amita Verma, eds. *Capturing Complexity: An Interdisciplinary Look at Women, Households and Development*. New Delhi: Sage, 1994.

Boserup, Ester. *Women's Role in Economic Development*. New York: St. Martin's Press, 1970.

Burawoy, Michael. 'The Functions and Reproduction of Migrant Labor: Comparative Material from Southern Africa and the United States.' *American Journal of Sociology* 5, 81 (1976): 1050-1087.

Burgos-Debray, Elisabeth, ed. *I, Rigoberta Menchu: An Indian Woman in Guatemala*. Translated by Ann Wright. London: Verso, 1984.

Centre for Science and Environment. *The Second Citizen's Report on the State of India's Environment*, 1984-1985, 179-182, Delhi.

Chakravorty, Shanti. 'Farm Women Labour: Waste and Exploitation.' *Social Change* 5, 12 (March/June 1975): 9-16.

Charlton, Sue Ellen M. *Women in Third World Development*. Boulder, Co: Westview, 1984.

Dandekar, Hemlata C. *Men to Bombay, Women at Home: Urban Influence on Sugao Village, Deccan Maharashtra, India 1942-1982*. Bombay: Popular Prakashan, 1989.

Datta, Satyabrata. 'Role of Indian Worker in Early Phase of Industrialization: A Critique of Established View, with Special Reference to Tata Iron and Steel Co. 1910-1930.' *Economic and Political Weekly*, Review of Management. 20, 48 (30 November 1985): 130-147.

Desai, Rajani X. *Women Migrants and Labour from Ratnagiri*. Geneva: International Labour Office, 1982.

Dixon, Ruth B. *Rural Women at Work: Strategies for Development in South Asia*. Baltimore: Johns Hopkins University Press, 1978.

———. 'Women in Agriculture: Counting the Labour Force in Developng Countries.' *Population and Development Review* 8,

3 (September 1982): 539-566.

Dixon-Mueller, Ruth. *Women's Work in Third World Agriculture*. Geneva: ILO, 1985.

Dumont, L. *Homo Hierarchichus*. Chicago: University of Chicago Press, 1980.

Dyson, Tim. 'Excess Male Mortality in India.' *Economic and Political Weekly*, 19, 10 (10 March 1981): 422-426.

Ganesh, Kamala, and Carla Risseeuw. 'Gender: Between Family and State.' *Economic and Political Weekly* 28, 43 (23 October 1993): 2332-2336.

Gold, Peggy, ed. *Women in the Field: Anthropological Experiences*, 2nd ed. Berkeley, University of California, 1986.

Gothoskar, Sujata, ed. *Struggles of Women at Work*. New Delhi: Vikas, 1992.

Gothoskar, Sujata, Nandita Gandhi and Nandita Shah. 'Maharashtra's Policy for Women.' *Economic and Political Weekly* 29, 48 (November 1994): 3019-3022.

Government of India. *Towards Equality: Report of the Committee on the Status of Women in India*. New Delhi: Department of Social Welfare, Government of India, 1974.

Government of Maharashtra. *Policy for Women*. Bombay: Government Central Press, 1994.

Gray, John N. 'Chetri Women in Domestic Groups and Rituals.' In *Women in India and Nepal*, edited by Michael Allen and S. N. Mukherjee. New Delhi: Sterling, 1990.

Gulati, Leela. 'Male Migration to the Middle East and the Impact on the Family; Some Evidence from Kerala.' *Economic and Political Weekly*, 18, 52/53 (24 December 1983): 2217-2226.

Gupte, Vasant. *Labour Movement in Bombay: Origin and Growth up to Independence*. Bombay: Institute of Workers' Education, 1981.

Hartmann, Heidi. 'Capitalism, Patriarchy, and Job Segregation by Sex.' In *Women and the Workplace*, edited by Martha Blaxall and Barbara Reagan, 137-169. Chicago: University of Chicago Press, 1976.

Islam, Shamima. *Exploring the Other Half: Field Research with Rural Women in Bangladesh*. Dhaka: Women for Women, 1982.

Jain, Devaki. 'Creation of Employment Opportunities for Women through Cooperatives.' New Delhi: National Cooperative Union of India, March 1976.

Jeffery, Patricia. *Frogs in a Well; Indian Women in Purdah*. London: Zed, 1979.

Jeffery, Patricia, Roger Jeffery, and Andrew Loyn. *Labour Pains and Labour Power: Women and Childbearing in India.* London: Zed, 1988.

Krishnaraj, Maithreyi, and Jyoti Ranadive.'The Rural Female Heads of Households: Hidden from View.' In *Women's Status and Development in India* edited by K. Murali Manohar. Warangal, AP: Society for Women's Studies and Development, 1984.

Krygier, Jocelyn. 'Caste and Female Pollution.' In *Women in India and Nepal*, edited by Michael Allen and S. N. Mukherjee. New Delhi: Sterling, 1990.

Kulkarni, Sumati. 'Dependence on Agricultural Employment.' *Economic and Political Weekly* 29, 51-52 (17-24 December 1994): 3260-3262.

Kumar, Nita, ed. *Women as Subjects: South Asian Histories.* Calcutta: Stree, 1994.

Lewis, Barbara. 'Women in Development Planning: Advocacy, Institutionalization and Implementation.' In *Perspectives on Power: Women in Africa, Asia, and Latin America*, edited by Jean F. O'Barr. Durham, NC: Duke University Center for International Studies, 1982.

Lingam, Lakshmi. 'Women-headed Households: Coping with Caste, Class and Gender Hierarchies.' *Economic and Political Weekly* 29, 12 (19 March 1994): 699-704.

Lokadhikar Chalwal Karyakarte. *Pudhech Ata Pudhech Pay.* Bombay: Maruti Kumbhar, 1982.

Marriott, McKim, ed. *Village India: Studies in the Little Community.* Chicago: University of Chicago Press, 1955.

Mencher, Joan P., K. Saradamoni, and Janaki Panicker.'Women in Rice Cultivation: Some Research Tools.' *Studies in Family Planning* special issue edited by Sondra Zeidenstein, 10, 11/12 (November/December 1979): 406-408.

Mencher, Joan, and K. Saradamoni. 'Muddy Feet, Dirty Hands: Rice Production and Female Agricultural Labour.' *Economic and Political Weekly*, Review of Agriculture, 17, 52 (December 1982): A149-167.

Mencher, Joan, P. 'Landless Women Agricultural Labourers in India: Some Observations from Tamil Nadu, Kerala, and West Bengal.' Paper presented at the conference on 'Women in Rice Farming Systems' at the International Rice Research Institute, Los Banos, Philippines, 26-30 September 1983.

Mencher, Joan, P. 'Women Agricultural Labourers and Landowners in Kerala and Tamil Nadu: Some Questions about Gender and Autonomy in the Household.' Paper presented at the conference on 'Women and the Household in Asia', New Delhi, 27-31 January 1985.

———. 'The Forgotten Ones: Female Landless Labourers in Southern India.' Paper presented at the AWID conference in Washington, D. C., April 1985.

Mies, Maria. *Patriarchy and Accumulation on a World Scale: Women in the International Division of Labour*. London: Zed, 1976.

———. 'Dynamics of Sexual Division of Labour and Capital Accumulation: Women Lace Workers of Narsapur.' *Economic and Political Weekly* 16 (annual number 1981): 487-500.

Mies, Maria, K. Lalita, and K. Kumari. *Indian Women in Subsistence and Agricultural Labour*. Geneva: ILO, 1986.

Miller, Barbara. 'Female Labour Participation and Female Seclusion in Rural India: A Regional View.' *Economic Development and Cultural Change* 30, 4 (July 1982): 776-793.

Mitra, Asok, Lalit P. Pathak, and Shekhar Mukherji. *The Status of Women: Shifts in Occupational Participation, 1961-1971*. New Delhi: Abhinav, 1980.

Murphy, Yolanda, and Robert Murphy. *Women of the Forest*, 2nd ed. New York: Columbia University Press, 1985.

Narayan, Kirin. 'Birds on a Branch: Girlfriends and Wedding Songs in Kangra.' *Ethos* (1986): 47-75.

'O Hanlon, Rosalind. *A Comparison Between Women and Men: Tarabai Shinde and the Critique of Gender Relations in Colonial India*. Madras: Oxford University Press: 1994.

Omvedt, Gail. 'Peasant Movements: Women and Rural Revolt in India.' *Journal of Peasant Studies* 5, 3 (April 1978): 320-403.

———. 'Textile Strike Turns Political.' *Economic and Political Weekly* 18, 35 (27 August 1983): 1509-1511.

Papa, Kondavati. *Women in Rural Areas*. Allahabad: Chugh, 1992.

Patwardhan, Raja. *Kokancha Raja*. Bombay: Stree Mukti Sanghatana, October 1987.

Raheja, Gloria, Goodwin. *The Poison in the Gift: Ritual Prestation and the Dominant Caste in a North Indian Village*. Chicago: University of Chicago Press, 1988.

Raheja, Gloria Goodwin. 'Women's Speech Genres, Kinship and Contradiction.' In *Women as Subjects: South Asian Histories*, edited by Nita Kumar. Calcutta: Stree, 1994.

Ram, Kalpana. *Mukkuvar Women: Gender Hegemony and Capitalist Transformation in a South Indian Fishing Community.* New Delhi: Kali for Women, 1992.

Ramasubban, Radhika, and Nigel Crook. 'Mortality Toll of Cities: Emerging Patterns of Disease in Bombay.' *Economic and Political Weekly*, 20, 23 (8 June 1985): 999-1005.

Ranadive, Joy R. 'Gender Implications of Adjustment Policy Programmes in India: Significance of the Household.' *Economic and Political Weekly* 29, 18 (30 April 1994): WS 12-18.

Reiter, Rayna R., ed. *Toward an Anthropology of Women.* New York: Monthly Review Press, 1975.

Rogers, Barbara. *The Domestication of Women: Discrimination in Developing Societies.* London: Routledge and Kegan Paul, 1980.

Rosaldo, Michelle Zimbalist, and Louise Lamphere, eds. *Women, Culture, and Society.* Stanford: Stanford University Press, 1974.

Rosenthal, Donald B. *The Expansive Elite: District Politics and State Policy Making in India.* Berkeley: University of California Press, 1977.

Rubin, Gayle. 'The Traffic in Women: Notes on the "Political Economy" of Sex.' In *Toward an Anthropology of Women*, edited by Rayna R. Reiter, 157-210. New York: Monthly Review Press, 1975.

Sen, Gita. 'Women Workers and the Green Revolution.' In *Women and Development: The Sexual Division of Labour in Ru₁al Societies*, edited by Lourdes Beneria, 29-64. New York: Praeger, 1982.

Shah, Nandita, Sujata Gothoskar, Nandita Gandhi, and Amrita Chhachhi. 'Structural Adjustment, Feminization of Labour Force and Organizational Strategies.' *Economic and Political Weekly* 29, 18 (30 April 1994): WS 39-48.

Sharma, Kumud. 'Gender Environment and Structural Adjustment.' *Economic and Political Weekly* 29, 18 (30 April 1995): WS 5-11.

Sharma, Ursula. *Women, Work and Property in North-West India.* London: Tavistock, 1980.

Singh, Gurbir. ' "Displaced" Textile Workers: Kotwal Report.' *Economic and Political Weekly*, 22, 13 (28 March 1987): 539.

Sinha, Amrita. 'Women's Local Space: Home and Neighbourhood.' In *Bridging Worlds: Studies on Women in South Asia*, edited by Sally J. M. Sutherland. Delhi: Oxford University Press, 1992.

Srinivas, M. N. *Caste in Modern India and Other Essays.* Bombay: Asia Publishing House, 1962.

Srinivas, M. N. *The Remembered Village*. Berkeley: University of California Press, 1976.

Srinivas, M. N, A. M. Shah, and E. A. Ramaswamy, eds. *The Field-worker and the Field: Problems and Challenges in Sociological Investigation*. Delhi: Oxford University Press, 1979.

Srinivasan, Amrit. 'Reform or Conformity? Temple "Prostitution" and the Community in the Madras Presidency.' In *Structures of Patriarchy: The State, the Community and the Household in Modernizing Asia*, edited by Bina Agarwal. London: Zed, 1988.

Tulpule, Bagaram. 'Rehabilitation Assistance to Closed Textile Mill Workers.' *Economic and Political Weekly*, 21, 41 (11 October 1986): 1780.

Vyas, V. S. 'New Economic Policy and Vulnerable Sections: Rational for Public Intervention.' *Economic and Political Weekly* 27, 10 (6 March 1993): 403-407.

Wiser, William H., and Charlotte Viall Wiser. *Behind Mud Walls: 1930-1960; with a Sequel: The Village in 1970*. Berkeley: University of California Press, 1971.

Zachariah, K. C. *Migrants in Greater Bombay*. Bombay: Asia Publishing House, 1986.

Zeidenstein, Sondra, ed. Special Issue. *Studies in Family Planning* 10 (November/December 1979).

Index